MIND
BEFORE
MATTER

**Visions of a New Science
of Consciousness**

First published by O Books, 2007
O Books is an imprint of John Hunt Publishing Ltd.,
The Bothy, Deershot Lodge, Park Lane, Ropley, Hants, SO24 0BE, UK
office1@o-books.net
www.o-books.net

Distribution in:

UK and Europe
Orca Book Services
orders@orcabookservices.co.uk
Tel: 01202 665432 Fax: 01202 666219 Int. code (44)

USA and Canada
NBN
custserv@nbnbooks.com
Tel: 1 800 462 6420 Fax: 1 800 338 4550

Australia and New Zealand
Brumby Books
sales@brumbybooks.com.au
Tel: 61 3 9761 5535 Fax: 61 3 9761 7095

Far East (offices in Singapore, Thailand, Hong Kong, Taiwan)
Pansing Distribution Pte Ltd
kemal@pansing.com
Tel: 65 6319 9939 Fax: 65 6462 5761

South Africa
Alternative Books
altbook@peterhyde.co.za
Tel: 021 447 5300 Fax: 021 447 1430

Design: Stuart Davies

ISBN: 978 1 84694 057 6

Printed in the US by Maple Vail

MIND
BEFORE
MATTER

Visions of a New Science
of Consciousness

Editors
Trish Pfeiffer & John E. Mack, M.D.

Associate Editor
Paul Devereux

Foreword: Larry Dossey, M.D.

BOOKS

Winchester, UK
Washington, USA

"Matter is derived from mind, and not mind from matter."
The Tibetan Book of the Great Liberation

"The stuff of the universe is mind-stuff."
Sir Arthur Eddington, Physicist

"This universe is a gradation of planes of consciousness."
Sri Aurobindo

"I believe that consciousness and its contents are all that exists. Space-time, matter and fields never were the fundamental denizens of the universe but have always been, from their beginning, among the humbler contents of consciousness, dependent on it for their very being."
Donald Hoffman, Cognitive Scientist, University of California, Irvine

Dedicated to the memory of John E. Mack,
friend and mentor to so many,
who wrote and spoke from a worldview of a living universe.

CONTENTS

COMMUNION 217

Introduction to the essays in this section

ACKNOWLEDGEMENTS

I want to express my deepest gratitude to my friend and co-editor, John Mack. Without his unfailing encouragement and support, invaluable advice and ideas, and his generous giving of time and thought, this book would never have come into being.

My heartfelt thanks to Larry Dossey for writing the foreword to this anthology, and likewise to the contributing authors for the great gift of their time, their visions, their enthusiasm and their patience.

Everlasting gratitude goes to my great friends, Paul and Charla Devereux: Paul stepped in at my request at a time of crisis with tremendous contributions, including assisting me in the difficult task of making the final selection of essays for this particular volume, structuring those into four sections, providing each section with a wonderfully concise introductory summary, functioning as an associate editor to ensure cohesion and clarity, and presenting the entire finished manuscript to the publisher. Charla functioned expertly as overall trans-Atlantic organizer and helped mightily with many extraneous problems dealing with the book's publication.

Additionally, I want to thank the following friends who helped in so many ways: Ronee and Norman Bank, Will Bueche, Michael Baldwin, Deborah Benson, Trish Corbett, Frank Don, Veronica Goodchild, Michael Grosso, Roger Jones, Veronica Keen, Gerard Koeppel, Anna Lemkow, Michael Mannion, Lillian Martino, Richmond Mayo-Smith, Jessica Salky, Mary Schmitt, Timothy Seldes, and Gillian Spencer.

Finally, to my daughter, Lisbeth, I wish to express my appreciation for her enduring interest in "how the world works", and to my husband, Bob, for his discerning eye and wise suggestions.

Trish Pfeiffer

Very special appreciation to Lynn Owens, whose dedication to the concept of consciousness as being primary, whose knowledge of publishing, and whose creative suggestions and donation of time, have been of great value to the entire book.

NOTES ON THE CONTRIBUTORS

John E. Mack, M.D. (1929 –2004) was a professor of psychiatry at
Harvard Medical School and a Pulitzer Prize-winning biographer
whose efforts to bridge psychiatry and spirituality were compared by
The New York Times to that of fellow Harvard professor William
James. Mack received his medical degree from Harvard Medical
School (Cum Laude) after undergraduate study at Oberlin (Phi Beta
Kappa). He was a graduate of the Boston Psychoanalytic Society and
Institute. His many books include the Pulitzer Prize-winning biogra-
phy, *A Prince of Our Disorder: The Life of T. E. Lawrence* (Little,
Brown & Co., 1976), and *Passport to the Cosmos: Human
Transformation and Alien Encounters* (Crown, 1999). The latter, his
final book, was a philosophical treatise connecting the themes of spir-
ituality and modern worldviews.

Trish Pfeiffer is a longtime student of consciousness and quantum
physics. As a researcher at the Parapsychology Foundation's lab in
New York City, she participated in the first generation of the many pro-
tocols still used in the investigation of anomalous phenomena. She was
founder and former director of the Center for Exploring New
Dimensions of Consciousness presenting 45 programs annually in Rye,
New York over a nine year period. She was Creative Director for
Superlearning, Inc. in New York City and a founder of the Marion
(Foundation) Institute co-creating programs exploring frontier science
and human potential. She is on the Advisory Board of the Friends of
the Institute of Noetic Sciences (FIONS). In 1999, Pfeiffer co-launched
(with Charla and Paul Devereux) 'The Consciousness Connection' to
promote convergence of thought within the field of consciousness
studies, opening with a conference at the Royal Society of Arts in
London which drew people from eleven countries.

* * *

Christopher Bache, Ph.D. Professor of religious studies at Youngstown State University and adjunct faculty at the California Institute for Integral Studies. For two years he was the Director of Transformative Learning at the Institute of Noetic Sciences. An award winning teacher, his work explores reincarnation and the philosophical implications of non-ordinary states of consciousness. Authored: *Lifecycles: Reincarnation and the Web of Life* (Paragon House, 1990), *Dark Night, Early Dawn: Steps to a Deep Ecology of Mind* (SUNY, 2000), and *The Living Classroom* (forthcoming).

Anne Baring Jungian analyst, author, lecturer. Currently writing two books: *The Dream of the Water* and *The Psychosis of War*. Authored: *The One Work: A Journey Towards the Self* (Vincent Stuart, 1961), *The Birds Who Flew Beyond Time* (Barefoot Books and Shambhala, 1993). Co-authored with Jules Cashford, *The Myth of the Goddess: Evolution of an Image* (Penguin, 1992); with Andrew Harvey, *The Mystic Vision* (Godsfield Press & HarperSan Francisco, 1995) and *The Divine Feminine* (Godsfield Press & Conari, 1996). Her website (www.annebaring.com) is devoted to the affirmation of a new vision of reality and the issues facing us at this crucial time of choice.

Paul Devereux Author, independent researcher, lecturer. Focus of work: consciousness studies, cognitive archaeology, and deep ecology. In addition to many articles and a range of peer-review academic papers, he has published 26 books between 1979 and 2003, including *Re-Visioning the Earth* (Fireside Books, Simon & Schuster, 1996), *The Sacred Place* (Cassell, 2000), *Haunted Land* (Piatkus, 2001), *Stone Age Soundtracks* (Vega, 2001), and *Spirit Roads* (Collins & Brown, 2007). Is currently working on *Cultures Collide – Extraordinary Experiences in Tribal Societies and their Challenge to Science*. A founding co-editor of the new, cross-disciplinary peer-review publication, *Time & Mind: Journal of Archaeology, Consciousness & Culture* (published by Berg; first issue: March 2008). Internet contact: pdevereux@onetel.com

4

Larry Dossey, M.D. Internist, consultant, lecturer and author of ten books on the interrelationship of consciousness, spirituality and healing. Executive editor of peer-reviewed *Explore: The Journal of Science and Healing.* Authored: *The Extraordinary Healing Power of Ordinary Things* (Random House, 2006), *Healing Beyond the Body: Medicine and the Infinite Reach of the Mind* (Shambhala, 2001), *Reinventing Medicine* (HarperSanFrancisco, 1999), and *Space, Time and Medicine* (Shambhala, 1982).

Duane Elgin, M.B.A., M.A. Researcher of the co-evolution of culture and consciousness for 30 years. Formerly a senior social scientist at the Stanford Research Institute (now SRI International). Authored: *Promise Ahead: A Vision of Hope and Action for Humanity's Future* (Wm. Morrow, 2000), and *Voluntary Simplicity: Toward a New Way of Life That is Outwardly Simple and Inwardly Rich* (Quill, 1998).

Amit Goswami, Ph.D. Professor of physics at the Institute of Theoretical Sciences at the University of Oregon for 34 years. His ground-breaking book, *The Self-Aware Universe: How Consciousness Creates the Material World* (Putnam, 1993; Tarcher, 1995), provided the first hard scientific evidence for the undergirding of the primacy of consciousness. His latest book is *Integral Medicine.*

Neal Grossman, Ph.D. His field of inquiry concerns whether scientific methodology can uncover empirical evidence for spiritual truths. Associate professor of philosophy at the University of Illinois at Chicago. Authored: *Healing the Mind: The Philosophy of Spinoza Adapted for a New Age* (Susquehanna University Press, 1993) exploring Spinoza's path to spiritual integration.

Michael Grosso, Ph.D. Philosophy doctorate from Columbia University. Taught at The City University of New York, Kennedy University, Mary Mount Manhattan College, and New Jersey City

University, and is currently teaching ancient philosophy at the Virginia School of Continuing Education, University of Virginia. Presents Wisdom Seminars on "practical philosophy for everyday life." Authored: *Experiencing the Next World Now* (Pocket Books, 2004), *Soulmaking* (Hampton Roads, 1997), and *The Millennium Myth* (Quest Books, 1995).

Bernard Haisch, Ph.D. Astrophysicist and Chief Scientific editor for the *Astrophysical Journal* and former editor-in-chief of the *Journal of Scientific Exploration*. Has been principal investigator on numerous NASA research projects. A visiting scientist at the University of Utrecht in the Netherlands, and a deputy director of the Center for EUV Astrophysics at the University of California, Berkeley. Doctorate from the University of Wisconsin, Madison and three years post-doctoral research at the Joint Institute for Laboratory Astrophysics at the University of Colorado. 20 years as staff scientist at the Lockheed Palo Alto Research Laboratory and the Lockheed Martin Advanced Technology Center working primarily on NASA-funded research projects. Has authored over 120 scientific articles and the book, *The God Theory: Universes, Zero-Point Fields and What's Behind It All* (Red Wheel/Weiser).

Will Keepin, Ph.D. is president and executive director of the Satyana Institute, a non-profit organization he co-founded to integrate spiritual wisdom into social-change leadership. Adjunct faculty member at the California Institute of Integral Studies in San Francisco. Originally trained as a physicist, he was a Hewlett Fellow at Princeton and a research scholar at the Royal Swedish Academy of Sciences, working on energy and environmental science.

David C. Korten, Ph.D. Author, lecturer, and engaged citizen. Co-founder and board chair of the Positive Futures Network, which publishes *YES! A Journal of Positive Futures* (www.yesmagazine.org), founder and president of the People-Centered Development Forum (www.developmentforum.net), a board member of the Business Alliance for Local Living Economies, and author of *The Great Turning: From Empire to Earth Community* from which his article is drawn. He is also author of the international best-selling *When Corporations Rule the World*, *The Post-Corporate World: Life After Capitalism*, and *Globalizing Civil Society*. He is an associate of the International Forum on Globalization and a major contributor to its study of *Alternatives to Economic Globalization*. He holds M.B.A. and Ph.D. degrees from the Stanford Graduate School of Business and was for several years a member of the Harvard Business School faculty. Website: www.davidkorten.org

Ervin Laszlo, Ph.D. One of the world's foremost exponents of applied systems theory and general evolution theory. Founder of the Club of Budapest. Authored: *The Whispering Pond: A Personal Guide to the Emerging Vision of Science* (Harper Collins UK, 1999) and *Science and the Akashic Field* (Inner Traditions, 2004). Co-authored: *The Connectivity Hypothesis: Foundations of an Integral Science of Quantum, Cosmos, Life, and Consciousness* (SUNY Press, 2003) with Ralph Abraham.

Corinne McLaughlin and Gordon Davidson Co-authors of *Spiritual Politics* (Ballantine Books, 1994; Foreword by the Dalai Lama), and *Builders of the Dawn* (The Book Publishers, 1985), and a forthcoming book on *Creators of a New World*. They are co-founders of The Center for Visionary Leadership, based in the Washington, D.C. and San Francisco areas, and co-founders of Sirius, an ecological village in Massachusetts. Corinne coordinated a national task force for President Clinton's Council on Sustainable Development. Gordon was formerly the Executive Director of the Social Investment Forum and of The Center for Environmentally Responsible Economies. They have both served on the adjunct faculty of The American University and the

University of Massachusetts, and are Fellows of The World Business Academy and The Findhorn Foundation. (Contact information: [USA] 472-2540; corinnemc@visionarylead.org ; www.visionarylead.org.)

Seyyed Hossein Nasr, M.S., Ph.D. University Professor of Islamic Studies at George Washington University. Authored: many books, including *Knowledge and the Sacred* (1990), *Islamic Art and Spirituality* (1987), and *Islamic Life and Thought* (1981), all State University of New York Press, and *The Heart of Islam: Enduring Values for Humanity* (Harper San Francisco, 2002). He is editor of *Expectation of the Millennium: Shi'ism in History* and *Shi'ism: Doctrines, Thought, and Spirituality* (SUNY).

Dean Radin, Ph.D. Psychologist and electrical engineer; studies the mind-matter interactions. Senior Scientist at the Institute of Noetic Sciences, Adjunct Faculty at Sonoma State University, and Distinguished Consulting Faculty at Saybrook Graduate School. Authored: *The conscious universe: The scientific truth of psychic phenomena* (1997), *Entangled minds: Extrasensory experiences in a quantum reality* (2006), and over 200 scientific and popular articles.

Elisabet Sahtouris, Ph.D. Evolution biologist, futurist, and consultant on Living Systems Design for businesses, governments and other organizations. She is a fellow of the World Business Academy, a member of the World Wisdom Council and travels around the world teaching sustainable business and globalization as natural evolutionary processes. Dr Sahtouris also works on foundations of science and the integration of science and sprituality. Her venues include The World Bank, Boeing, Siemens, Hewlett-Packard, Tokyo Dome Stadium, Australian National Govt, Sao Paulo's leading business schools, State of the World Forums (NY & San Francisco) and the World Parliament of Religions. Her books include: *Earth Dance: Living Systems in*

Evolution (Universe, 2000); *Biology Revisioned* (North Atlantic, 1998), co-authored with Willis Harman, and *A Walk Through Time: From Stardust to Us* (John Wiley, 1998). Websites: www.sahtouris.com and www.ratical.org/lifeweb .

Mary F. Schmitt, Ph.D. Neurophysiologist on the faculty of John F. Kennedy University and the Sophia Center of Holy Names College. Lectures on the emerging science of "wholism", the study of consciousness in nature and the role of human consciousness in evolution.

Richard Tarnas, Ph.D. A Professor of philosophy and psychology at the California Institute of Integral Studies, where he founded the graduate program in philosophy, cosmology, and consciousness. He also teaches archetypal studies and the history of western culture at Pacifica Graduate Institute. Authored: *The Passion of the Western Mind: Understanding the Ideas That Have Shaped Our World Views* (Harmony, 1991; Ballantine, 1993) and a sequel, *Cosmos and Psyche: Intimations of a New World View* (2006).

Rose von Thater-Braan Of Tuscarora/Cherokee ancestry. Has spent most of her adult life exploring the transformative power of communication. As the Director of Education at U.C. Berkeley's Center for Particle Astrophysics, she led collaborative efforts to increase cultural competency and cultivate a scientific community that values diversity of perception, thought and expression. She is co-founder of The Native Science Academy, a circle of indigenous scholars engaged in developing a center for the study of native science and is the Director of Silver Buffalo Consulting. Prior to entering the scientific realm, she worked extensively in both the theatrical and corporate worlds. She trained and worked in theater (the American Conservatory Theater) and television (KQED-TV) and with the writer/critic/producer Ralph J. Gleason (co-founder of Rolling Stone magazine).

Hank Wesselman, Ph.D. Former university and college professor, zoologist and paleoanthropologist involved in expeditionary field research in search of human origins in eastern Africa's Great Rift Valley. In addition to his scientific publications, he is the author of *Spiritwalker* (Bantam, 1995), *Medicinemaker* (Bantam, 1998) and *Visionseeker* (Hay House, 2001), an autobiographical trilogy focused upon spontaneous anomalous experiences that took him deep into the shamanic worlds of magic and meaning. His most recent books include *The Journey to the Sacred Garden* (Hay House, 2003) and *Spirit Medicine* (Hay House, 2004, with Jill Kuykendall.) Website: www.sharedwisdom.com

ASSOCIATE EDITOR'S NOTES

Paul Devereux

I have placed each of the essays selected from those Trish Pfeiffer and John Mack received into one of four sections – Science, Philosophy, Psi, Communion – as seems to best fit its content. However, let it be noted that the essays tend to be so wide-ranging this has had to be something of a token exercise. Nevertheless, it does, hopefully, give some structure to this volume. Also, rather than trying to shoehorn each essay into the bland uniformity of either British or (more often) North American English, I have allowed the native usuage of English by each author to stand with the minimum of modifications, and those merely to aid clarity and a measure of overall standard presentation.

These essays, these visions, while sometimes overlapping and at other times slightly contradicting one another, carry some recurring messages and ideas, and it is with these that the common wisdom of the contributors comes to the fore. Perhaps the most generally underlying thought is that mainstream Western science will simply have to find room for the subjective, for human experience. It needs to understand consciousness as being "inside" of the objective universe. Without it, our Western model of reality will forever be incomplete, and danger-ously so. I will leave the reader to note the recurrence of other common themes – there are many, some apparent, others more subtle.

While I suspect most readers will be familiar with the majority of the terms used by our essayists, two belonging to quantum physics might cause some difficulty for general readers. One is "entanglement" or non-locality. This refers to the curious but experimentally confirmed fact that if two quantum elements (photons, say) are emitted from a suitably prepared source in opposite directions a change in one will be mirrored instantaneously in the other of the pair, irrespective of the distance between them. This entanglement, this "spooky action at a distance" as Einstein called it, does not happen merely faster than the speed of light but *infinitely* fast, precluding the transfer of energy or information between the photons. The other quantum term, the "electromagnetic vacuum" (or "zero-point energy" or "zero-point field"), is even more difficult to comprehend. As it is invoked by a number of our contributors I have asked one of them who is particularly well informed in this matter, astrophysicist Bernard Haisch, to give us a definition of it:

The electromagnetic vacuum, also known as the electromagnetic zero-point field, is a sea of virtual photons at every point in the universe, whose existence is a result of the Heisenberg uncertainty principle. Physical manifestations include the Casimir force and Lamb shift. A speculative physics theory proposes a connection between the quantum vacuum and the origin of mass. Far more speculative ideas abound, however, which have no connection whatsoever to the quantum vacuum or zero-point field as defined by physics, but rather use the term in an undefined catch-all fashion.

If that doesn't help, then take it as the cue to consult sources on the World Wide Web – or *even* books – to explicate the terms used by Haisch to better understand the mysterious, infinitesimally small sub-atomic world that is the quantum realm, lying at the heart of what we consider to be the physical reality surrounding us. It is, after all, part of our modern cosmology.

Those who already believe that consciousness is the prime foundation of reality will find that the visions in these pages broaden that understanding; sceptics are urged to read all the essays in this anthology before hardening their viewpoint. This book represents the start of a discussion, not some kind of "last word". What it is intended to do is to inspire, challenge and provoke the reader, leading to further, ever-deepening discussion. The hour is late, and it is past time we spoke together.

PROLOGUE

Purpose, Vision and Inspiration
Trish Pfeiffer

As long as I can remember, I felt a strong and persistent need to find out "how the world works". I was puzzled and annoyed that the adults I came in contact with were seemingly uninterested in pondering such questions with me. So, in my growing-up years I became a voracious reader, hoping to find in books clues to this fascinating universe in which I found myself.

I came upon my first "Aha!" in my early teens. It was just a single sentence in Ouspensky's *Tertium Organum:* "The drop is contained in the ocean, and the ocean is contained in the drop." Although I couldn't understand how the ocean could be contained in the drop, I found the words immensely exhilarating as though they held great secret knowledge. In the years that followed I kept coming across the same idea in unexpected places, and my surprise and delight knew no bounds. For instance, in physics, there it was in Bootstrap's theorem – "Every particle contains every other particle"; in Lao-Tse's commentary on the Tao: "The greatest is within the smallest", and in ancient philosophy, where Plotinus declares: "Each Being contains in itself the whole world – each is therefore All and All is each." And I came to learn that in holography the smallest particle contains all the information of the whole. This same basic notion became an insistent message beating on my awareness, like waves of a deep ocean crashing repeatedly on the shore.

Then, in my early twenties, I had an experience that forever changed my idea of reality. I had looked up from writing a letter, and was idly watching a dust particle drifting and planing in a shaft of sunlight when I was overwhelmed by a sense of simply *knowing* that everything that exists, from the tiniest particle to the farthest reaches of the cosmos, is somehow *conscious* and *alive,* and that reality is *composed* of consciousness. For months afterwards I spent many hours trying to absorb the implications of this experience, and felt increasingly driven to find some way to stimulate everyone's thinking generally about consciousness, and specifically about this insight I felt I had received directly – through the heart rather than via my intellect. But back in those days no one seemed interested in consciousness, which was looked upon by most scientists as a kind of chemical fluke produced by the brain, and was treated virtually as a non-subject. Behaviorism was all the rage, and one could deal with mind only obliquely rather than as a vital topic worthy of study in its own right. But times eventually began to change and the nature of mind came back onto the cultural agenda.

By the early 1990s, conferences started to be held and articles written themed on the subject of consciousness, consciousness studies gained momentum, and physicist Amit Goswami formulated a physics identifying consciousness as being primary, as being the building block of everything – a theme he explored in a technical paper published jointly by the Institute of Noetic Sciences (IONS) and the Fetzer Institute, and then in a 1993 book (with Richard E. Reed and Maggie Goswami), *The Self-Aware Universe: How Consciousness Creates the Material World*. In 1999, Harvard professor John Mack, the psychiatrist, lecturer and Pulitzer prize-winning author, invited me to co-chair with him the board of his Center for Psychology and Social Change. When I discussed with John the concept of the primacy of consciousness, and my long-held dream of getting it more widely circulated and discussed, he was most enthusiastic. He urged me to start figuring out how this might be accomplished.

After discarding various ideas, I suggested to John that one way of trying to get discussion going would be to publish a collection of essays in which the writers envisioned what life would be like in a world that believed consciousness was primary. John volunteered to contact those of his many friends he thought might make valuable contributions, and I did likewise, listing authors of books that had meant so much to me. The invitation letter we sent out to prospective essayists included the following excerpts:

We are inviting you to participate in what we feel is an exciting and timely project. Its purpose is to increase awareness of the … concept that consciousness, and not matter, is ultimate reality, the ground of all being. We believe this could be an … important, and intriguing collection of contributions from penetrating thinkers in diverse fields describing what they think the world would look like from this perspective and how our lives would be changed…

We are inviting you to play with this concept and imagine the implications for our planet, and the ways in which our lives, thinking and society itself might change should this notion be enabled to take hold … the fundamental threat to human survival derives from a materialistic worldview that is altogether inadequate.

In short, we were asking potential contributors to turn the old paradigm, that only matter is real, on its head, and to begin with the assumption instead that consciousness is the primary reality and creative force and to write about the transformation, individual and collective, we can imagine flowing from such a figure/ground reversal of virtually everything we think we know.

This really should not now be so terribly controversial. The advent of quantum physics has presented us with a worldview in sharp contrast to the classical one we inhabit in which we assume that matter is the primary reality. "The stuff of the universe is *mind-stuff*," declared Sir Arthur Eddington, one of the founding fathers of the new physics. Yet, outside the circles of quantum physics, how many are aware today of the implications of this scientific revolution that began nearly a century ago? How many are aware of the staggering implications of the work of John Bell and Alain Aspect, establishing that the universe at its most basic level is non-local – that information doesn't travel from A to B, because it does not need to travel at all – *it exists everywhere.* This interpretation presents us with the vision of a participatory universe in which everything is interconnected and interdependent; a seamless whole. For all its mathematical complexities, the implications of quantum physics are only what I directly sensed when observing the dust mote floating in that long-ago sunbeam. It is the very antithesis of the present materialistic, clockwork worldview.

We wanted the collection of essays to present a flux of views as to *what would a world be like based on a mindset that understood that all is One and interconnected?* My own mind teems with questions. How soon could the knowledge that we live in a participatory world initiate change in our thinking about war, and our desecration of the planet? Would a world aware of the primacy of consciousness be akin to the world as seen by some of the indigenous peoples? Would we then see the cosmos as a living presence; and the whole universe, and all of nature, as intelligent? Would we come to think of thought itself as only a small portion, perhaps, of what the mind is capable of, as physicist David Peat has suggested. Following the insights of mystics and scientists, like Sri Aurobindo and Rupert Sheldrake respectively, would we discover that the physical laws of the universe were "habits", evolving rather than immutable? Would we begin to sense other realities and other dimensions? When we realized that time and space are not fundamental dimensions underlying reality, would it change forever our ideas about death? Would we strive for unconditional love? How would human relationships, social justice, poverty, science, medicine, politics, the government, and the military be reframed according to consciousness-primary perspectives?

These questions are a long way from being answered, but it is at least a hopeful sign that the idea that consciousness as not localized in time or space, and therefore ubiquitous, is being discussed now by an ever-increasing number of scientists and thinkers. This new vision signals an approach to the nature of reality more profound, meaningful and beautiful than is ever imagined in our present culture.

The potential contributors John Mack and I approached responded with enthusiasm, and there has been space here in this single volume to include only some of the essays we received. I hope circumstances will allow for further volumes to be published, but I will feel satisfied if this anthology can help to stimulate further thinking and discussion in which the new insights of cutting-edge science and thought can impinge on the current worldview, leading to perceptions and explorations that take us along a better, more informed path than we currently tread. Maybe the voices in these pages will reach the ears of someone who, on gazing at a speck of dust drifting in sunlight, will feel inspired to go on and change the world.

INTRODUCTION

Why Worldviews Matter
John E. Mack

Worldviews – and the ways of knowing that produce and sustain them – structure our perceptions and define how we experience ourselves in relation to the universe. They determine how we relate to each other and to the Earth itself, how we find satisfaction, and how we come to terms with the ultimate questions of living and dying. For these reasons, there is no matter of greater significance than which worldview, or paradigm, is ascendant in our society.

The dominant worldview in our culture for the past three centuries has been scientific materialism, or Newtonianism. (Tulane philosopher Michael Zimmerman aptly calls it "anthropocentric humanism.") In this worldview matter and energy are primary: the universe came into being through a kind of gigantic accident (the Big Bang) and has evolved according to fixed laws. This cosmos is devoid of any indwelling spirit or soul, or inherent meaning, and man stands at the pinnacle of its intelligence hierarchy. The scientific method – the way of knowing that sustains the materialist worldview – relies exclusively on empirical tools and rational understanding.

The alternative worldview is more fluid and evolving. In this perspective, a universal consciousness – or some sort of eternal, intelligent principle – pervades the cosmos and *participates* with humanity in the evolution of reality. Knowledge to support this worldview comes not only from observable phenomena but also from experiential, subjective, and intuitive knowing. From this standpoint, soul and spirit are not vestiges of abandoned religiosity but living realities that can be experienced through the direct knowing of the heart.

Recent discoveries in physics, biology, consciousness research, comparative religion, and transpersonal psychology, together with increasing recognition of the value of traditional (indigenous) and spiritual ways of knowing, show that the materialist paradigm provides a far too limited view of reality. Furthermore, careful analysis of the major political, economic, social, and ecological problems afflicting the world today suggests that they can be traced to the dominance of the materialist philosophy.

Rather than create another volume debating alternative worldviews, Trish Pfeiffer and I decided to ask a selection of leading scientists, philosophers, and psychologists to envision a world in which consciousness is given primacy, and knowledge of a divine intelligence is "restored" to the cosmos. The responses of these thinkers reveal that they, too, have discovered that the materialist paradigm has become untenable. They offer increasing evidence from a variety of disciplines to support the emerging worldview. Far from perceiving a conflict between "heart-knowing" or "spiritual-knowing" and the scientific method, they recognize that what is of value in the scientific paradigm can be readily subsumed within this broader worldview.

The essays included in this anthology reflect a diversity of views. But readers may be surprised to discover how many leading scientific thinkers agree with theologian Huston Smith that "the greatest problem the human spirit faces in our time is having to live in the procrustean, scientistic worldview that dominates our culture." The contributors to this volume show us an alternative: a universe of abundance that offers an opportunity to participate in its infinite, self-organizing creativity.

The expanded sense of ourselves that grows out of recognizing our vital connection with all living things – and even with non-animate matter – can act as a kind of insurance policy for our survival. As we begin to appreciate our identity with all beings and with the Earth itself, inevitably our destructive proclivities are curbed.

Today we find increasing concern over the dark pall that hangs over our planet, as a result of war, poverty, disease, environmental desecration, and abuse in many forms. *Mind Before Matter* is intended to help liberate human life from the constrictions of the materialist worldview.

[*John Mack died before he could expand upon this draft.*]

FOREWORD

Nonlocal Mind: Why It Matters
Larry Dossey

Human history is largely a reflection of "what ifs." What if we could make fire, our ancestors wondered? Craft a wheel? Domesticate wild animals? Grow grain? Sail around the world? Fly? Split an atom? Go to the moon? In this book, we are considering the most important "what if" ever conceived: What if consciousness is fundamental in the universe? What if it is elemental, irreducible to anything more basic? What would be the consequences?

For nearly all of recorded history, it was taken for granted that consciousness is indeed fundamental and real in its own right. People saw evidence for this belief everywhere. With the ascendancy of empirical science, however, this view was rejected, and consciousness was increasingly considered a fiction, an imaginary ghost in the body's machinery, a derivative of the brain. As Nobelist Sir Francis Crick, the co-discoverer of the structure of DNA, said in his 1994 book *The Astonishing Hypothesis: The Scientific Search for the Soul,* "The Astonishing Hypothesis is that, 'You,' your joys and your sorrows, your memories and your ambitions, your sense of personal identity and free will, are in fact no more than the behavior of a vast assembly of nerve cells and their associated molecules. As Lewis Carroll's Alice might have phrased: 'You're nothing but a pack of neurons.' This hypothesis is so alien to the ideas of most people today that it can truly be called astonishing."[1] This view is not just alien, it is disastrous for the things that have always mattered to humans, issues such as volition, meaningful choice-making, personal responsibility, soul, spirit, and survival of bodily death. After an awkward interlude, however, the idea that consciousness is real, fundamental, and irreducible is returning. That's what this book is all about.

In 1989 I introduced the term "nonlocal mind" in my book

Recovering the Soul[2] because of the abundant evidence supporting this particular view of consciousness. Since then evidence has continued to accumulate.

If we unpack "nonlocal mind," we can see why this idea is crucial for human existence.

The street meaning of "nonlocal" is, literally, not local. If something is nonlocal, it is not localized or confined to a specific place in space and time. "Nonlocal," therefore, is another word for "infinite." The implications for consciousness are profound, for, if something is nonlocal or infinite in space, it is omnipresent; and if nonlocal or infinite in time, it is eternal or immortal.

There are compelling scientific, historic, and experiential reasons for believing that consciousness behaves nonlocally or infinitely in space and time, that it is spatially unconfineable to brains and bodies, and that it is temporally unconfineable to the present. This evidence, too vast to be reviewed here, suggests that space and time are simply not applicable to certain operations of consciousness. Consciousness is both trans-spatial and trans-temporal; it is not in space and time.[3]

Nonlocality is a concept also applied by physicists to a class of events whose definition relates to the speed of light.[4] But physics does not own nonlocality, nor do physicists enjoy a monopoly on nonlocal events and the language that describes them. People were routinely experiencing nonlocal manifestations of consciousness millennia before quantum physics was invented in the twentieth century, and we are not obligated to cede nonlocality to scientists who have chosen to nuance the term differently.

In contemporary neuroscience, consciousness is equated with the workings of the brain, a local and finite view. This implies that when the brain dies consciousness is annihilated; nothing survives death. In striking contrast, the idea of nonlocal mind affirms ancient concepts such as "soul," "spirit," and "Buddha nature" that designate an ongoing something that survives the death of the physical body. In short, nonlocal mind not only makes room for immortality, it mandates it.

Why? Temporal nonlocality does not mean "for quite a while" or "a long time," but *infinitude* in time: eternality or immortality.

Immortality has been ridiculed in science in the twentieth century, and the results have been disastrous. As author George Orwell put it, "The major problem of our time is the decay of belief in personal immortality."[5] This is not admitted within science. Even addressing the topic of immortality in many scientific circles is considered a sign of intellectual weakness or of "going mystic." Yet the old rivers run deep within the psyche, and merely declaring the yearning for immortality dead does not make it so.

Make no mistake: the fear of death is humanity's Great Disease, the terror that has caused more suffering throughout history than all of the physical diseases combined. Nonlocal mind is the Great Cure for this affliction, because it assures us that the most essential aspect of who we are cannot die, even though the physical body perishes.

It is only a matter of time before a nonlocal view of consciousness is accepted in science. No other view is capable of explaining research findings in the field of distant healing and prayer. Currently, twenty controlled clinical trials of remote, intercessory prayer and healing intentions in humans have been conducted.[6 - 25] Eleven demonstrate statistically positive results, far more than would be expected by chance. Eight systematic or meta-analyses of this body of research have been done; seven report positive findings.[26 - 33] Humans can also influence the physiology of each other at a distance, even when the distant individual is unaware that the effort is being made.[34 - 36] In addition to these human studies, scores of experiments reveal that human intentions can act remotely to influence cellular function,[37] microbial growth,[38 - 40] the growth of tumors in animals,[41,42] the germination of seeds and the growth of plants,[43] and the kinetics of biochemical reactions.[44 - 46] These studies in biological systems are buttressed by hundreds of experiments in non-biological settings in which human intentions exert statistically significant effects.[47 - 50]

Close examination of the studies in distant healing and prayer reveals that nonlocal mind is intimately connected with love, compassion, and deep caring, just as healers throughout history have maintained.[51,52] This is one of the great lessons of the healing experiments: love, operating through nonlocal mind, can literally change the world.

The experiments in nonlocal, distant and healing prayer show that the prayers of all religions appear to be effective. Even non-theistic prayer, as in some forms of Buddhism, results in healing, as do secular and so-called pagan intentions that are not associated with any traditional religion. These findings are of utmost importance. They democratize and universalize healing intentions and prayer. These studies reveal that no religion enjoys a monopoly on the nonlocal effects of prayer, and they are therefore the enemy of religious intolerance.[53]

Attention to nonlocal mind will eventually transform modern medicine.[54,55] Currently the type of medicine that prevails in our culture could be called Temporal Medicine, because it assumes linear, flowing time with its inevitable correlates of aging, infirmity, disease, and death. But nonlocal mind makes possible another approach, Eternity Medicine, based on the evidence of a temporally infinite aspect of consciousness.[56,57] Eternity Medicine comes into play anytime we honor our boundless, eternal, nonlocal nature. Eternity Medicine recognizes that something, however named, endures beyond the death of the physical body. The beginning assumption of Temporal Medicine is death and annihilation; Eternity Medicine assumes immortality, not as something to be acquired, cultivated, or engineered, but as innate and fundamental. This transforms the fatalistic premise of modern science. As a result, fear relents, the pressure eases, the future brightens. A lightness and perhaps a sense of humor enter. Life, not death, is now our birthright and a condition of our being.[58 - 60]

If mind is genuinely nonlocal, then it is boundless and boundaryless. This means that individual minds cannot be separated and walled off from one another. In some dimension, minds come together and form what Nobel physicist Erwin Schrödinger called the One Mind, and what our ancestors called the Universal Mind.[61] Shared mind has enormous ethical implications, because it implies that what we do to others we do to ourselves, and vice versa. This leads to a re-formulation of the Golden Rule, from "Do unto others as you would have them do unto you," to "Do good unto others because in some sense they *are* you."

Our poor, tortured world is aflame with the countless hatreds of a thousand sects, and "me against you" has become the order of the day. Nonlocal mind is the enemy of this madness. It enlarges the compass of existence and opposes barriers, boundaries, and bigotry.[62] It is an imprimatur for humans to behave kinder and gentler toward one another and to the Earth and all of its creatures.

It is difficult to imagine anything more important.

References

1. Crick, F., *The Astonishing Hypothesis*, New York, NY: Scribner's, 1994; p. 3.

2. Dossey, L., *Recovering the Soul: A Scientific and Spiritual Search*, New York, NY: Bantam, 1989.

3. Clarke, C.J.S., The nonlocality of mind, *Journal of Consciousness Studies*, 1995; 2(3) 231-240.

4. Nadeau, R., Kafatos, M., Over any distance in "no time": Bell's Theorem and the Aspect and Gisin Experiments, *The Non-local Universe*, New York, NY: Oxford University Press, 1999; pp. 65-82.

5. Orwell, G., Quoted in: John Banville, "Good Man, Bad World." *The New York Review*, November 6, 2003; L(17), 62-65.

6. Byrd, R., Positive therapeutic effects of intercessory prayer in a coronary care unit population, *Southern Medical Journal*, 1988; 81(7), 826-9.

7. Sicher, F., Targ, E., Moore, D., Smith, H.S., A randomized double-blind study of the effect of distant healing in a population with advanced AIDS – report of a small-scale study, *Western Journal of Medicine*, 1998; 169(6), 356-363.

8. Harris, W., Gowda, M., Kolb, J.W., Strychacz, C.P., Vacek, J.L.,

Jones, P.G., Forker, A., O'Keefe, J.H., McCallister, B.D., A randomized, controlled trial of the effects of remote, intercessory prayer on outcomes in patients admitted to the coronary care unit, *Archives of Internal Medicine*, 1999; 159(19) 2273-2278.

9. Cha, K.Y., M.D., Wirth, D.P., Lobo, R., Does prayer influence the success of in vitro fertilization-embryo transfer? Report of a masked, randomized Trial, *J. Reproductive Medicine*, September 2001; 46(9), 781-787.

10. Krucoff, M.W., Crater, S.W., Green, C.L., Maas, A.C., Seskevich, J.E., Lane, J.D., Loeffler, K.A., Morris, K., Bashore, T.M., Koenig, H.G., Integrative noetic therapies as adjuncts to percutaneous intervention during unstable coronary syndromes: Monitoring and Actualization of Noetic Training (MANTRA) feasibility pilot, *American Heart Journal*, 2001; 142(5), 760-767.

11. Aviles, J.M., Whelan, S.E., Hernke, D.A., Williams, B.A., Kenny, K.E., O'Fallon, W.M., Kopecky, S.L., Intercessory prayer and cardiovascular disease progression in a coronary care unit population: A randomized controlled trial, *Mayo Clinic Proceedings*, December 2001; 76(12), 1192-1198.

12. Bentwich, Z., Kreitler, S., Psychological determinants of recovery from hernia operations. Paper presented at Dead Sea Conference, June 1994; Tiberias, Israel.

13. Beutler, J.J. *et al*, Paranormal healing and hypertension, *Br Med J* (Clin Res Ed), 1988; 296(6635), 1491-1494.

14. Matthews, W.J., Conti, J.M., Sireci, S.G., The effects of intercessory prayer, positive visualization, and expectancy on the well-being of kidney dialysis patients, *Alternative Therapies in Health and Medicine*, 2001; 7(5), 42-52.

15. O'Laoire, S., An experimental study of the effects of distant, intercessory prayer on self-esteem, anxiety, and depression, *Alternative Therapies in Health and Medicine*, 1997; 3(6), 39-53.

16. Achterberg, J., Cooke, K., Richards, T., Standish, L., Kozak, L., Lake, J., Evidence for correlations between distant intentionality and

25

briefbrain function in recipients: A functional magnetic resonance imaging analysis, *Journal of Alternative and Complementary Medicine*, 2005; 11(6), 965-971.

17. Tloczynski, J., Fritzsch, S., Intercessory prayer in psychological wellbeing: Using a multiple-baseline, across-subjects design, *Psychological Reports*, 2002; 91 (3Pt 1), 731-741.

18. Palmer, R.F., Katerndahl, D., Morgan-Kidd, J., A randomized trial of the effects of remote intercessory prayer: interactions with personal beliefs on problem-specific outcomes and functional status, *Journal of Alternative and Complementary Medicine*, 2004; 10(3), 438-448.

19. Leibovici, L., Effects of remote, retroactive intercessory prayer on outcomes in patients with bloodstream infection: a randomized controlled trial, *British Medical Journal*, 2001; (323),1450-1451.

20. Astin, J.A., Stone, J., Abrams, D.I., Moore, D.H., Couey, P., Buscemi, R., Targ. E., The efficacy of distant healing for human immunodeficiency virus – results of a randomized trial, *Alt Ther Health Med*, 2006; 12(6), 36-41.

21. Mathai, J., Bourne, A., Pilot study investigating the effect of intercessory prayer in the treatment of child psychiatric disorders, *Australasian Psychiatry*, 2004; 12(4), 386-389.

22. Benson, H. *et al*, Study of the Therapeutic Effects of Intercessory Prayer (STEP) in cardiac bypass patients: A multicenter randomized trial of uncertainty and certainty of receiving intercessory prayer, *Am Heart J*, 2006; 151, 934-42.

23. Krucoff, M.W., Crater, S.W. *et al*, Music, imagery, touch, and prayer as adjuncts to interventional cardiac care: the Monitoring and Actualization of Noetic Trainings (MANTRA II) randomized study, *Lancet*, 2005; 366, 211-217.

24. Walker, S.R., Tonigan, J.S., Miller, W.R., Corner, S., Kahlich, L., Intercessory prayer in the treatment of alcohol abuse and dependence: a pilot investigation, *Alternative Therapies in Health and Medicine*, 1997 Nov; 3(6), 79-86.

25. Harkness, E.F., Abbot, N.C., Ernst, E., A randomized trial of distant healing for skin warts, *American Journal of Medicine*, 2000; 108, 507-8.

26. Abbot, N.C., Healing as a therapy for human disease: a systematic review, *Journal of Alternative and Complementary Medicine*, 2000; 6(2), 159-169.

27. Astin, J.A., Why Patients Use Alternative Medicine: Results of a National Survey, *JAMA*, 1998; 279(19), 1548-1553.

28. Benor, D.J., Survey of spiritual healing research, *Complementary Medical Research*, 1990; 4(1), 9-33.

29. Benor, D.J., *Spiritual Healing*, Southfield, MI: Vision, 2002.

30. Crawford, C.C., Sparber, A.G., Jonas, W.B., A systematic review of the quality of research on hands-on healing: clinical and laboratory studies, *Alternative Therapies in Health and Illness*, 2003; 9(3), A96-A104. See also: Jonas, W.B., Crawford, C.C., *Healing, Intention and Energy Medicine*, New York, NY: Churchill Livingstone, 2003; xv-xix.

31. Jonas, W.B., The middle way: Realistic randomized controlled trials for the evaluation of spiritual healing, *The Journal of Alternative and Complementary Medicine*, 2001; 7(1), 5-7.

32. Jonas, W.B., Crawford, C.C., Science and spiritual healing: A critical review of spiritual healing, "energy" medicine, and intentionality, *Alternative Therapies in Health and Medicine*, 2003; 9(2), 56-61.

33. Schlitz, M., Braud, W., Distant intentionality and healing: assessing the evidence, *Alternative Therapies*, 1997; 3(6), 62-73.

34. Wiseman, R., Schlitz, M., Experimenter effects and the remote detection of staring, *Journal of Parapsychology*, 1997; 61, 197-208.

35. Wiseman, R., Schlitz, M., Experimenter effects and the remote detection of staring: an attempted replication, *Proceedings of Presented Papers: Parapsychological Association 42nd Annual Convention*, 1999; 471-479.

36. Sheldrake, R., *The Sense of Being Stared At*, New York, NY:

Crown, 2003.

37. Braud, W., Distant mental influence of rate of hemolysis of human red blood cells, *Journal of the American Society for Psychical Research*, 1990; 84 (1), 1-24.

38. Barry, J., General and comparative study of the psychokinetic effect on a fungus culture, *Journal of Parapsychology*, 1968; 32, 237-243.

39. Rauscher, E.A., Human volitional effects on a model bacterial system, *Subtle Energies*, 1990; 1(1), 21-41.

40. Grad, Bernard R., PK effects of fermentation of yeast, *Proceedings of the Parapsychological Association*, 1965(b); 2, 15-16.

41. Bengston, W.F., Krinsley, D., The effect of the "laying on of hands" on transplanted breast cancer in mice, *Journal of Scientific Exploration*, 2000; 14(3), 353-364.

42. Grad, Bernard R., The laying-on of hands: Implications for psychotherapy, gentling and the placebo effect, *Journal of the Society for Psychical Research*, 1967; 61(4), 286-305. (Also reproduced in: Schmeidler, Gertrude (Ed.), *Parapsychology: Its Relation to Physics, Biology, Psychology and Psychiatry*, Metuchen, NJ: Scarecrow Press,1976).

43. Grad, Bernard R., A telekinetic effect on plant growth: III. Stimulating and inhibiting effects, *Research brief, presented to the Seventh Annual Convention of the Parapsychological Association*, Oxford University, Oxford, England, September 1964(b).

44. Bunnell, Toni., The effect of "healing with intent" on pepsin activity, *Journal of Scientific Exploration*, 1999; 13(2), 139-148.

45. Muehsam, D.J., Markov, M.S., Muehsam, P.A., Pilla, A.A., Shen, R., Wu, Y., Effects of qigong on cell-free myosin phosphorylation: Preliminary experiments, *Subtle Energies*, 1994; 5(1), 93-108.

46. Rein, G., 1986. A psychokinetic effect on neurotransmitter metabolism: Alterations in the degradative enzyme monamine oxidase. In: Weiner, Debra H. and Radin, Dean (Eds.): *Research in Parapsychology 1985*, Metuchen, NJ: Scarecrow Press, pp.77-80.

47. Yan, X., Lin, H., Traynor-Kaplan, A., Xia, Z-Q., Lu, F., Fang, Y., Dao, M., Structure and property changes in certain materials influenced by the external *qi* of qigong, *Material Research Innovations*, 1999; 2(6), 349-359.

48. Schlitz, M.J., May, E., Parapsychology: Fact or fiction? Replicable evidence for unusual consciousness effects. In: Hameroff, S.R., Kaszniak, A.W., Scott, A.C. (Eds.), *Toward a Science of Consciousness: II. The Second Tucson Discussions and Debates*, Cambridge, MA: MIT Press, 1998; 691-700.

49. Radin, D.I., Nelson, R.D., Evidence for consciousness-related anomalies in random physical systems, *Foundations of Physics*, 1989; 19, 1499-1514.

50. Radin, D., *The Conscious Universe*, San Francisco: HarperSanFrancisco, 1997.

51. Levin, J., "The Power of Love" [Interview] *Alternative Therapies in Health and Medicine*, 1999; 5(4), 78-86.

52. Levin, J., "A Prolegomenon to an Epidemiology of Love: Theory,
Measurement, and Health Outcomes." *Journal of Social and Clinical Psychology*, 2000; 19, 117-136.

53. Dossey, L., *Healing Words: The Power of Prayer and the Practice of Medicine*, New York, 1993.

54. Dossey, L., *Reinventing Medicine*, San Francisco, Calif: HarperSanFrancisco, 1999.

55. Jonas, W.B., Crawford, C.C., *Healing, Intention and Energy Medicine: Scientific Research Methods and Clinical Applications*, New York: Churchill Livingstone, 2003.

56. Dossey, L., Eternity Medicine. In: *Reinventing Medicine*, San Francisco, CA: HarperSanFrancisco, 1999; 2-3-226.

57. Dossey, L., Era III Medicine. In: *Meaning & Medicine*, New York: Bantam, 1989; pp. 189-193.

58. Tart, C.T., *Body, Mind, Spirit: Exploring the Parapsychology of Spirituality*. Charlottesville, VA: Hampton Roads, 1997.

59. Stoeber, M., Meynell, H. eds., *Critical Reflections on the Paranormal*, Albany, NY: SUNY Press, 1996.

60. Griffin, D.R., *Parapsychology, Philosophy, and Spirituality: A Postmodern Exploration*, Albany, NY: SUNY Press, 1997; p. 264.

61. Dossey, L., Erwin Schrödinger, *Recovering the Soul*, New York: Bantam, 1989; pp. 125-137.

62. "You people: Intolerance and Alternative Medicine." *Alternative Therapies in Health and Medicine*, 1999; 5(2), 12-17, 109-112.

SCIENCE

The six essays in this section explore aspects of the history, philosophy and development of science, and try to gauge its potential for eventually accommodating the idea of consciousness being the kernel or "inside" of the so-called objective, material universe that mainstream science currently insists is the totality of reality. In their individual ways, our contributors argue that at its deepest, quantum-level roots, the material universe dissolves into a sea of energies and pure potential or virtuality, and that an abstract notion of matter isolated from consciousness is, essentially, an illusion. Our knowledge of reality is by definition subjective – the only way we know the universe is through the prism of consciousness, and even our scientific instruments are part of that process.

Matter is apprehended by mind, not the reverse.

INTRODUCTION TO THE ESSAYS IN THIS SECTION

AMIT GOSWAMI: *From Information to Transformation*
Physicist Goswami meditates on mental information processing, on mental and emotional intelligence, and describes their limitations. He argues for a greater use of what he refers to variously as "transformational intelligence" or, citing Sri Aurobindo, "supramental intelligence". This faculty allows a person to move "in the domain of archetypes" and even to transcend physical laws – to literally perform miracles. He complains that a deterministic materialistic worldview skews our understanding, relegating consciousness to the mere epiphenomenon of matter, concluding this to be a "faulty ideology". He associates supramental intelligence with the principles of quantum physics, and claims that though we all naturally possess supramental intelligence we allow it to lie dormant for one reason or another. He gives the reader some simple exercises to try out.

BERNARD HAISCH: *Reductionism and Consciousness*
After describing how modern science is beginning to glimpse "a deep connection between life and the universe", astrophysicist Haisch goes on to note that despite the fact that consciousness is "the *sina qua non* of human existence" many scientists can nevertheless manage to argue that it does not exist. He suggests that this "reductionist materialism" is effectively a dogma, thus impervious to evidence. Haisch reminds us what modern science is actually telling us, invoking the electromagnetic quantum vacuum, and links it with the sum of human experience and wisdom. He concludes by challenging the scientific skeptics to cease denying the evidence of phenomena and experiences that contradict the reductionist-materialist paradigm, while at the same time issuing a request to the mainstream institutions of religion to stop replacing the search for truth with "dogma and fairy tales and pat answers".

MARY F. SCHMITT: *If All is Consciousness, What Then is my Body?*
In seeking answers to the question posed in her essay title, neurophysiologist Schmitt takes us along with her down, down and down into the very fabric of the body and thus the very fabric of matter. She finds that the amount of "matter" that comprises her body could easily fit on the head of a pin. She then takes us down, down, down into the heart of that speck of matter to the truth that is at the end of all our journeys inwards.

DUANE ELGIN: *Living Universe: Toward a New Perceptual Paradigm*
The author provides a historical perspective to support his belief that the present time offers the potential to be a moment of cultural paradigm shift. He explains how the properties of the universe now being seen at the frontiers of modern science show it to be exhibiting the characteristics of all life – "unity, regeneration, freedom, sentience." He argues that consciousness is present throughout.

ERVIN LASZLO: *Elements of the New Concept of Consciousness*
Laszlo feels that claiming all is consciousness or that all is matter are *both* reductionist viewpoints. Rather, he argues that both elements are fundamental from the beginning, that the universe is "bi-polar", that mind and matter could be "distinct but complementary aspects of it". He observes that this "principle of complementarity" is recognized in quantum physics. In his view, the mental and physical aspects of the universe were "present in the primordial quantum vacuum", the "pre-space of the observed universe". A body and brain is seen as matter from the outside but experienced as consciousness from the inside. While tellingly pointing out that "contrary to widespread belief, there is no solid evidence that consciousness would be limited to an organism with an evolved brain", he does not deny that the complex human brain has a highly evolved consciousness with "articulated images,

thoughts and feelings". He remarks that the human brain "has enormous and as yet unused information processing capacity" that promises a yet higher evolution of consciousness.

ELISABET SAHTOURIS: *Prologue to a New Model of a Living Universe*
This final essay in this section provides us with the bridge to the next. Paying close attention to the root meanings of words such as "science", "physics", and "cosmos", Sahtouris gives a clear and concise view of the relationship between science and philosophy, detailing how the reductionist, materialistic modern model of the universe originated, developed and maintains itself. She highlights the paradox of eliminating the inventor of the machine-like universe in the materialistic approach. Although the "new sciences" of quantum physics and cosmology are refuting this view, the paradigm shift is still awaited. She lambasts science's "lack of moral accountability". She goes on in some detail to promote an "orderly model of the universe" – the very meaning of the word "cosmos" – a model that includes – *all* human experience.

FROM INFORMATION TO TRANSFORMATION
Amit Goswami

Some politicians love to say that this is the information age. They believe that processing information in such large scale as we are capable of today is the ultimate in our achievement and, therefore, the information age is the golden age of our civilization. This is a very narrow view of the human potential.

What is information? If you don't have any information about the answers to a problem, then all answers are equally probable, a not-so-desirable situation. With information, the probability of particular answers grow, and your chance of the getting the appropriate answer improves. So information is certainly useful. But information does not make you happy. Sure it can be exciting to use the e-mail to communicate extensively around the world and gather a large amount of information in a short time. And that may help to keep our worrying mind at bay. It is also an occasionally effective medicine against boredom to go surfing on the internet for information that may come in handy later. But is your worry gone because you gained information? Is your boredom gone from your extensive exploration of even more information? Hardly. The worrying mind gets anxious about the next item of worry. Stop net surfing, and the suffering called boredom is back again with gusto. The busy mind has to be kept busy or else it will be unhappy.

You can say that the intelligent use of information surfing is not to avoid boredom, but to amass power and money which can bring you happiness. But examine the life of people who have amassed power or money, those very innovative entrepreneurs of dot.com enterprises. Happiness is enjoying a relaxed moment, doing nothing. Are these entrepreneurs doing that? No, they are not capable of enjoying life, of being happy.

I am not saying that information processing is bad, just that it is a quite limited achievement. It gets boring after a while anyway. Surely, you can intuit that there must be more to being human than what power computers bring us. And it's not just about mental suffering or boredom. Look around you. There are environmental problems, a by-product of our search for money and power. We are running out of cheap energy! Violence, overcrowding, health care, there are problems galore, and surely you recognize that these problems are not tractable even with the best of information processing.

If information processing cannot give us tangible answers to questions of physical and mental health, of environmental pollution, of energy shortage, of violence and deterioration of society, is there another way to proceed that will give us tangible answers? I am saying that there is another way. Loosely speaking, it is the way of transformation. But the way is subtle and throughout human history it has been much misunderstood.

What is transformation? There are certain qualities of life that we all intuit. Happiness is such a quality. Health is another; beauty, truth, justice, love, are other such qualities. Transformation is that which gives us effortless access to these qualities of living. Consider an example. You see somebody's purse lying on the floor of a deserted waiting room of a airport. The thought may come to look inside and take any money or valuables that may be there. But this thought may be followed by other thoughts: what if the owner comes running to recover the purse; or, stealing is not a good thing, I shouldn't steal; or, it would not be fair to the person to take her valuables. So as a result of these thoughts, and a little wrestle with your conscience, you leave the purse alone. This is quite normal behavior. But there are people to whom the thought of looking into the purse, or picking it up (except for the purpose of finding the owner) would not even occur. Not stealing, not hurting another person unjustly, would come effortlessly to them.

Transformation enables us to effortlessly live qualities of life that we all covet: happiness, love, and all that. Now here is the confusion that we used to have in our past. In the past, up till now, transformation was considered the goal of human life. Life was regarded as suffering; so as you transcend suffering and become happy, what else is there?

You are liberated from this earthly existence. You have earned your place in heaven. But in a new worldview called the quantum worldview, this interpretation of the goal of transformation can easily be seen to be shortsighted. In the quantum view, heaven is existence, but only in possibility; it is not manifest existence. So the question becomes pertinent, can we bring heavenly perfection to manifest existence, to Earth? Can we use the power of the transformed mind to deal with the impossible societal problems of violence, energy shortage, ecological destruction, and, most of all, physical and mental health?

There is already talk about ageless body and timeless mind. How do we approach ageless body and timeless mind?[1] I submit that no amount of information processing will get you there. Sorry, fella; information processing is space bound, is time bound. You need to transform. But if we have ageless body and timeless mind, isn't that going to contribute to our overpopulation problem, to say the least? Myopic thinking again. The cosmos is very big. So far, advances in our materialist technology not withstanding, we have been exploring it very locally, as timebound people are apt to do. When we extend our being beyond time and space, we have the potential to really become players in the entire cosmic game. Sounds like science fiction? Well, truth can be even stranger than fiction.

The truth is, the information age, despite all the hype, is already passé. The age of transformation is the next great wave of the future. Want to ride it? Then be prepared to explore a new kind of intelligence, *supramental* intelligence.

Supramental Intelligence

What is intelligence? It is the capacity to respond appropriately to a given situation. People who gave us the IQ (intelligence quotient) test tell us that all our problem solving capacities are mental in nature; they are logical-rational, algorithmic capacities, and, as such, they are also measurable. So the intelligence quotient that IQ tests measure relates to our mental intelligence. Information processing is algorithmic, so people who tout rationalism are quite happy with IQ and rational-logical mental intelligence as the only measure of people's intelligence. Is there intelligence aside from and beyond mental intelligence? In the West, some people have long recognized the fashionableness in the culture to suppress emotions. We, men specially, are taught to suppress emotions because when emotions cloud our psyche, mind and mental logic cannot function very well, and even the best IQ is not of much help. Only by suppressing emotions, can we retain control, or so we are told. The problem with this approach is that if we become emotion suppressors, we not only suppress those negative emotions (such as anger) that are detrimental to appropriate action that demands reason, but we also tend to suppress positive emotions (such as love) that we covet, that we intuit add to the quality of life. What kind of intelligence is that that reduces the quality of life instead of enhancing it?

If you like science fiction, you can see the ongoing theme of the famous *UStar Trek* shows here: reason versus emotion. Reason is efficient, reason enables you to better function in a crunch, but without emotion where is any reason to live for? So in recent years, there has been much talk about emotional intelligence – intelligence that enables you to appropriately respond to emotions. But emotional intelligence is a funny beast. Suppose there is anger in your environment and you are caught up in it. Yet you are not suppressing it (that would be the approach of mental intelligence). But if you also express your anger as everybody else in the environment, wouldn't the situation only get worse?

Okay, so you neither express nor suppress, what happens? Have you tried it? If you have, you will have discovered very soon that it takes tremendous effort and discipline. So people of limited ability to exert effort and discipline would succumb to either suppression (in the West) or expression (in the East). Practices as espoused in popular books[2] buys you a little bit of leeway in dealing with emotion, but not much. Again it boils down to transformation. True emotional intelligence requires transformation. Can we transform so that staying with equanimity in the face of anger becomes effortless? Mental intelligence is useless here. Is there an intelligence that enables us to do that? There are also other situations when mental intelligence is useless, and information processing is useless. Mental information processing always takes place within given contexts of thinking. If the problem you are looking at requires a brand new context you are stuck, there is no amount of mental thinking or net surfing that is of help.

Toward the end of the nineteenth century, Einstein was trying to integrate two seemingly contradictory theories of physics, one by Newton, another by the nineteenth century great Clerk Maxwell, but to no avail for about ten years. Then one fine morning, he realized that he was thinking about time in an old accepted context (as all information or mental processing does) and that was the trouble. In an inspired moment he realized the context-shifting insight that contrary to then accepted dogma that time was absolute, independent of motion, time is actually relative, it changes with motion. This shift of context of thinking about time, led him to a new integrated physics from which came the famous formula $E = mc^2$. Einstein's was an act of what we now call fundamental creativity – discovery of a new context of thinking.[3] Einstein himself said later, I did not discover relativity by rational thinking alone. First came the insight, then rational thinking to help manifest the insight.

I submit that there is a new kind of intelligence that is involved in the case of both emotional equanimity and fundamental creativity: I will call it supramental intelligence following the lead of philosopher-sage Sri Aurobindo.[4]

Are there still other situations that call for supramental intelligence? How do you discriminate between good and evil? Logic, fear of retribution, this kind of thing can help you some, but that is (a) always too much effort, and (b) sometimes there may not be any guidance available at all from known information. What do you do then? I submit that this ability to discriminate between good and evil requires supramental intelligence.

There is still another situation calling for supramental intelligence. If you have been in a relationship, especially a romantic love relationship, then you know that there is a great challenge toward developing a truly satisfying relationship – it is the ability to achieve unconditional love. What is unconditional love? Again as the words indicate, it is love without reason, without the imposition of conditions that reason demands. This man must support me in order for me to love him. This woman must keep me sexually satisfied in order for me to love her. But impositions of this kind of mental/logical demand only constrains the relationship, and it goes nowhere. Unconditional love is of supramental origin. It is a signature of supramental intelligence.

There are other instances of supramental intelligence which are more controversial. Among these, one I need to mention: miracles. There are examples of people in all cultures around whom miracles, in apparent violation of physical laws, take place. So people of supramental intelligence potentially even have control over physical laws.

Fundamentally then, supramental intelligence is the ability to move in the domain of consciousness that involves the contexts of thinking and feeling, and even those of physical laws. Plato called this the domain of archetypes. The psychologist Carl Jung recognized this as the domain from whence comes our intuition.

Supramental Intelligence and the Quantum

UI stated earlier that there is much misunderstanding about transformation. Similarly, although Sri Aurobindo introduced the idea of the supramental many decades ago, this idea also has been much misunderstood. I submit that we have to use concepts of quantum physics in order to truly understand transformation and its vehicle, supramental intelligence.

Does quantum physics apply to us? It was originally discovered through the study of the motion of elementary particles at the atomic and subatomic level, and many people still cannot get over the prejudice that quantum thinking must be confined to only when we deal with the submicroscopic world. The same people also think that the world is fundamentally made of matter, the world is objective, local and rational, and deterministic. In other words, these people cannot rise beyond their IQ mental intelligence in their belief system, although many of them take regular forays into supramental intelligence when they creatively discover the solutions to their scientific problems. But their relationship with the world outside their profession is seriously handicapped because of their faulty belief system: they usually live a loveless life, they cannot discriminate between good and evil consequences of their scientific or social work (they are not bothered by their developing the atomic bomb or such things), and happiness and equanimity escape them but they don't know why. The problem with a worldview that is strictly objective, deterministic, and materialist (such a worldview is formally called material realism) is that it gives us a highly skewed view of us, our consciousness, our conscience, and our values. In materialism, everything is made of matter; thus consciousness (and all subjective phenomena related to it such as conscience) are relegated to mere epiphenomena of matter (as a gold ornament is an epiphenomenon of gold) without causal efficacy. If consciousness has no causal efficacy, how can we transform? How can we apply the dictates of our conscience? How can we love?

But science is changing and some scientists are realizing that they have to take a transformative path in order to develop a twenty-first century science that can deal with transformation.[5] These scientists are using supramental intelligence consciously. It is as a result of their work that today a scientific treatment can be given of transformation and supramental intelligence that removes all confusion on this subject.

Once you understand the quantum principles, it greatly facilitates your entry to supramental intelligence. The truth is, you (and everybody) already have it; you just don't use it for one reason or another. The materialist scientist does not use it optimally because of faulty ideology in which he or she has vested interest. What is your reason?

With help from quantum principles, as explained below, I am convinced your reasons for avoiding supramental intelligence will dissipate and you will be able to move on to the transformative path, leaving behind the so-called information superhighway to nowhere. The world and its twenty-first century problems need you and your supramental intelligence.

You probably like to dance occasionally. Dancing has a unique spontaneity that sometimes surprises you; the dancing seems to happen by itself, effortlessly. When supramental intelligence manifests in us, it is like this, it is dancing in the world all the time. Will you, won't you, will you, won't you, won't you join the dance?

The Quantum Tools for Supramental Intelligence and Transformation

Why is transformation a relatively rare commodity? The psychologist Abraham Maslow who did one of the first definitive studies of trans- formed people (Maslow's term for this people was people of positive mental health) estimated that maybe five percent of all people are transformed. What is the explanation of this rarity?

Let's put it in a different way, following the mystic philosopher Jiddu Krishnamurti. Krishnamurti used to chide people (I will para- phrase): why can't you change? Why can't you embrace nonviolence? Great teachers have given you the message of nonviolence for millen- nia, and good recipes, too. You all have tried to follow them. But why do you fail? Why does a vast majority of people fail? Because you try to be nonviolent in a continuous way. You think, today I will be little less violent, and tomorrow even less. It doesn't work like that!

So how does transformation work, if not through continuous effort, if not by applying rational intelligence? Can any movement, any change be discontinuous? There are two reasons that people tend to be skeptic about discontinuous change. One is that they seldom experience a discontinuous movement of consciousness. Generally, our experiences are continuous. We look outside, close our eyes or go to sleep; when we open our eyes or wake up from sleep, we see the same outside world. Continuity seems to prevail. If we look inside, we find thoughts and feelings that seem to make up a stream of consciousness. The second reason for skepticism is the brainwashing that goes on today under the guise of scientific education in favor of rationality, in favor of continuous algorithmic answer to every problem. But quantum physics from its very inception is telling us about the validity of the concept of discontinuous movement. Consider Niels Bohr's picture of the discontinuous movement of the electron in the atom. In the atom, the electrons go around the nucleus, the core of the atom, in orbits; this part of the electron's movement is continuous, one little bit at a time. But when the electron jumps from one orbit to another, something it does whenever there is emission of light from the atom, the electron never goes through the intervening space. A moment it is here; and then it is there instantly. This quantum leap, Bohr style, remains a good example of discontinuous movement in nature even today.

Can we describe the movement of quantum leap via continuous algorithms, via mathematics, via causal logic, via mechanical modeling? No. So where does the doctrine of continuity (which underlies determinism; if motion can be determined even in principle, continuity must prevail so we can calculate at least in principle) stand now? The doctrine of continuity has to be given up!

The realist can still hope that maybe quantum physics is not the final theory of physics, or maybe quantum physics can be reformulated in such a way that continuity prevails. But quantum physics' success seem to indicate the futility of this kind of hope. Alternatively, the realist can hope that although discontinuity undeniably prevails in the submicroscopic world, maybe it does not make it to the macroworld of our experience. Maybe when the movement of jillions of submicroscopic objects are involved, all discontinuity gets wiped out and continuity prevails once more. But this hope also does not hold up.[6]

And as for your lack of personal experience of discontinuous movement of consciousness – relax. It is not as foreign to you as you think. Have you seen the cartoon, *The Physics Teacher*, by Sidney Harris ? Einstein stands before a blackboard trying to discover his law $E = mcP^2$. He writes $E = maP^2$ and crosses it out. Next he tries $E = mbP^2$ and crosses it out. The caption says, "The creative moment". Why do you laugh when you see the cartoon? Because intuitively you know that creative discoveries do not involve step-by-step continuity; instead they are the product of discontinuous insight. The truth is, when you were a child you used to take such discontinuous quantum leaps of thought quite regularly. That's how we learn things that require new contexts of thinking, such as a new mathematical concept, reading meaning in a story, abstract thinking for the first time, and so on. And if childhood is too remote, think of those moments when you intuit something. What happens? What is intuition? Why do you call certain thoughts intuition? Because there is no rational continuous explanation for such thoughts; there is no contextual precedent for such thoughts. An intuition is your glimpse at a quantum leap.

Transformation involves the same kind of discontinuous quantum leap in the movement of consciousness as acts of creativity in science, math, art, music. I call the latter acts of outer creativity and the former inner creativity for this reason.

So the first quantum tool of supramental intelligence is discontinuous quantum leap. There are others. Before we delve into them, let's consider a few practices for quantum leaping.

Exercise: exploring gaps in the stream of conscious thinking

Sit quietly and comfortably with back straight. Close your eyes and watch your thoughts as they come into awareness and fade away from awareness. Try not to be partial to any particular thought; regard all of them as the same passing show. The analogy of watching clouds may help. When you start this meditation, you will notice how one thought is quickly replaced by another. Your mind is racing. After a while, especially with practice, you will see your mind slowing down and successive thoughts will seem to appear with distinct gaps between them. Don't get too excited. You have not discovered "no thought" or emptiness of mind because even in the gap your subject-object split of awareness remains. However, this is a good place to be because quantum leaping is much facilitated from such a place.

Exercise: exploring sudden involuntary phenomena
When you are in the midst of seemingly sudden involuntary phenomena such as a sneeze or an orgasm, be intensely aware. Practice to see if you can stop yourself right before sneezing or right before an orgasm. Again, a sneeze or even a sexual orgasm is not a quantum leap or a true discontinuity. But being aware in such moments is a proven recipe for the facilitation of a quantum leap.

Exercise: exploring the gap between sleep and wakefulness
Watch carefully if you can remain aware right down to the junction of wakefulness and sleep. From this awareness also quantum leaping is a distinct possibility. You may have heard how many creative people get their idea while in a reverie; this is precisely your objective.

If you want more practices like this with the same objective of quantum leaping, read the appendix of Paul Reps' book on Zen; they are called the 112 meditation techniques of Siva.[7]

Quantum Nonlocality
Consider now another important principle of the realist's worldview, locality. Locality is the idea that all influences that cause movement or change travel through space and time continuously, a little bit at a time. So influences that are in the local vicinity have more effect; the influences further away are less effective. An example derives from how a wave affects an object. When the object is close, the power of the wave reaching out to the object is strong. But at twice the distance, this power attenuates to only one fourth of the previous strength. Furthermore, Einstein proved with his relativity theory (and experimenters have verified Einstein's relativity many times over) that

influences can propagate in space and time only subject to a speed limit, the speed of light (300,000 km/second). This is also part of the locality principle.

But for quantum objects, the locality principle does not hold. Ironically, Einstein, whose relativity theory was instrumental for establishing the locality principle, was the first to see (along with two other collaborators Nathan Rosen and Boris Podolsky) that if two quantum objects interact they become so correlated that their mutual influence persist unabated even at a distance, even when they are not interacting via any local force or exchanging any local signals. The experimental verification of the idea came via the work of physicist Alain Aspect and his collaborators. They watched two photons emitted with quantum correlation from the same calcium atom continuing their correlated dance even when separated by distance, even when no signals were exchanged between them.

Quantum nonlocality has now been directly verified even for human subjects (correlation between brains), leaving no doubt that quantum physics does apply to us, to the macroworld under suitable subtle situations. Let us go into this experiment in some detail. Two subjects meditate with the intention of direct communication without signals. After twenty minutes, they separate in two different electromagnetically isolated chambers while still continuing their meditative intention of direct communication. Both subjects' brains are connected to individual electroencephallogram (EEG) machines. Now one subject is shown a series of light flashes; his or her brain responds with electrical activity which is measured by the EEG and is called an evoked potential. The other subject doesn't see any light flashes, nor has even the knowledge when light flashes are going to be displayed to the first subject. In spite of this, the EEG of the second subject shows (in roughly twenty-five percent of cases) an unmistakable electrical activity so similar in strength and phase to the evoked potential of the first subject that it can only be interpreted as a *UtransferredU* potential – electrical activity passed nonlocally from the first subject.[8]

Nonlocal connections between humans have been known to exist for millennia in such phenomena as mental telepathy. What is special about the experiment above is that it is objective and the role of meditation and intention is so clearly seen. Indeed control subjects who do not meditate together or cannot hold the intention of direct communication never show a transferred potential.

Our mind ordinarily works with local stimuli, either from the physical environment or from memory. In nonlocal communication, we transcend the local mind and use supramental intelligence. Like creatives who (somewhat unconsciously) use supramental intelligence in their professional field, psychics are people who display the supramental ability (again somewhat unconsciously) in the area of nonlocal communication. Quantum physics makes the idea of nonlocal communication of information scientifically feasible. But to see this, we have to clearly understand the role of consciousness in quantum nonlocality which is discussed in the next section. In the meantime, here are a couple of exercises for you to practice supramental intelligence via quantum nonlocality.

Exercise: distant viewing exercise

Sit with a friend who has in hand an object, which you know nothing about, hidden in a closed box. Meditate together with the intention of direct communication for about twenty minutes and maintain this meditative intention during the rest of the exercise which is distant viewing. You will try to "see" nonlocally without visual signals what's inside that box while your friend will visualize the thing inside the box. For best result, write down and draw pictures of what will appear to "pop" into the mind distinct from stream-of-consciousness thinking. After the exercise, compare your drawing etc with the physical object.

Exercise: meditation with a group of other meditators

To start with get a reference point by meditating about ten minutes by yourself. Then meditate another ten minutes with a group of other meditators. Notice if the quality of meditation is deeper. Repeat for a few days. If group meditation is consistently better for you than meditation individually, you are getting the hang of quantum nonlocality. Your supramental intelligence is being enhanced.

Exercise: quantum brainstorming or dialoging

You may know about brainstorming or dialoging. The idea is to communicate freely with another, listening without judgment and with attention and respect. In quantum dialoging, you also include speaking from a silence to give nonlocality a chance to work its magic. Take any topic, for example transformation, and have a quantum dialog with a friend. Write down the result. If the dialoging begins to produce new insights of discontinuous thought, it is a tell-tale sign of growing supramental intelligence.

Aside from discontinuity and nonlocality, quantum physics gives us two more tools for cultivating supramental intelligence: downward causation or freedom of choice and tangled hierarchy.

Downward Causation and Tangled Hierarchy

The most important of all the tools that quantum physics gives us for understanding and using supramental intelligence is downward causation. Mastering this one leads to transformation. What is downward causation? I mentioned before how quantum physics describes the movement of objects as possibilities, more exactly, as waves of possibility. Quantum mathematics gives us the algorithms to determine these possibilities and their individual probabilities as instances of *upward causationU* from the interactions of elementary particles to atoms, to molecules, to cells, all the way to our brain; but quantum physics is silent about what converts the possibilities into actual events of experience. It makes sense to think that we, consciousness, in the process of looking, choose the unique actuality from the myriad possibilities that quantum dynamics and upward causation creates. But if we think of consciousness as brain epiphenomenon as materialists do, then there is a paradox, the quantum measurement paradox. The paradox is resolved by turning the materialist metaphysics upside down – recognizing that consciousness is the ground of all being, and matter, including the brain, are the epiphenomena. [9]

So consciousness collapses the quantum possibility waves into actual events of experience; this is called downward causation. A little analysis shows that downward causation is (1) discontinuous, and therefore acausal and consists of free choice; (2) nonlocal; the consciousness that collapses is not the localized individual consciousness that we ordinarily experience, but is nonlocal, cosmic; and (3) self-referential leading to subject-object split; the self-referential nature of downward causation is the result of a tangled hierarchical dynamics of the quantum measurement in the brain. Our individuality arises from conditioning. [10]

These ideas of quantum physics resolves a fundamental problem of taking supramental intelligence seriously – dualism. How does the supramental domain of archetypes, nonphysical as it must be, interact with the physical? In the quantum view, the movements in the physical, the mental, and the supramental, all are possibilities within consciousness. Consciousness creates its manifest experience by collapsing correlated possibilities in each of these domains. The supramental determines the context, the mental gives meaning, and the physical makes representations of the mental meaning. [11]

The realization that consciousness mediates the nonlocal communication between people also solves the problem of information transfer. It is sometimes argued, via mathematical logic, that information transfer using quantum nonlocality is impossible. But when consciousness is in the game, the mathematics does not extend to consciousness and the argument against information transfer with quantum nonlocality falls through. [12]

So a fundamental component of the user's manual of supramental intelligence is the ability to act with creative freedom using downward causation. The crucial task is to learn to access the universal consciousness, also called the quantum self. The oriental system of yoga, which means union, is a technique to jump into the quantum self wherein lies our power of creative downward causation and supramental intelligence.

Self-referential collapse that gives us the subject-object split in an experience, is tangled hierarchical as opposed to simple hierarchical. What does this mean? In a tangled hierarchy, the levels of the hierarchy are codependent, each has causal efficacy over the other, and yet, the causal efficacy is only an appearance, coming from an inviolate level. In the case of the subject-object split, the causal efficacy is neither in the subject nor in the object, but in the consciousness beyond the subject-object split. When we learn to love tangled hierarchically, we have an opportunity to fall into the quantum self beyond the simple hierarchy of the ego. This gives another path to supramental intelligence.

I will end this discourse offering you a practice of creative downward causation that will help with your aspiration of supramental intelligence and lead you to transformation sooner or later.

Exercise: creative and transformative intention

Sit comfortably and quietly. An intention must start with the ego, that's where you are. So at the first stage, intend for yourself; be forceful, try to manifest your intention. At the second stage, recognize that you can have what you want in two ways, having it all by yourself, or having it because everybody (which includes you) gets it. So now intend for everyone. In the third stage, your intention must become a prayer: if my intention resonates with the intention of the whole, then let it come to fruition. At the fourth stage, the prayer must pass into silence, become a meditation.

References

1. Chopra, D., *Ageless Body, Timeless Mind*, NY: Harmony Books, 1993.

2. Goleman, D., *Emotional Intelligence*, NY: Bantam, 1997.

3. Goswami, A., *Quantum Creativity*, Kreskill, NJ: Hampton Press, 1999.

4. Aurobindo, Sri., *The Synthesis of Yoga*, Pondicherry, India: Sri Aurobindo Ashram, 1955.

5. Harman, W. and Clark, J. (eds.), *New Metaphysical Foundations of Modern Science*, Sausalito, CA: Institute of Noetic Sciences, 1994.

6. Goswami, A., *The Self-Aware Universe*, NY: Tarcher/Putnam, 1995.

7. Reps, P., *Zen Flesh, Zen Bones*, NY: Doubleday, 1957.

8. Grinberg-Zylberbaum, J. *et al.*, *Physics Essays*, 1994; 7, 422-428.

9. Goswami, A., Ibid, 1995.

10. Ibid.

11. Goswami, A., *The Visionary Window*, Wheaton, IL: Quest Books, 2000.

12. Ibid.

REDUCTIONISM AND CONSCIOUSNESS
Bernard Haisch

The perspective on consciousness within the mainstream community of physical scientists is in direct opposition to the possibility that consciousness may be primary, rather than being merely an epiphenomenon of the brain. Indeed, from my vantage point within that community I would guess that many of my fellow scientists would be quite unable to even comprehend how a "primacy of consciousness" perspective could be soberly articulated, the very idea appearing to most as supernatural mumbo-jumbo. Yet at the same time, glimpses are beginning to be seen within modern physics and astrophysics of remarkable coincidences of physical constants such as to permit the evolution of life and of a deep connection between properties of matter and an underlying sea of quantum energy, the latter being reminiscent of the role of light in the creation process of metaphysical cosmogonies.

It is quite amazing how two people, even within the same culture, can look at the identical thing and yet "see" something as different as black and white. To make the point, let me give a perhaps emotionally charged example. In 1996, California voters approved a proposition establishing a medical marijuana law, giving people the right, by state law, to grow and use cannabis to alleviate medical problems, as attested by a statement from a physician. To provide a safe supply – you don't want sick people having to hit the streets in search of pot dealers – numerous "clinics" sprang up across the state which grew marijuana plants and processed the products, in many cases working closely with local authorities to establish acceptable rules of operation. Of course, by federal law this remained strictly illegal. To show its authority, the federal government eventually began to selectively raid these clinics. In one particularly public confrontation, the mayor of Santa Cruz, along with five out of six City Council members and other local officials, gathered in the City Hall courtyard and passed out cannabis prod-

ucts (tinctures, cannabis-laced milk and muffins, buds for smoking) to
patients coming forward – according to the *San Francisco Chronicle* –
"in wheelchairs, on canes and with emaciated legs." All the while an
unmarked green helicopter hovered persistently overhead. Clearly the
city officials saw these people as patients and themselves as do-good-
ers helping the sick. How did the Drug Enforcement Agency see these
people? According to an official statement by their spokesman (who
shall remain anonymous): "We see them as victims of their traffick-
ers." A truly amazing black and white difference of perspective within
a common culture.

A corollary of this dichotomy is that it is virtually impossible for
each side not to regard the other as irrational and to experience strong
emotions in connection with this judgment. I confess, it makes me pretty angry to see the needs of sick people subordinated to politically-
motivated policies: demonstrating a vote-getting tough-on-drugs
stance by accusing the handicapped grannie in the wheelchair with her
Alice B.

Toklas brownie of being a criminal. I may have given away my perspective, but the point is made: if the subject is serious enough we get
quite angry with the perceived idiocy of the other side.

If there is anything that every non-comatose human being shares
with every other it is the experience of consciousness. Indeed, consciousness is the *sine qua non* of the human experience. I could not
write this, you could not read this, and we would not even be thinking
about what we are thereby missing without the existence of consciousness. The experiences of life are like waves riding upon the ocean of
consciousness. I would argue that Descarte already skipped the first
step when he wrote "Cogito, ergo sum" because I certainly sense that
even when I do succeed in suppressing any conscious thoughts, the
background hum of consciousness drones on in the gaps. And since I
am an ordinary human being and I sense that, I expect that everyone
else senses that too. But what is it that we are sensing?

The perspective on consciousness is no less dichotomous than the legal one. It seems to me to be the fundamental inner experience. I would regard my own consciousness as more certain than any rational knowledge I might possess. For while I could imagine being put into some delusional state in which I might deny the reality of the outer physical world, try as I might I cannot imagine denying my own consciousness. Is there logically even any way to consciously deny one's own consciousness? It is just there, and so I regard it as utterly fundamental, tied to, but even more basic than, my physical body. I regard the knowledge of my consciousness as a root knowledge, incapable of being taken away any more than you can have an ocean without the water.

And yet a very opposite perspective reigns in the field in which I have practiced a research career for a good many years. Modern western science regards consciousness as an epiphenomenon that cannot be anything but a byproduct of the neurology and biochemistry of the brain. I have written "cannot be anything but" rather than "is" because while this perspective is viewed within modern science as a fact, it is in reality far stronger than a mere fact: it is a dogma. Facts can be overturned by evidence, whereas dogma is impervious to mere evidence.

Philosopher Neal Grossman published a paper in the *Journal of Near Death Studies* called "Who's Afraid of Life After Death?" (the answer being modern western science, by the way) in which he relates a conversation with an academic colleague on the topic of the Near Death Experience. After the colleague is finished cavalierly dismissing the evidence of accurately reported details by near-death experiencers as coincidences and lucky guesses, he is asked by an exasperated Grossman: "What will it take, short of having a Near Death Experience yourself, to convince you that it is real." Rising to the occasion in a fashion, the colleague responds that "even if I were to have a Near Death Experience myself, I would conclude that I was hallucinating, rather than believe that my mind can exist independently of my brain." And then to dispose of the annoying evidence once and for all the colleague confidently states that, after all, it has been proven that the concept of mind existing independently of matter has been shown to be a false theory, and there cannot be evidence for something that is false. Grossman goes on to write that: "This was a momentous experience for me, because here was an educated, intelligent man telling me that he will not give up materialism, no matter what."

This conversation was a revelation to Grossman about the true nature of the concept of materialism within modern science: rather than being "an empirical hypothesis about the nature of the world which is amenable to evidence one way or the other" it is in actuality a dogma, an ideology.

The ideology of modern science is that of materialism, or more accurately reductionist materialism. There is a physical universe consisting of matter and energy which is governed by the four fundamental forces: electromagnetism, strong and weak interactions, and gravity. It gets fairly complicated in that matter can convert into energy and vice versa, in that gravity is regarded as a spacetime curvature according to General Relativity, and so on. And it is assumed that reductionism is the only way to analyze and understanding the origin of phenomena: you understand the machine by looking at the pieces and their functions and relationships. Now admittedly things get rather fuzzy when things get sufficiently complex: chaos theory shows how unpredictable macro effects can arise from micro causes, for example. And things, of course, get very fuzzy indeed in the quantum realm. Then it gets even more complicated when you take into account that, according to current theory, mini-dimensions orthogonal to our four-dimensional space are postulated to exist and superstring theory involves concepts and mathematics that even most competent physicists who are not specialists would admit to not grasping (at least perhaps to a colleague over a few post-colloquium beers). The details of the modern scientific view of reality are in thousands of books and literally millions of research papers and are only touched upon here, my point being simply that reality is regarded as something material, that is to say physical, built out of fundamental particles (called leptons and quarks which may actually be superstrings, and so on) and elementary processes which are utterly unconscious. The operative word is *unconscious*: whatever we are experiencing as consciousness can in actuality be nothing greater than a complicated form of unconsciousness, because after all, we are ultimately no more than the sum of our pieces and these are, indeed cannot be anything but, unconscious.

Now recognition is growing that the details of the laws of physics seem to be finely tuned so as to make our existence possible. Numerous authors have written about this in recent years, but the book *Just Six Numbers* by British Astronomer Royal Sir Martin Rees makes the point particularly well. He presents cogent arguments that it is a mere six numbers (specifying the strengths of physical constants, such as the ratio of gravitational to electrical attraction) that determine the nature of our universe and if their values were only slightly different, life would not be possible here.

One such number involves the strength of the force between two nucleons, and in particular the role of this number in the formation of carbon. All life on Earth is based on carbon. Astronomer Fred Hoyle identified a specific resonance that allows carbon to be built up in the three-step process that goes on inside stars, which is where the carbon we are made of ultimately came from. Even a few percentage points change in the strength of the nucleon-nucleon interaction determining this resonance would "severely deplete the amount of carbon that could be made" according to Rees, who cites the critical value for a habitable universe as four percent. In fact, a recent paper "Fine-Tuning Carbon-Based Life in the Universe by the Triple-Alpha Process in Red Giant Stars" by Heinz Oberhummer of the Vienna University of Technology and collaborators find this criterion to be ten times more stringent still. They conclude that, "Even with a change of 0.4 percent in the strength of the N-N force, carbon-based life appears to be impossible, since all the stars then would produce either almost solely carbon or oxygen, but could not produce both elements."[astro-ph/9908247] Regardless of whether it is four percent or four-tenths of one percent, this particular physical constant really is close to being just right, and in any event, there are five other constants that may not have to be just as goldilockian but have to at least be pretty good for us to exist, and when you multiply six small probabilities together the odds get tiny indeed, like rolling six dice and getting six of the same number.

I would say that most scientists who ponder such issues would call these arguments, about these just-right physical laws, pretty credible in terms of their impact on a habitable universe. Based on that, one might naively assume that since the universe seems finely-tuned in just such a way as to enable life to exist, it must have been tailor-made for that purpose. But no, that is not the conclusion the modern scientist comes to. The only acceptable conclusion is one compatible with the ideology of reductionist materialism and that has to be something along the following lines.

We reject *a priori* the possibility of a designed universe and so we assume that the just-right universe we are living in was created by chance. How can that be? Simple. We assume that instead of just one, there must be a huge, perhaps even infinite, number of other universes, in other hyperspaces, in other times, in other dimensions, in other somewheres. Then if so, by the law of probability one has to be just right, purely by chance. Of course since that is the only one we can exist in, that's the one we see around us.

An infinite number of utterly unconscious universes in which one turns out to be purely by chance just right for the evolution of beings whose material brains evolve enough neuro-chemical complexity to create the illusion of consciousness is preferable to the notion of a conscious creator making a physical universe in order for conscious beings to experience physical existence. Two radically different perspectives indeed.

What arguments can each side muster for its position? On the side of mainstream science, the next best thing to facts is a good theory, and indeed a theory of cosmic inflation has been developed over the past two decades. Originally proposed to explain the remarkable uniformity of our own Universe in all directions, it has since been expanded, if I may use that term, to justify the assumption of an unlimited ensemble of universes springing into existence spontaneously. Consider the original theory of inflation to be like blowing a bubble (our Universe). The surface of a bubble is pretty much the same all over when you blow it up and this is the desired analogy to a homogenous (on the largest scale) universe. The expanded theory of inflation is founded on the realization that the same inflationary process (if real) would let new bubbles form spontaneously and blow themselves up on the surfaces of old bubbles, and this would yield a kind of infinite foam of ceaseless bubble expansion and creation, each bubble in

the foam being a new, and perhaps totally different kind, of universe. It is difficult to assess the strength of this idea because there are several variations of this theory, all based upon observations and first principles in a fairly *ad hoc* fashion. I would characterize the competing ensemble of inflation theories as highly mathematicized conceptualization of how hypothesized fields of positive and negative energies together with quantum laws can allow for an unending spin-off of universes from each other. In other words, if you really want to believe in an infinite number of random universes, inflation theory can reconcile that with the laws of physics we know today.

I would say that the most substantive evidence for the other perspective comes from the inner experiences that countless people have had through the ages, including the Near Death Experience. Of course adherents of the reductionist-materialist belief immediately try to trump this by dismissing such evidence as merely subjective, hence by their pejorative interpretation of subjective, unreal. But this ploy amounts to no more than trying to win your argument by claiming you are right. If consciousness underlies the universe and our own consciousness is capable of seeing into or communicating with other levels of consciousness, then what people, especially mystics, have seen and experienced constitutes real data. Constructing a synthesis from the vast amount of data is the problem of course, this having been tackled by philosophers and theologians (as well as one particularly visionary German shoemaker) throughout history. Two books which I think are of particular value in this regard are *The Perennial Philosophy* by Aldous Huxley published in 1944 and still widely available, and *The Great Secret* by Belgian Nobel-laureate playwright Maurice Maeterlinck published in 1922 and difficult to find today.

It may not be very evident from within mainstream science, but it does appear that overall the idea that consciousness may be fundamental and matter secondary is gaining ground. The challenge for science is going to be to free the tools, experiments, observations and logic of the scientific method from the shackles of a reductionist-materialist ideology which cannot tolerate the concept of a real consciousness and especially any consciousness that would be primary over matter. Nonetheless it is possible – indeed I would say it is desirable – to think like a scientist without believing in the present-day physical model of reality as all there is and all there can be.

Over the last few years I have been privileged to be involved in scientific research that is strongly suggestive – to me at least – of an intersection between a concept deeply rooted in esoteric traditions and fundamental physics. One does not have to be a rocket scientist to discover that light is claimed to play a critical role in the creation process, the most obvious example in western literature being the opening lines of Genesis. Being an astronomer myself, I immediately spot a difficulty in that ancient account, of course, since the Creator is said to have made light a few "days" prior to creating the Sun and the stars. It is also written that he looked upon this and proclaimed it good, but to me as an astronomer it does not look very good at all, for the obvious reason that the God of Genesis seems to have successfully flipped the light switch before he got around to inventing the bulbs. Even if I were willing to let the "days" problem pass as a metaphor for some kind of passage of time which could be eons, the illogical sequence of events had always seemed to me to be the show stopper. But one day I happened to run across the following commentary on that problematic creation account in a Kabbalistic book called the *Haggadah*: "The light created at the very beginning is not the same as the light emitted by the sun, the moon and the stars. God concealed it, but in the world to come it will appear to the pious in all its pristine glory." (It also says, by the way, in a concept reminiscent of cosmic inflation: "Nor is the world inhabited by man the first of things earthly created by God. He made several worlds before ours, but he destroyed them all, because he was pleased with none until he created ours.")

Digging a bit more deeply into Kabbalistic literature one finds the claim that the origin of our universe was the result of a conscious act involving creation of some kind of void and a primordial light which filled that void and which led, *somehow*, to the manifestation of a "world" spawning a series of ever denser (i.e. less spiritual and more material, whatever that really means) "worlds", the last and lowest of which is our physical world of matter. This final manifestation of the lowest, physical world viewed from the inside is presumably the Big Bang. It is that *somehow* that I will come back to, but for the moment and for whatever it may be worth, I will risk a venture into deep waters by speculating on what the conceivable rationale might be behind this.

What would one do with infinite potential, some literally unlimited ability to do anything? Or to back up and put it in more prosaic, but more easily comprehensible, terms, imagine having a billion dollars in your bank account. Would this give you pleasure or satisfaction if you could never spend a penny of it? I doubt it. The joy of wealth is in the usage of it. What I picture in my limited human capacity is an unlimited conscious being of infinite ability whose ideas become our laws of physics. Now some ideas are mutually compatible – as in the six numbers scenario discussed above – and would result in created universes where evolution can take place and beings can live; whereas other ideas just wouldn't work together, resulting in pure chaos or inability to manifest at all owing to mutual contradictions. A square-circle universe is probably a non-starter. But infinity being what it is, there are probably an endless number of congenial combinations yielding universes with characteristics that may be utterly unimaginable to us, but which would still allow the essential purpose to be fulfilled: for the consciousness of the Creator to enter into whatever physical life form may be possible within that universe governed by its particular set of ideas-become-laws. In this way, the infinite Creator gets to "spend the billion dollars": by experiencing that which would otherwise be only sterile potential. And the punch line, it seems to me, is that the manifestations of the Creator in this particular physical universe are none other than all of us. The Creator experiences himself through us because he and we are one. At some level we all know this to be true because our consciousness is a part of the Creator's consciousness. In some literal sense we made our own universe and then entered into it, but it is better to not be fully aware of that because the experience of physicality has far greater possibilities if we do not consciously know all these details. It is a richer experience if we can live our lives as if they were all there is – what sense of satisfaction would there be for a scientist to make discoveries if she really already consciously knew all the laws of physics, having been part of their creation. It's no fun to discover the buried treasure if you already know where you hid it, but if you can contrive to forget where you hid it, the game is on. And to the objection that some lives seem to be patently unfair, or be the agent or victim of evil, I would say: think about whether it makes any sense to assume that a given consciousness only enters into physical life once. Our Universe is about fifteen billion years old and is expected to continue for many billions more. Why would an individualized spark of divine consciousness choose to limit its experience of physical existence to only, say, eighty years of life in some town? There is plenty of time in our Universe for karma to balance the good and the bad, the high and the low if that is how it works. Perhaps it may be useful to think of the law of karma as the analog for consciousness of the law of conservation of mass-energy or momentum for matter.

Returning to the *somehow* pertaining to the creation of a Universe of matter, I bring up a concept that may shed some light (literally) on this by perhaps giving us a bottom-up view from inside the physics laboratory of what may be going on, as opposed to lofty top-down cosmogonical speculation. I – and colleagues – have spent much of the last several years investigating the electromagnetic quantum vacuum, which is essentially the same concept as the zero-point field (which contains zero-point energy). Having been funded by NASA and by Lockheed Martin to do this, and having published papers in top-notch research journals on this topic, I am less than happy to see the concept of "zero-point field" claimed to underlie all manner of free energy gadgets and gizmos and well-intentioned but fuzzy New Age musings based on lack of understanding of what the zero-point-field concept actually is in physics.

Putting it in greatly simplified terms, what my colleagues and I have shown – using the analysis techniques of a discipline in physics called stochastic electrodynamics – is that the property that really makes matter the substantive stuff that it is, the property of mass, has a plausible origin in the electromagnetic quantum vacuum. Since this essay is not a physics paper, I am going to use the term "dense matter" in the sense that someone like Rudolf Steiner might have, to say that our concept suggests that dense matter is not as real as it looks. This is no attempt to foolishly deny the obvious. Certainly matter exists, it is just that it is not the dense massive stuff that we generally think of and that Newton built his mechanics on. When you sit in an airplane and it starts its take-off roll down the runway and you feel yourself pressed back against the seat, it is, we suggest, not some innate inertia of your body that is responsible, it is the mathematically derivable effect that the electromagnetic quantum vacuum is acting like a molasses. In our papers we showed in some detail that this molasses effect turns on when any bit of matter is accelerated and becomes stronger in direct proportion to the acceleration. A similar effect appears to underlie gravitational forces, and yes, this can be reconciled with the formalism of General Relativity. We are not interested in any Einstein bashing, especially since our entire approach is based upon Special Relativity.

The deep connection between physics and metaphysics that I see glimpses of in this work lies in the fact that the electromagnetic quantum vacuum is a form of light. It is an underlying sea of energy, predicted by the Heisenberg Uncertainty Principle, that permeates every tiny volume of space, from the emptiest intergalactic void to the depths of the Earth, the Sun, or our own bodies. In this sense, our world of matter is like the visible foam atop a very deep ocean of light. And it is worth noting that from the perspective of a beam of light, there is no space and time. Special Relativity is quite clear on this point: if an observer could ride a light beam, space would be infinitely contracted and time would be infinitely dilated. We astronomers talk about a photon from the Andromeda galaxy taking 2.2 million years to make the trip from there to our telescopes, and this is true from our vantage point. But the little photon does not see it that way at all. Its experience, if I may anthropomorphise a photon, is one instantaneous hop from its point of creation – most likely some star in the Andromeda galaxy – to its destruction in the detector at the end of the telescope. There is a profound hint here of how space and time become possible only when you slow down from the light reference frame.

These are indeed barely more than glimpses of deep connections, but they do address a heretofore unsuspected relationship grounded in theoretical physics between light and matter, a relationship which is paralleled but has never been articulated in such a promising way in esoteric metaphysics. Finally, I suggest that it is no accident that the thing that human consciousness encounters over and over again in the Near Death Experience is light.

This essay may strike some as emphasizing spiritual notions over those having to do with consciousness. Frankly I do not see how one can separate the two. If consciousness is indeed primary, then the "traveler's reports" of mystics who have accessed higher levels of consciousness absolutely must be taken seriously, and those leave no doubt that there is some universal consciousness transcending space and time in which we share. I think it is little more than cultural or social preference whether one uses the term God or universal consciousness, though I can appreciate how the seemingly endless problems traceable to bearded, patriarchal deities whose fantasized commands are quite un-godly can sour one on the first term.

The challenge for the institution of modern science is to be true to its foundational commitment to examining evidence and to resist the temptation to explain away evidence, such as the Near Death Experience, because it contradicts the reductionist-materialist paradigm. There is, however, a very similar challenge for the institutions of religion to replace dogma and fairy tales and pat answers with a genuine, unfettered search for the truth. Interestingly, in my opinion, the institutions of religion will have succeeded if they can eventually put themselves out of business, having helped humanity to achieve a level of consciousness that no longer requires a middleman. But on the other hand, I think we will practice some form of science forever – provided science can evolve beyond the constraints of its reductionist-materialist ideology – since curiosity seems to be an essential trait of consciousness.

(This essay is a version of a chapter in Bernard Haisch's book, *The God Theory: Universes, Zero-Point Fields and What's Behind it All.*)

IF ALL IS CONSCIOUSNESS, WHAT THEN IS MY BODY?

Mary F. Schmitt

If I look at my body in a full-length mirror (and depending upon the importance I give to my ego's assessment), I may see it as something to be liked and appreciated, or something that definitely needs work. But we are talking in these essays about the emerging paradigm that sees all that is as *consciousness*. So, what, then, *is* my body?

Agreeing on an understanding of what we mean by "consciousness" is imperative. Most people think of this word as applying only to the human type of awareness we experience during wakefulness. But the great Twentieth-Century scientist and mystic, Pierre Teilhard de Chardin, spoke of all matter as having a "within" as well as a without. The latter is what we study in all our sciences, but all matter, down to the tiniest subatomic component, he says, has a free, conscious, feeling, and spontaneous within. Alfred North Whitehead's radical revisioning of modern ontology, and the postmodern approach of "panpsychism" speak similarly. Consciousness, then, is in all matter, including every cell and organelle in my body.

But our problem here is that we tend to anthropomorphize this consciousness, and therefore to see such things as the "feelings" of a tree to be like our own. It must be a totally different subjective event for the simple reason that a tree has no limbic brain to process emotions, and therefore its feelings will probably have a very different quality from ours. Nevertheless it *is* conscious, *and* feeling. The Eskimos have some thirty-three words for "snow" and the native people of Hawaii have even more for "wave". We need at least that many for our understanding of the word "consciousness". In fact, we need a whole new language to grasp its fractal nature, and all its many states and nuances.

To really begin to understand the awesomeness of the mystery that is Me looking back at me, I must first consider the body's many dimensions. A woman's thumbnail, say, is approximately a centimeter across. If I divide that width into tenths, then divide one of those tenths into tenths, and do that four more times, I am at a level of magnification seen by the electron microscope, in the range of a millionth of a centimeter. In that domain, the body appears more like a vast sea, inhabited by many types of creatures. Ocean caves (pores of the skin) seem to be inhabited by various sea creatures (bacteria); nerve receptors in the inner ear look like sea anenomes, and the taste buds as beautiful floral arrangements. Schools of minnows are really sperm; seaweed flowing with the tides are the fallopian tubes, and if it is the right time of the woman's cycle, they would be welcoming a new egg. Sea snakes piggybacking giant sea lions are actually muscle tissue with nerve fibers running along their surface – and on and on. These beautiful beings are all meaningfully communicating with one another, and are vibrating, dancing, at their own natural rhythm, thousands of times a second, following an exquisitely timed choreography. One finds, when one looks and listens carefully, that each component is carrying on intelligent conversations with its neighbors, using a syntax and semantics that is specific to its role.

At each level of self-organization, then, information is being passed on, so that intelligent communication can happen in all of the body's complex interrelationships. For this to take place, subsystems at each level, and in every moment, will be encoding or decoding the data. For example, a cell must be able to carry on a conversation within its boundaries, and then encode that salient data into a form that can be understood at the next higher level of organization. Heart cells as an example, communicate within and among themselves in one language, and then encode the data into a language understood by the heart as a whole. The organ of the heart must first *de*code that data received from its cells so that it can use it, and then follow a similar *en*coding process to enable the entire cardiovascular system to understand, and on up the line of self organization. Therefore, there are a multitude of conversations going on within me using unique languages of biochemistry, at each level of complexity and at every moment of time. *This is my body!*

Yet we are still talking and thinking of the body as solid matter, which can be touched and seen, however many times it is to be magnified. But, if we continue that process of magnification from a millionth of a centimeter to approximately one hundred millionth that size (ten to minus 14 cm), we are at a domain where all semblance of solidity is gone. We are now viewing each atom of the body itself, and if we should enlarge its nucleus to about the size of a speck of dust, the electrons, when they do manifest, (because it is believed that the mind of an observer – some relationship – must be involved for that to happen) are hundreds of yards away. Everything else is emptiness. And yet, this is *me*. If I were to get rid of all the emptiness within me, I could easily sit on the head of a pin, with room left over. I am ninety-nine percent void!

As I continue the process of magnification, even referring to myself as "matter" is problematic. The hundreds of subatomic fragments of the protons and neutrons of the nucleus, such as leptons, mesons, quarks, though spoken of as particles, are not so much "entities", as intelligent, vibratory patterns of interacting, communicating energies. Some of these so-called "particles" can go backward in time, go into and out of existence – yet that is still *me*, the being looking back at me in the mirror. In the world of quarks, leptons, bosons, one can more readily speak of oneself as a "fire" person, an "earth" or "air" person, where these qualities of earth, air, fire, water refer, not to such things as dirt, H_2O, or nitrogen and oxygen, but to qualities of personality. It's how I am predisposed to relate to the world. These are qualities of *consciousness* or *mind,* not so much matter. Outwardly, they are understood as the equations, the force fields of quantum mechanics, while "within" they are the subjective expressions of the intelligence, the dynamics of my psyche.

In all of these comments, we have been speaking of this mysterious body in all its many dimensions – whether in size, or in subtlety – as *having* intelligence, or consciousness. But if we continue magnifying until we get to 10 to the minus 33rd centimeters, we are in the realm of Planck's length – as tiny as nature seems to want to go. At this point, we can no longer speak of space or time, or even of manifest reality. We are in "the Implicate Order", as David Bohm refers to it, where nature (including ourselves) does all her creating, holds all her memories (morphogenetic fields) and where what exists is infinite possibility – infinite potential. We are in the realm of "The Unified Field". There are probably an infinite number of implicate orders, each one more inclusive and subtle than the one before it. And I exist in all these domains – I simply don't know it yet. The whole challenge of my personal evolution is to bring that reality to my consciousness. Here, there is no distinction between myself as observer, what I am observing, or the act of observation itself – I am one with all that is in a timeless domain of infinite complexity but utter simplicity!

Back in the 1960s, a major change began to take place in our collective human consciousness, at least to that part of us that we might call "the left brain" of Mother Earth, that which is represented by western culture. Prior to this time, the materialistic, reductionistic, myopic thinking of the West left no room for intuitive insight, for learning in other states of consciousness, no awareness of realms in ourselves other than those opened by the rational mind, the logical intellect, or by what the limited senses, so hypnotized by our cultural beliefs, could absorb. So there was little probability, for the majority of us, of knowing any of these realms of ourselves. But then we discovered psychedelic drugs. While these are not the better means for opening doors of our psyche, there can be no doubt that they gave us access to other dimensions of our consciousness, and allowed us to begin to see what Stan Grof has called "the cartography of the psyche". More importantly, and synchronistically, our culture also began to listen to the great, especially eastern, spiritual masters, and learned to practice meditation. In doing so, we realized that we could access these other dimensions in a way that was not only healthier, but more under the mastery of our own inner wisdom. Furthermore, parapsychological research became a reputable science. Out-of-the-body, and near-death experiences seemed to happen to more and more people, and 'astral travel', clairvoyance, telepathy, and intuitive awareness were commonly accepted as valid. What was happening was that the realms of the quantum domain which were being opened to us *objectively* by science, were also opening to us, more and more *subjectively*, in the experience of these other realms of our awareness.

It is accepted by many today, even some scientists, that mind and body are the same thing, that they are two sides of the same coin. The body is the outer expression of self, and the mind is the inner experience of the same reality. In a similar way, we might say that the many domains of our consciousness is one side, and the quantum realm, interpreted by science in all its mathematical formulations is the other.

The challenge before me is to bring awareness to these hidden domains of my consciousness and to love, unconditionally, the truth, the whole truth, that is me. Numerous modern scholars have stated that the future of evolution is not the development of new, more exotic physical forms of plants and animals, or larger brains, but rather the *inward evolution of* consciousness, becoming aware that we are awareness, consciousness, itself. Intelligence, ego, emotion, soul, spirit are not "things" or "parts" of me. As the physicist David Bohm has said, "There is no such thing as a noun, only slow verbs." I am a "Becoming", more than a "Being". These are all dynamics of Self in the ever broadening, evolving, self-aware realms of Who I Am. My greatest challenge in life is to bring my awareness to these domains *which already exist*, and not only learning its language, but learning to converse on each of its many levels. I simply don't know or personally experience yet, that that is possible and important, nor do I have the wisdom or courage needed to open myself to the truth of All That I Am.

Ultimately, I *am* Consciousness, I *am* the "Jewel in Indra's Net" that reflects all jewels, I *am* one with the Void that is Everything, the Infinite Domains of the Implicate Order, the Unified Field , God Becoming.

The next time I see myself in the mirror, perhaps after shaking my head in disbelief, I can wink at the person I see, smile with my reflection, throw myself a kiss and most importantly, love unconditionally that Mystery I see before me.

LIVING UNIVERSE:

Toward a New Perceptual Paradigm
Duane Elgin

I believe that the most far-reaching trend of our times is an emerging shift in our shared view of the universe – from thinking of it as dead to experiencing it as alive. In regarding the universe as alive and ourselves as continuously sustained within that aliveness, we see that we are intimately related to everything that exists. This insight – that we are cousins to everything that exists in a living, continuously regenerated universe – represents a new way of looking at and relating to the world, and overcomes the profound separation that has marked our lives. From the combined wisdom of science and spirituality is emerging an understanding that could provide the perceptual foundation for the diverse people of the world to come together in the shared enterprise of building a sustainable and meaningful future.

Fundamental shifts in perception happen slowly, are subtle, and often seem inconsequential or even go unnoticed by the majority of people living through them. Yet such shifts amount to nothing less than revolutions in our sense of ourselves, our relationships with others, and our view of the universe. Only three times in human experience has our view of reality been so thoroughly transformed.

The first transformation occurred when humanity "awakened" roughly 35,000 years ago. The archeological record shows that the beginnings of a reflective consciousness emerged decisively at this time as numerous developments were occurring in stone tools, burial sites, cave art, and migration patterns. Because we were just awakening to our capacity for "knowing that we know," we were surrounded by mystery at every turn. Nonetheless, human culture was born in these first glimmerings of personal and shared awareness.

The second time our view of reality and human identity changed dramatically was roughly 10,000 years ago when our ancestors shifted from a nomadic life to a more settled existence in villages and farms. Mid-way during the agrarian period, roughly 5,000 years ago, we see the rise of city-states and the beginnings of civilization.

The third time that our perceptual paradigm transformed was roughly 300 years ago, following the scientific revolution, when the stability of agrarian society gave way to the radical dynamism and materialism of the industrial era. Each time that humanity's prevailing paradigm has changed, all aspects of life have changed with it, including the work that people do, the ways they live together, how they relate to one another, and how they see their role in society and place in the universe.

We are now living at a time when humanity's perceptual paradigm is again undergoing one of its rare shifts, and that shift has the potential to dramatically transform life for each of us. A paradigm shift is much more than a change in ideas and how we think. It is a change in our view of reality, identity, social relationships, and human purpose. A paradigm shift can be felt in the body, mind, and soul.

At the heart of the new paradigm is a remarkable idea: Our cosmos is not a fragmented and lifeless machine (as we have believed for centuries) but is instead a unified and living organism. Although it is new for our times, the idea that the universe is alive is an ancient one. More than 2,000 years ago, Plato described the universe as "one Whole of wholes" and "a single Living Creature that encompasses all of the living creatures that are within it." What is unprecedented is how this notion is being informed today by both modern science and the world's diverse spiritual traditions (see Note: "The Mother Universe").

Scientific Evidence of a Living Universe

Less than a hundred years ago, when Einstein was developing his theory of relativity, he considered the universe a static, unchanging system no larger than the cloud of stars we now know to be our galaxy. Today, we know that the universe is expanding rapidly and contains at least a hundred billion galaxies, each with a hundred billion stars, or more. Our cosmos embodies an exquisitely precise design. Researchers have calculated that if the universe had expanded ever so slightly faster or slower than it did (even by as little as a trillionth of a percent), the matter in our cosmos would have either quickly collapsed back into a black hole or spread out so rapidly that it would have evaporated.

It is reasonable to assume that if our cosmos is alive it would exhibit specific properties characteristic of all life – unity, regeneration, freedom, sentience, and a capacity for self-reproduction. These in fact are among the properties of our universe emerging from the frontiers of modern science. The cosmos is a unified system. Physicists once viewed our universe as composed of separate fragments. Today, however, despite its unimaginably vast size, the universe is increasingly regarded as a single functioning system. Because other galaxies are millions of light years away, they appear so remote in space and time as to be separate from our own. Yet experiments show that things that seem to be separate are actually connected in fundamental ways that transcend the limitations of ordinary space and time. Described as "nonlocality," this is one of the most stunning insights from quantum physics.

Although scientists working in this domain hold divergent views about the implications of quantum mechanics for our everyday lives, physicist David Bohm says that ultimately we have to understand the entire universe as "a single undivided whole." Instead of separating the universe into living and nonliving things, Bohm sees animate and inanimate matter as inseparably interwoven with the life-force that is present throughout the universe, and that includes not only matter, but also energy and seemingly empty space. For Bohm, then, even a rock has its unique form of aliveness. Life is dynamically flowing through the fabric of the entire universe.

Our home galaxy – the Milky Way – is a swirling, disk-shaped cloud containing a hundred billion or so stars. It is part of a local group of nineteen galaxies (each with a hundred billion stars), which in turn is part of a larger local supercluster of thousands of galaxies. This supercluster resembles a giant many-petaled flower. Beyond this, astronomers estimate that there are perhaps a hundred billion galaxies in the observable universe. Scientists and spiritual seekers alike ask the question: If this is a unified system, then could all this be but a single cell within a much greater organism?

The cosmos is continuously regenerated. For decades, the dominant cosmology in contemporary physics has held that creation ended with the Big Bang some fourteen billion years ago and that, since then, nothing more has happened than a rearranging of the cosmic furniture. Because traditional physicists think of creation as a one-time miracle from "nothing," they regard the contents of the universe – such as trees, rocks, and people – as being constituted from ancient matter. In sum, the dead-universe theory assumes creation occurred billions of years ago, when a massive explosion spewed out lifeless material debris into equally lifeless space and has, by random processes, organized itself into life forms on the remote planet-island called Earth.

In striking contrast, the living-universe theory proposes that the cosmos is completely recreated at each moment, and is maintained, moment by moment, by an unbroken flow-through of energy. Imagine the cosmos as the vortex of a tornado or a whirlpool, as a completely dynamic structure. David Bohm calls the universe an "undivided wholeness in flowing movement." In this view, our universe has no freestanding material existence of its own. The entire cosmos is being regenerated at each instant in a single symphony of expression that unfolds from the most minute aspects of the subatomic realm to the vast reaches of thousands of billions of galactic systems.

It overwhelms the imagination to consider the size and complexity of our cosmos with its billions of galaxies and trillions of planetary systems, all partaking in a continuous flow of creation. How can it be so vast, so subtle, so precise, and so powerful? "We are not stuff that abides, but patterns that perpetuate themselves; whirlpools of water in an ever-flowing river," states the mathematician Norbert Wiener. Physicist Max Born, adds: "We have sought for firm ground and found none. The deeper we penetrate, the more restless becomes the universe; all is rushing about and vibrating in a wild dance." Physicist Brian Swimme tells us, "The universe emerges out of an all-nourishing abyss not only twelve billion years ago but in every moment."

The foundation of the cosmos is freedom. Traditional physicists have seen the cosmos as being like a clockwork mechanism locked into predetermined patterns of development. By contrast, the new physics maintains that the cosmos has the freedom and spontaneity to grow in unexpected ways. Uncertainty is so fundamental that quantum physics describes reality in terms of probabilities, not certainties. No one part of the cosmos determines the functioning of the whole; rather, everything seems to be connected with everything else, weaving the cosmos into one vast interacting system. Everything that exists contributes to the cosmic web of life at each moment, whether it is conscious of its contribution or not. In turn, it is the consistency of interrelations of all the parts of the universe that determines the condition of the whole. We therefore have great freedom to act within the limits established by the larger web of life within which we are immersed.

A living universe is a learning system in which we are free to make mistakes and to change our minds. "Through us, the universe questions itself and tries out various answers on itself in an effort – parallel to our own – to decipher its own being," writes the philosopher Renee Weber.

Consciousness is present throughout. Consciousness, a capacity for feeling or knowing, is basic to life. If the universe is alive, we should therefore find evidence of some form of consciousness operating at every level. Renowned physicist Freeman Dyson writes about consciousness at the quantum level: "Matter in quantum mechanics is not an inert substance but an active agent, constantly making choices between alternative possibilities ... appears that mind, as manifested by the capacity to make choices, is to some extent inherent in every electron." This does not mean that an atom has the same consciousness as a human being, but rather that an atom has a reflective capacity appropriate to its form and function.

Dyson thinks it is reasonable to believe in the existence of a "mental component of the universe," and that, if so, "then we can say that we are small pieces of God's mental apparatus." While it is stunning to consider that every level of the cosmos has some degree of consciousness, that seems no more extraordinary than the widely accepted view among scientists that the cosmos emerged as a pinpoint some twelve billion years ago as a "vacuum fluctuation" – where nothing pushed on nothing to create everything.

The cosmos is able to reproduce itself. A remarkable finding from the new physics is that our cosmos may very well be able to reproduce itself through the functioning of black holes. In his book, *In the Beginning: The Birth of the Living Universe*, astrophysicist John Gribbin proposes that the bursting out of our universe in the Big Bang may be the time-reversed mirror image of the collapse of a massive object into a black hole. Many of the black holes that form in our universe, he reasons, may thus represent the seeds of new universes: "Instead of a black hole representing a one-way journey to nowhere, many researchers now believe that it is a one-way journey to somewhere – to a new expanding universe in its own set of dimensions." Gribbin' s dramatic conclusion, reflecting the work of many physicists and cosmologists, is that "our own Universe may have been born in this way out of a black hole in another universe." He explains it in this way: If one universe exists, then it seems that there must be many – very many, perhaps even an infinite number of universes. Our universe has to be seen as just one component of a vast array of universes, a self-reproducing system connected only by the "tunnels" through space-time (perhaps better regarded as cosmic umbilical cords) that join a "baby" universe to its "parent." Gribbin suggests not only that universes are alive, but also that they evolve as other living systems do: "Universes that are 'successful' are the ones that leave the most offspring."

The idea of many universes evolving through time is not new. David Hume noted in 1779 that many prior universes "might have been botched and bungled throughout an eternity ere this system."

In the light of recent scientific findings, our universe is revealing itself to be a profoundly unified system in which the interrelations of all the parts, moment-by-moment, determine the condition of the whole. Our universe is infused with an immense amount of energy, and is being continuously regenerated in its entirety, while making use of a capacity or consciousness throughout. As an evolving, growing, and learning system, it is natural that freedom exists at the quantum foundations of the universe. It even appears that the universe has the ability to reproduce itself through the mechanism of black holes. When we put all of these properties together, it suggests an even more spacious view of our cosmic system. Our universe is a living system of elegant design that was born from and is continuously regenerated within an even larger universe. We are living within a "daughter universe" that, for twelve billion years, has been living and growing within the spaciousness of a Mother universe. The Mother Universe may have existed forever, holding countless daughter universes in its grand embrace while they grow and mature through an eternity of time. [1]

Implications of the Living Universe Paradigm

Like any paradigm shift, the idea and experience of a living universe is transformative. In addition to changing our view of the universe, it can alter our sense of identity, our sense of purpose, how we relate with others. Let's consider a few of its many implications.

A rebirth of connectedness in all aspects of life

The ways American Indians perceive and experience the world is instructive. Their culture provides a clear window into the experience of living with an infusing aliveness that is an intimate part of everyday life. Author Luther Standing Bear expresses the wisdom of indigenous peoples around the world when he says that, for the Lakota Sioux, "there was no such thing as emptiness in the world. Even in the sky there were no vacant places. Everywhere there was life, visible and invisible, and every object gave us a great interest in life." Since a life force was felt to be in and through everything, all things were seen as being connected and related. Because everything is an expression of the Great Spirit, everything deserves to be treated with respect.

The awakening of cosmic identity

In the industrial era paradigm, we are no more than biological beings, ultimately separate from others and the rest of the universe. The new findings from physics, however, reveal that we are intimately connected with the entire cosmos. Our actual identity or experience of who we are is vastly bigger than we thought – we are moving from a strictly personal consciousness to a conscious appreciation of ourselves as integral to the cosmos. Technically, we humans are more than homo sapiens or "wise" – we are homo sapiens sapiens or "doubly wise." In other words, whereas animals "know," humans have the capacity to "know that we know." In this new paradigm, our sense of identity takes on a paradoxical and mysterious quality: We are both observer and observed, knower and that which is known. We are each completely unique yet completely connected with the entire universe. There will never be another person identical to any one of us in all eternity – we are absolutely original beings. At the same time, since our existence arises from and is woven into the deep ecology of the universe, we are completely integrated with all that exists. Awakening to the miraculous nature of our identity as simultaneously unique and interconnected with a living universe can help us overcome the species-arrogance and sense of separation that threaten our future.

Living lightly in a living universe

In a dead universe, consumerism makes sense; in a living universe, simplicity makes sense. If the universe is unconscious and dead at its foundations, then each of us is the product of blind chance among materialistic forces. It is only fitting that we the living exploit on our own behalf that which is not alive. If the universe is lifeless, it has no larger purpose or meaning, and neither does human existence. On the other hand, if the universe is conscious and alive, then we are the product of a deep-design intelligence that infuses the entire cosmos. Our sense of meaningful connection expands to the entire community of life, including past, present, and future generations. Every action in a living universe is felt to have ethical consequences as it reverberates throughout the ecosystem of the living cosmos. The focus of life shifts from a desire for high-consumption lifestyles (intended to provide both material pleasures and protection from an indifferent universe) toward sustainable and simple ways of living (intended to connect us with a purposeful universe of which we are an integral part).

Living with purpose in a living universe

The shift to a new paradigm also brings a shift in our sense of evolutionary purpose. We are shifting from seeing our journey as a secular adventure in a fragmented and lifeless cosmos without apparent meaning or purpose, to seeing it as a sacred journey through a living and unified cosmos whose purpose is to serve as a learning system. Our primary purpose is to embrace and learn from both the pleasure and the pain of the world. If there were no freedom to make mistakes, there would be no pain. If there were no freedom for authentic discovery, there would be no ecstasy. In freedom, we can discover our deeper identity and purpose within a living cosmos.

Living ethically in a living universe

A form of natural ethics accompanies our intuitive connection with a living universe. When we are truly centered in the life current flowing through us, we tend to act in ways that promote the well-being and harmony of the whole. Our connection with the Mother Universe provides us with a sort of moral tuning fork that makes it possible for individuals to come into collective alignment. An underlying field of consciousness weaves humanity together, making it possible for us to understand intuitively what is healthy and what is not, what works and what doesn't. The new paradigm will usher us into an era in which people will be inclined to live ethically because they understand that everything they do is woven into the infinite depths of the Mother Universe. When we discover that all beings are part of the seamless fabric of creation, it naturally awakens in us a sense of connection with and compassion for the rest of life. We broaden our scope of empathy and concern when we realize that we are inseparable from all that exists. We no longer see ourselves as isolated entities whose being stops at the edge of our skin, and whose empathy stops with our family, or our race, or our nation. We see that, because we all arise simultaneously from a deep ocean of life-energy, a vital connection always exists among all beings.

The living universe paradigm is not simply a lateral shift from one set of values to another; it is a contextual shift from one cultural atmosphere to another, from one perceptual environment to another. It transforms the human story. After fourteen billion years of evolution, we stand upon the Earth as agents of self-reflective and creative action on behalf of the universe. We see that we are participants in an unceasing miracle of creation. This recognition brings a new confidence that our potentials are as exalted, magnificent, and mysterious as the living universe that surrounds and sustains us.

Note

1. *The Mother Universe*

When our cosmos blossomed into existence from an area smaller than a pinpoint some twelve billion years ago, it emerged out of "somewhere." Modern physics is beginning to speculate on the nature of this generative ground. Distinguished Princeton astrophysicist John Wheeler describes space as the basic building block of reality. He explains that material things are "composed of nothing but space itself, pure fluctuating space ... that is changing, dynamic, altering from moment to moment." Wheeler goes on to say that, "Of course, what space itself is built out of is the next question ... The stage on which the space of the universe moves is certainly not space itself ... The arena must be larger: superspace [which is endowed] with an infinite number of dimensions." What Wheeler calls "superspace," I am calling the "Mother Universe."

The idea of a "superspace" or Mother Universe is not simply a creation of theoretical physics. It is a reality that can be directly experienced and has ancient roots in the world's meditative traditions. For example, more than twenty centuries ago, the Taoist sage, Lao-tzu, described it this way: There was something formless and perfect before the universe was born.

> It is serene. Empty.
> Solitary. Unchanging.
> Infinite. Eternally present.
> It is the mother of the universe.
> For lack of a better name,
> I call it the Tao.

Regardless of what the Mother Universe is called, all wisdom traditions agree that it is ultimately beyond description. Nevertheless, many attempts have been made to describe her paradoxical qualities. Here are six of the key attributes of the Mother Universe as seen by both East and West: (i) *Present everywhere* – The clear, unbounded life-energy of the Mother Universe is present in all material forms as well as in seemingly empty space. She is not separate from us, neither is she other than the "ordinary" reality continuously present around us. Other universes, besides ours, grow in other dimensions of her unimaginable spaciousness. (ii) *Non-obstructing* – The Mother Universe is a living presence out of which all things emerge, but is not herself filled or limited by these things. Not only are all things in her; she is in all things. There is mutual interpenetration without obstruction. (iii) *Utterly impartial* – The Mother Universe allows all things to be exactly what they are without interference. We have immense freedom to create either suffering or joy.

(iv) *Ultimately ungraspable* – The power and reach of the Mother Universe is so vast that she cannot be grasped by our thinking mind. As the source of our existence, she is forever beyond the ability of our limited mental faculties to capture conceptually.

(v) *Compassionate* – Boundless compassion is her essence. To experience the subtle and refined resonance of the Mother Universe is to experience unconditional love.

(vi) *Profoundly creative* – Because we humans do not know how to create a single flower or cubic inch of space, the creative power of the Mother Universe to bring into existence and sustain entire cosmic systems is utterly incomprehensible.

Christians, Buddhists, Hindus, Jews, Muslims, Taoists, mystics, tribal cultures, and Greek philosophers have all given remarkably similar descriptions of the universe and the life force that pervades it. Here are just a few examples:

"The Tao is the sustaining Life-force and the mother of all things; from it, all things rise and fall without cease." Taoist tradition of China

"Jesus was asked, 'When will the kingdom come?' He replied, 'It will not come by waiting for it ... Rather, the Kingdom of the Father is spread out upon the earth, and men do not see it.' Gospel of Thomas, Gnostic Gospels

"My solemn proclamation is that a new universe is created every moment." D. T. Suzuki, Zen scholar and teacher

"All Hindu religious thought denies that the world of nature stands on its own feet. It is grounded in God; if he were removed it would collapse into nothingness." Huston Smith, scholar of the world's sacred traditions

"God is creating the entire universe, fully and totally, in this present now. Everything God created ... God creates now all at once." Meister Eckhart, Christian mystic

These are more than poetic and metaphorical descriptions. Because we find the notion of a living universe emerging across cultures and millennia as well as from modern science, there is compelling evidence that it forms the basis of a powerful perceptual paradigm – one that will open up enormous opportunities for the human family as we are pressed to create a sustainable future for ourselves.

ELEMENTS OF THE NEW CONCEPT OF CONSCIOUSNESS

Ervin Laszlo

A new concept of consciousness is surfacing at the leading edge of contemporary science and philosophy. Two elements of the new concept are discussed here: one relates to its origins, and the other to its transpersonal aspect.[1]

1. The Cosmic Co-evolution of Consciousness

The new view emerging from a sustained scrutiny of the implications of leading-edge research in the physical, cosmological, and biological sciences goes beyond the traditional alternatives of materialism and idealism, which can be defined as follows.

Materialism. The matter-energy particles that populate space and time are the basic elements of reality. Consciousness in the universe is an epiphenomenon, a local and temporary by-product of the evolution of some species of matter-energy systems constituted of these particles.

Idealism. The matter-energy systems that populate space and time are a secondary phenomenon: local and temporary carriers of the consciousness that constitutes basic reality. The essential feature of the universe is the consciousness that pervades it.

Neither the materialist nor the idealist concept lacks experiential support. Those who take the position of external observers find only matter-energy particles and systems of particles and the forces and fields that surround them: for them the universe consists exclusively of these elements. They can conclude that reality is material, mind and consciousness are epiphenomena. Introspective subjects, in turn, find exclusively perceptions, volitions, feelings, and intuitions – their entire stream of experience is made up of these elements of consciousness. For them all of reality is in the form of mind; the rest is a human construction of conscious experience.

A categorically monistic position espouses one of these viewpoints to the exclusion of the other. These, however, are reductionist positions: one states that there is "nothing but, matter"; the other that there is "nothing but, consciousness." They collapse the distinction between the mental and the physical and constitute an oversimplification of the nature of reality. Both mind and matter may be fundamental elements of the universe and both may have existed from the beginnings of the cosmic process. This does not require the adoption of classical Cartesian dualism, for mind and matter could be complementary aspects of the same reality. Matter may not be limited to particles, and mind to organisms. The universe could be "bipolar": *matter* (in the form of matter-like bound-energy entities) and *mind* (as manifested in the stream of lived experience), could be distinct but complementary aspects of it.

The principle of complementarity is borrowed from quantum physics. Nils Bohr suggested that the wave- and the corpuscular-aspects of a particle are complementary: whether the one or the other comes to the fore depends on the kind of questions one asks and the kind of observations one makes. Independently of whether or not the complementarity principle fully accounts for the properties of the quantum, an analogous principle offers an adequate account of the physical and the mental properties of the universe. Complementarity in this regard means that, whether the physical or the mental aspect emerges for an observer depends on the viewpoint assumed by that observer. In the perspective of the external observer, it is the physical aspect that emerges: even the brain of the observer, seen from the "outside," is a system of neurons embedded in gray matter. In the perspective of introspection, on the other hand, it is the mental aspect that appears: not only the observer herself, but the widest reaches of the cosmos are experienced as elements of consciousness, only interpreted as elements of physical reality. The mental and the physical, *psyche* and *physis*, are both fundamental in the universe.

In light of current cosmological and cosmogonical theories, it is reasonable to assume that the potential for the evolution of the universe's mental and physical aspects was present in the primordial quantum vacuum, the pre-space of the observed universe. Both aspects emerge in the course of the universe's evolution, through the initial creation of the particles that populates space-time through the Big Bang and the subsequent condensation of the initial radiation-field into galaxies, stars, and stellar systems. The mental aspect is realized corresponding to the level of evolution attained by the resulting matter-energy systems. A comparatively evolved system such as the human has a correspondingly evolved mental aspect, experienced as an articulated form of consciousness.

Matter-energy systems exist throughout the universe. An evolved form of consciousness is likely to be associated with all evolved varieties of systems including, but not limited to, advanced biological organisms. Contrary to a widespread belief, there is no solid evidence that consciousness would be limited to an organism with an evolved brain. Clinical and experimental evidence speak only to the fact that brain function and state of consciousness are correlated, so that when brain function ceases, consciousness ceases as well. (This is not always the case: in some well-documented cases patients suffering cardiac arrest in a hospital had detailed and subsequently clearly recalled experiences during the time their EEG showed a complete absence of brain function.) The evidence says little about how the human brain's network of neurons would actually produce the qualitative sensations that make up human consciousness. Functional MRI and other techniques show only that when particular thought processes occur, they are associated with metabolic changes in specific areas of the brain. They do not show how the cells of the brain, which produce proteins and electrical signals, could also produce sensations, thoughts, emotions, images, and other elements of consciousness.

The fact that a high level of consciousness, with articulated images, thoughts, feelings and rich subconscious elements, is associated with complex neural structures is not a guarantee that such consciousness is produced in and by these structures. Both matter and mind could be ubiquitous in nature; they could both have evolved into what they are today. What we call "matter" is what we apprehend when we look at a person, a plant, or a molecule from the outside; "mind" is what we apprehend when we look at the same thing from the inside. Apart from mystical and other transpersonal experiences, the inside view is available to humans only in regard to their own brain. This view yields the stream of human consciousness, with its sights and sounds, feelings and intuitions, and its manifold subconscious elements.

The usual limitation of the inside view to one's own brain is not a valid reason to deny the existence of an analogous view in regard to other things. Both views could be present not only for humans, but for quarks and particles, atoms and molecules, and cells and all species of organisms. The level of articulation of the inside view would correspond to the level of information-processing capacity of the given systems. The articulated consciousness of *Homo* is made possible (even if it is not the product of) a large and complex brain, the result of an extended evolutionary history.

While the articulated consciousness associated with the human brain is made possible by the evolution of that brain, the already attained evolution of the hominid brain is likely to allow a further evolution of the consciousness associated with it. The human brain has enormous and as yet unused information-processing capacity and sufficient flexibility to accommodate diverse forms and levels of consciousness. A further evolution of consciousness should be possible even in the absence of the evolution of the neural structures that underlie it. Some elements of this evolution may be manifest in our lifetime. There is increasing attention focused on the phenomenon of consciousness, and a growing tendency to reexamine the nature of today's dominant consciousness. This may catalyze a qualitative leap in the tenor of the consciousness of a segment of contemporary humanity.

Ideas about a hierarchy of levels of consciousness, with progressive evolution from the lowest to the highest, have been present in all major spiritual traditions. A number of thinkers attempted to define the specific steps or stages of human consciousness evolution. Sri Aurobindo spoke of superconsciousness as the next step in the development of human-species consciousness; in a similar vein, Jean Gebser described the emergence of four-dimensional integral consciousness from the prior stages of archaic, magical, and mythical consciousness. Richard Bucke portrayed cosmic consciousness as the next evolutionary stage of human consciousness, following the simple consciousness of animals and the self-consciousness of contemporary humans. Ken Wielder's six-level evolutionary process leads from physical consciousness, pertaining to nonliving matter-energy, through biological consciousness associated with animals and mental consciousness characteristic of humans, to subtle consciousness which is archetypal, transindividual and intuitive. Subtle consciousness gives rise to causal consciousness and is conducive in the final step to the ultimate consciousness Wilber calls "Consciousness as Such." And this writer, together with Stanislav Grof and Peter Russell, discussed the nature, the possibilities, and the evidence for the evolution of consciousness at the present time and concluded that there is something like a "consciousness revolution" already under way.[2]

The insight emerging from the above considerations can be framed in a simple but basic proposition: *Consciousness is a fundamental element of the reality of the cosmos, it is ubiquitous in space and time, and it evolves together with the matter-energy systems with which it is associated.*

2. The Physical Foundations of Transpersonal Consciousness

The transpersonal dimension of human consciousness has been known for millennia, but in western science it was dismissed as an illusion. The empiricism that held sway in the western world denied reality to any information entering consciousness that is not conveyed by eye and ear or another sensory organ. In recent decades, however, controlled experiments in parapsychology, consciousness, and alternative healing research have demonstrated the reality of nonsensory information transmission, and the experience of psychotherapists with patients in altered states of consciousness reinforced the findings.

Human consciousness, it appears, is open to flows of information that reach the brain from beyond the organism even when the information is not passing through the exteroceptive organs. This writer suggested that such information is mediated by a cosmically extended nonclassical field in the quantum vacuum.[3] The admission of such a field, or of any scientifically acceptable physical basis for the transpersonal communication of information would make for a fundamental shift in the dominant concept of reality. The shift can be portrayed by an updated "meta-physics" theory that follows from the new physics and uses it as a basis to construct the first principles of the emerging understanding.

In the new metaphysics reality is unitary, but it is analytically segmentable into two principal domains. One is the manifest domain of directly or instrumentally observable matter-energy particles and systems of particles; the other the virtual domain of the quantum vacuum, the energy sea from which the particles arise. The latter domain is intrinsically unobservable, but it is inferable through its effects on the observable domain. The former constitutes the "manifest domain," and the latter the "virtual domain" (In this context "virtual" is not opposite to "real," but to "observable.") The interaction of the two domains generates the observable entities, the matter-energy particles and systems of particles, of the universe.

Quantized particles and the systems built of them are the furnishings of the manifest domain. Their apparent materiality does not represent derivation from a categorically disjunctive element of physical reality denoted "matter." Manifest entities are merely matter-like: they are vibrating nodal points (distillations or crystallizations) of the energies of the virtual domain. Virtual energies become manifest, that is, emerge from the virtual into the manifest domain, upon the "excitation" of the virtual domain by an intrinsic instability (as in the universe-creating explosion known as the Big Bang) or by the influx of a significant level of energy (as in ordinary pair-creation). They are sustained in the manifest domain by interaction with each other. In the absence of interaction, particles do not exhibit the corpuscular properties that hallmark the manifest domain: they remain part of the underlying virtual domain without unique location in space and time.

At various levels of evolution the manifest entities of the universe are matter-energy particles, systems of particles, and higher-order systems of systems of particles. They are similar to Whitehead's "actual entities" and "societies of actual entities".[4] They bind the energies emerging from the virtual domain in quantized packets. As Whitehead affirmed, the emerging particles and systems are internally related to each other and to the rest of the universe.

The virtual domain is the quantum vacuum, with its vectorial electromagnetic and nonvectorial scalar component. The latter conveys information without conveying physical force. In consequence the matter-energy particles and systems of particles of the manifest domain receive from other particles and particle-systems (1) vectorial-energy signals, and (2) nonvectorial information. Nonvectorial information is the formative element in the evolution of matter-energy systems: it is the (physically real) equivalent of Plato's "Forms" and Whitehead's "eternal objects". This information is not given a priori, but results from the interaction of the universe's manifest domain with its virtual domain, i.e., the interaction of matter-energy particles and systems of particles with the scalar field of the quantum vacuum.

Thus in regard to the formative element of the cosmos, the indicated metaphysics departs from that of Whitehead, and also from the philosophy of Plato, which was Whitehead's inspiration. The a priori given of the universe is not a set of formative patterns, but a two-fold potentiality present in the quantum vacuum. It is the potentiality of that virtual energy-domain to (1) create manifest matter-energy particles, and (2) convey information among the existent matter-energy particles and systems. As just noted, matter-energy systems apprehend and process both vectorial radiations and nonvectorial information. In biological organisms apprehending and processing the former requires biochemical sensitivity ("irritability") or an evolved sensory apparatus, while the latter occurs through the coherence of the living organism as a macroscopic quantum system with the quantum fields that embed it. As this writer has argued in detail elsewhere, *the quantum coherence of the human brain with the scalar field of the vacuum lends human consciousness the observed transpersonal dimension.*[5] It provides the hitherto missing physical foundation for transpersonal phenomena.

The new "cartography of the human mind",[6] must include items received through sensory perception as well as through the quantum coherence of the brain with the surrounding vacuum field. The latter does not require mediation by sensory organs and is repressed in modern societies. It surfaces primarily in altered states of consciousness such as dreaming and meditative states, moments of intense creativity, and trance-states induced by prayer, fasting, and other visionary-consciousness inducing practices. The repression of non-sensory information impoverishes the mental universe of modern people, reducing it to elements consistent with the dominant materialist worldview, one that grasps only certain varieties of matter-energy processes and ignores the rest. However, evidence for information of a non-sensory origin in consciousness is accumulating. More and more people are awakening to the possibility that some of their dreams, visions, and subtle intuitions are not illusory, even if they do not come through the eye and ear. They are seeking ways old and new to access these sources of information, through meditation, yoga and other time-honored methods, as well as by finding new ways of entering altered states of consciousness, such as biofeedback, psychotherapy, and newly discovered or rediscovered spiritual practices.

The importance of subtle non-sensory information will increase with the discovery that it is not a figment of the imagination but has a scientific foundation. People will be able to seek the information reaching their consciousness without fear of being looked at askance and considered strange and esoteric. When they admit this information to their waking consciousness they will realize that they are linked to each other and to nature in more profound ways than they had recognized. When a critical mass comes to this realization, Jung's collective unconscious will break through into the world of everyday experience, and the integral, cosmic, or super-consciousness of Sri Aurobindo, Jean Gebser, Richard Bucke, Ken Wilber, Stanislav Grof and Peter Russell will become the norm rather than the exception.

The next evolution of human consciousness could be, and if we are wise or fortunate enough will be, from ego-bound to transpersonal consciousness. This would be a major, indeed a momentous evolution but, like all previous evolutions, it will not happen all at once. The consciousness of individuals can transform instantly, through a sudden insight or revelatory experience, but the consciousness of the species is likely to take time to spread in society. There are people today who live with a traditional or a medieval consciousness, and a few with the consciousness of Stone Age tribes. In the same way there will be humans in the next generation who will achieve transpersonal consciousness, while others, the great majority at first, will persist in the ego-bound consciousness that characterized most of the 20th Century.

In time, however, a more evolved consciousness is likely to spread over the six continents. It will spread by a form of contagion. An evolved mind is "infectious," it affects less evolved minds, just as the thinking, personality, and consciousness of an advanced teacher "infect" the thinking, personality and consciousness of the disciples. A more evolved consciousness will motivate people to develop their own consciousness, it will transform humanity's collective unconscious. Unless we produce a major societal or ecological catastrophe, most of our species will eventually graduate to transpersonal consciousness, and the next step in the evolution of human consciousness will be achieved.

This prospect is a source of great hope in our critical times. An evolved transpersonal consciousness is important not only for individuals: it is vital for the entire species. We need to achieve a higher level of solidarity, empathy, and responsibility if we are to survive on this precious but highly exploited planet. *Participating in the currently unfolding consciousness revolution is both a personal growth imperative, and an imperative of the assured continuation of human life on Earth.*

* * *

Farther horizons

The affirmation that the potential for the mental and physical aspects of the universe was given in its pre-space raises questions that go beyond the accepted horizons of science. One of these questions concerns the origins of the universe's self-evolving potential. How did it originate? We know that Gödel's incompleteness theorem forbids deriving all elements of a system from the system itself. Translated into the real world this means that we cannot account for the evolutionary potential of the cosmos by the evolution that results from that potential. We can, of course, deny that the evolutionary potential was specifically selected, it could have come about randomly in the pre-space of the universe. But this is highly improbable. The universe we inhabit is so finely tuned to the evolution of complex systems that it is extremely unlikely that it would be the result of mere chance. According to Roger Penrose's calculations, the probability of hitting on a universe such as ours by a random selection from among the alternative possibilities is one in $10^{10^{123}}$. Is it more reasonable, then, to assume the work of a transcendent agency that is analogous to, even if not the same as, Aristotle's and Newton's "unmoved" or "prime" mover?

Although this question cannot be answered definitively, it is clear that if the universe with its finely tuned constants and laws did not come about through chance processes, then it was selected by an agency that was in some sense above or beyond the universe itself. This assumption is not open to empirical scrutiny, but it is implied by the ensemble of the empirically known facts. It is an assumption

93

scientists are compelled to entertain regarding the ultimate nature of the reality they investigate. But beyond the selection of the universe's laws and constants, the facts disclosed by observation and experiment do not require recourse to transcendental agency. (This is equivalent to the theological position known as Deism: the tenet of an initial creative act without continuing divine intervention. Theologians generally reject it, since it conflicts with the doctrines of the major religions, most of which uphold the actuality, or at least the possibility, of ongoing divine intervention.) Given a proper selection of universal constants and natural laws, science can in principle account for the evolution of the universe and of all things in it, from the primordial explosion that gave rise to matter-energy particles, to the evaporation of the last supergalactic black hole that marks the disappearance of matter-energy particles and systems in space and time.

The presence of consciousness in the universe calls, however, for a further specification of the above assumption. If the mental aspect of the universe is just as fundamental as its physical aspect, the basic givens of cosmic evolution must include the potential for both aspects. This suggests that perennial intuitions regarding a cosmic conscious-ness of which individual consciousness would be an emanation or reflection (articulated in the Indian Vedic tradition, as well as by Plotinus, Berkeley, Spinosa, and Hegel) are both timely and true. The consciousness that pervades the cosmos may originate in, and emanate from, the quantum vacuum, the virtual energy domain that underlies the manifest domain of space and time. The zero-point field of the vacuum, with its electromagnetic and scalar components, may be a cosmically extended field of consciousness.

The above tenet is consistent with the complementarity thesis out-lined here. Viewed from the "outside," as human observers ordinarily (if only indirectly) do, the vacuum is a field of virtual particles and cor-responding energy fields and radiations. But viewed from the "inside," as some humans appear to do when they attain the deepest layers of trance, prayer or meditation, the vacuum would assume the aspect of an immense and unfathomable field of consciousness, a cosmic void that is also an essential fullness. This, at any rate, is the recurrent experience of individuals who are committed to seek the ultimate grounds of existence, and their experience lends a variety of empirical substance to the perennial thesis of a field of consciousness that pervades the cosmos.[7]

References

A fuller treatment of these issues is in the author's *The Connectivity Hypothesis: Foundations of a Unified Theory of Quantum, Cosmos, Life, and Consciousness*, Albany: State University of New York Press, 2003.

Laszlo, E., Russell, P., and Grof, S., *The Consciousness Revolution: A Transatlantic Dialogue*, Shaftesbury and Boston: Element Books, 1999.

Laszlo, E., *The Connectivity Hypothesis,* op. cit., and by the same author, *The Creative Cosmos,* Edinburgh: Floris Books, 1993; *The Interconnected Universe*, Singapore and London: World Scientific, 1994; and *The Whispering Pond,* Shaftesbury and Boston: Element Books ,1996.

Alfred North Whitehead, *Process and Reality,* London: MacMillan, 1927.

cf. *The Connectivity Hypothesis,* op. cit., chapter 7.

cf. Grof, S., *Psychology of the Future,* Albany: State University of New York Press, 2000.

Grof, S., *Psychology of the Future,* op. cit.

PROLOGUE TO A NEW MODEL OF A LIVING UNIVERSE

Elisabet Sahtouris

Introduction

The ancient Greek word for science was philosophy – *philos sophias*, the love of wisdom. This name was intended to set science on a course of searching for wisdom, for practical guidance in human affairs through understanding the natural order of the cosmos to which we belong.

Science and philosophy, originally one and the same pursuit, were separated when western science adopted its materialist stance of positivist reductionism, yet the first part of the *Cambridge English Language Dictionary*'s definition of philosophy is still "The use of reason in understanding such things as the nature of reality and existence" (including epistemology and moral judgment). Thus, over the past several centuries, science and philosophy have remained inextricably intertwined on the subject of understanding reality, though philosophy shared morality with religion and got exclusive rights to epistemology – the "study of, or a theory of, the nature and grounds of knowledge, especially with reference to its limits and validity". In other words, what can we know and how do we know that we know?

From my perspective, this separation of science and philosophy such that science was no longer concerned with how it knew what it knew or with exercising moral judgment about the consequences of its discoveries and pronouncements has led to fundamental scientific errors in the first case and a misplaced lack of accountability in the second.

Western science assumed the existence of an objective material universe that can be formally modeled through objective observation and measurement. Thomas Ehrich describes objectivity as follows:

Objectivity is commonly taken to mean, "freedom from idiosyncrasies." An idea is objective to the extent that it is unpolluted by the individual's beliefs or presuppositions; a critique is objective to the extent that the person making the criticisms and suggestions ignores their own personal feelings and biases. Objectivity in this sense is often defined as the negative of personal subjectivity, or as the opposite of personal opinion.[1]

Science set out not only to eliminate idiosyncrasy and bias by decreeing the separation of subjectivity (our inner world) from objectivity (our outer world), but to create a comprehensive and detailed model of the outer world as a universe independent of any individual human conception of it (whether revelatory or observed) and independent of human participation within it, an undisputed, public model of a "reality" entirely independent of our thoughts and actions. This heroic exercise (never seen as an act of creation) depended in both conception and practice on the prior creation of two formal languages abstracted from natural language. It was mathematics and logic, together with their "translation" into physical machinery, that inspired the western scientific model of a physical universe.

The symbols of logic and mathematics have no intrinsic real-world meaning, even though Aristotle devised logic for ordering human thought around the same time that Euclid devised geometry (literally, the measurement of Earth) to order the physical world. Engineers assigning real-world meaning to mathematics made it possible to translate that formal language into physical buildings, bridges, ships and all sorts of mechanisms, or machinery. Similarly, European scientists, heirs to Arabic and Greek math and logic, found mathematical patterns to be very useful in modeling those aspects of nature they could quantify (measure).

European scientists thus adopted the positivist stance that reality is made up only of measurable things, and that their description as natural mechanisms provides the only possible uncontaminated knowledge of reality. Machinery, having been invented and assembled from parts by man, could be totally understood by man. Formalizing nature as machinery was intended to make it equally understandable.

The task of positivist science was thus twofold: to discover what the parts of natural mechanisms are, and to see how the mechanisms work through the movement of these parts in relation to each other. Scientists took things apart in order to see how they were constructed as well as how they 'ticked' within the great Cosmic Clockworks. This method of reducing things to their parts came to be known as the *reductionist method* of positivist science.

Renaissance and Enlightenment Era mathematical models of the cosmos followed from Plato's insistence that God was a mathematician and from Descartes' conception of God as more than mathematician, as the *Grand Engineer* of Nature's mechanisms. Although Descartes, in his famous recognition "*I think, therefore I am*," came very close to recognizing consciousness as fundamentally self-evident, therefore axiomatic to any model of the universe conceived by humans, he became a "double dualist" by seeing God as the external Creator of Nature's mechanisms and Man as the external creator of his own simpler machinery by virtue of God's gift to him of godlike consciousness. (I call this kind of creation *allopoietic* to distinguish it from self-creation, which is *autopoietic*. See later.) Descartes claimed that man could eventually learn to make his bejeweled wind-up nightingales as complex as God's feathered ones. This belief underlies the whole of robotics, man-machine interface, artificial intelligence (AI) and artificial life (AL) today, and contributes to our failure to understand life as *autopoietic*.

Logically complete, if not satisfying in a contemporary world, Descartes' scheme was adopted, though its logic was soon destroyed when scientists decided they had no need for the hypothesis of God in their conception of Nature. *It was utterly illogical to eliminate the inventor engineer while keeping the concept of nature as mechanism.* Any dictionary defines mechanism as the purposive (invented) assembly of parts. Having no inventor for the mechanical universe, scientists were forced into the bizarre stance that nature's complex machinery had arisen accidentally, that the universe is a vast *purposeless* mechanism filled with smaller purposeless mechanisms, all running down by entropy (as machinery does). Western science is still devoted to rationalizing this illogical model taught to new scientists in every university.

The Axioms of Western Science

With Nature reduced to mechanism, and no proposal of some life force deemed acceptable in lieu of God, positivism arrogated to the physics of non-life the responsibility for modeling the universe. The fundamental assumptions, the "self evident truths" or axioms, underlying this positivist science include (a) that the universe exists objectively (not subjectively) as matter located in three-dimensional space and linear time, (b) that the universe is non-living, measurable and describable in familiar mechanical terms of matter and energy, (c) that the universe has linear causal order discoverable through the science of physics, using mathematical measurement and logical reason (including induction and deduction), (d) that the material universe is accidentally assembled from the smallest physical units into larger structures and interactive patterns through the workings of discoverable natural laws, (e) that large structures can be understood by reducing them to their component parts, and (f) that life is a rare and peculiar emergent phenomenon in a non-living universe, possibly restricted to a single planet's surface and ultimately subject to the laws of physics.

The most fundamental laws of physics were formulated on the basis of these axiomatic "truths" in contained laboratory experiments and then extrapolated from laboratory to cosmos. They are well known as Newton's laws, including inertia, energy conservation and entropy, the dissipation of working energy, and with it the disintegration of order, along the "arrow of time."

Much, of course, has happened in the world of physics since these axioms were formulated and the laws "discovered," but despite later understanding of light and the broader electromagnetic spectrum, Big Bang theory, Einstein's equivalence of matter and energy and adjustments to laws of time and motion, the dissolution of hard particles into quantum waves, string theories, multi-dimensional worlds, zero point energy, non-locality and many candidates for a Grand Unified Theory, all together seeming to push for a fundamental change in worldview, a true paradigm shift in physics is yet to happen (or at least to be accepted).

The word "physics" is taken literally from the Greek word for nature: *physis*. European scientists from Galileo onwards assumed that physics in its modern meaning, including astronomy, *was* the true science of nature, while life sciences from organic chemistry to biology, evolution biology and psychology, were (and still are) deemed secondary. Natural laws are still limited to the physics of a non-living universe, into which biologists are expected to fit their explanations of life. Toward this end, the concept of *negentropy* was coined as a kind of swimming upstream that could increase order locally within the overall river of entropy. Negentropy is credited with the descent of man, according to Darwin, his predecessors and his followers, as the natural creature of an evolutionary process billions of years long.

Biological evolution has become virtually axiomatic in the scientific worldview, though its recognition of man as a naturally evolved creature has had questionable social benefits, giving him scientific license to exploit fellow humans, often cruelly, along with the rest of the natural world now suffering a degree of devastation that threatens even human survival. The lack of moral accountability of science for social interpretations of Darwinian descent by natural selection, along with its failure to see the grave errors in the Darwinian hypothesis, has led to social ills from chaining children to machines for the sake of profits to the Holocaust and even to the current capitalist tyranny of the quarterly bottom line competition. The entrenched belief that man is doomed to perpetual hostile competition, the scientific belief underlying these social ills, is, as I will attempt to show, a serious misinterpretation of the evolutionary record.

The fundamental concept of a cold and lifeless, meaningless

universe running down by entropy made decidedly poor inspiration for man to become the good and moral creature Darwin personally hoped he would become by overcoming his evolutionary heritage. One can argue that the marvels of engineering this mechanical scientific worldview did inspire had a great deal to do with the social attitude of scientific industrialism to "get what you can while you can" as things deteriorate. It is interesting to note that the one species that believes in the prevailing rule of one-way entropy has visibly created such entropy by destroying ecosystems and degrading Earth's atmosphere, waters and soils to the level of previous extinctions. Man standing on the Moon sees, as the only mark of his presence on Earth, its deserts. Biologically, we are a desert-making species.

New Assumptions for an Integral Science

An alternative scientific worldview or model cannot be justified on moral grounds, but what if we can construct a model of the universe that fits the data of human experience, including scientific experiment, better than the prevailing one *and* leads to morality, wisdom and health for humanity and other life forms, as in the original Greek intention?

Consider what might have happened had Galileo looked down through a microscope into a drop of pond water teeming with gyrating life forms instead of up through a telescope into the heavens, already conceived in his time as celestial mechanics – might biology, rather than physics, have become the leading science into whose models all others must fit themselves? Might scientists then have seen life not as a rare accidental occurrence in futile struggle to build up syntropic systems against the inevitably destructive tide of entropy, but as the fundamental nature of an exuberantly creative universe?

Instead of projecting a universe of mechanism without inventor, assembling blindly through particular, atomic and molecular collisions a few of which came magically to life and further evolved by accidental mutations, I propose that there is reason to see the whole universe as alive, self-organizing endless fractal levels of living complexity as reflexive systems learning to play with possibilities in the intelligent co-creation of complex evolving systems. I propose that it is actually more reasonable to project our life onto the entire universe than our non-living machinery, which is a derivative of life, a truly *emerging* phenomenon, rather than a fundamental one. I propose that it is possible to create a scientific model of a living universe, and that such a model is not only scientifically justified but can lead to the wisdom required to build a better human life on and for our planet Earth as the ancient Greeks intuited it should.

The current revolution, the impending paradigm shift, in science is forcing reconsideration of its most fundamental assumptions, that is, of the worldview described above, of the basic beliefs supporting the current scientific model of our universe or cosmos and ourselves within it. *Cosmos* is defined as "the universe as an orderly construct," so because I am proposing an orderly model of the universe, I will usually prefer the word *cosmos*.

In eliminating those aspects of the perceived world that are not measurable, western science relegated them variously to subjective, mental, mythological, imaginary, storytelling, fictional, spiritual and other categories identified as *unreal*. A few aspects of our world, such as taste, smell and electromagnetism were shifted from unreal to real as ways of measuring them were discovered. My model of the cosmos includes *all* human experience. The goal of this proposed new framework for science is (a) to model a coherent and self-consistent cosmos as a public reality conforming as much as possible to necessarily private individual realities, and (b) to interpret this model for the purpose of orienting humanity within the cosmos and thus permitting it to understand its particular role within the greater cosmos. Toward that end, I propose the following:

(i) The scientific definition of reality should be the collective human experience of self, world and universe as inner and outer worlds perceived from individually unique perspectives. (We have no other legitimate basis for creating cosmic models.)

(ii) Consciousness (awareness) shall be axiomatic for the simple and obvious reason that no human experience can happen outside it.

(iii) Formal experiments have as their purpose the creation of publicly shareable models of reality that permit common understanding and prediction.

(iv) *Autopoiesis* (continuous self-creation) shall be adopted as the core definition of life. Since galaxies, stars, planets, organisms, cells, molecules, atoms and sub-atomic particles all fit this definition, this implies that life is the fundamental process of the cosmos, a self-creating living whole with self-creating living components in co-creative interaction.

(v) Nature shall be conceived in fractal levels of holons in holarchy, holons defined as relatively self-contained living entities such as those listed in (iv) and holarchy defining their embeddedness and co-creative interdependence on energy, matter and information exchange.

Beginning with these few assumptions and definitions as a conceptual framework for an integral science, we can reassess the past findings of science based on previous models, discover past errors and redesign experiments as necessary. We can also look for new patterns of regularity. (I shall avoid the term *laws* because of its implication of a law-giver.)

Reality as Direct Human Experience

The idea of defining reality in terms of human experience may seem strange to any western scientist accustomed to firm belief in a firm firmament that includes our Earth and humanity but exists separately from human experience of it. Yet the whole edifice of a separate, objective world has been built on a belief in objectivity that has been discredited by philosophers of science and increasingly by scientists themselves. If the claim of basing science on reason, on experiment (a word derived from *experience*) and on rational argument is to be upheld, then *we cannot postulate a world that is not within human experience as long as we have no way to be outside human experience.* The simplest case for conceiving reality as human experience, as stated above, is that we have no other legitimate basis for creating cosmic models. Note that this conception happily eliminates the need to define nonreality. *Merriam Webster Dictionary* defines reality as:

> **1**: the quality or state of being real, **2a** (1): a real event, entity, or state of affairs (2): the totality of real things and events; **b**: something that is neither derivative nor dependent but exists necessarily.

The first three definitions tell us nothing as they define reality in terms of *real*. Only the final definition begins to tell us something meaningful, that reality "is neither derivative nor dependent but exists necessarily." The only thing fitting this latter definition is direct perception, for once any perception is reported to another, whether by a three-year-old, a scientist or a theologian, it clearly becomes derivative.

The *Cambridge English Language Dictionary* adds: "existing in fact; not imaginary" to its definition of reality, but a perusal of its definition of *fact* tells us: "something which is known to have happened or to exist, esp. something for which proof exists, or about which there is information."

The only way to truly *know* that something has happened or exists is to have direct experience of it, as we just determined. This clearly implies that truth can only be subjective. Unfortunately, western science has denied subjective (direct) experience as a valid reality in maintaining that the objective practice of science is the only way to demonstrate it. This belief is still strong among scientists though philosophers of science have long held that science cannot reach truth but only useful hypotheses.

The way in which hypotheses are determined to be useful or not lies, of course, in testing them experimentally. If the experimental outcome predicted by the hypothesis is found, they are considered useful. The validity of extrapolation beyond the experiment itself can only be judged in terms of consistency with our direct experience of the world.

It has now been shown in very careful research, for example by Elisabeth Targ[2] and Marilyn Schlitz[3,4] that remote intention and experimenter expectation clearly influence experimental outcome despite laboratory controls. The repercussions of such research have only begun to be felt, but certainly threaten to undermine the basic premises of western science if not its results.

More generally, the objectivity so sacred to western science has proved logically impossible. As Gregory Bateson noted decades ago, philosopher of science Alfred Korzybski warned us (in discussing the relationship between scientific models and reality) that "the map isn't the territory and the name is not the thing named." As Bateson himself put it, "there are no pigs or coconuts in the brain."[5]

No human has ever had a direct (real) experience except in the eternally present Now; all the rest can only be stories that weave particular and more general past experience into the present. We cannot directly experience the past or the future. Whatever we are experiencing, from whatever combination of inner or outer sources, *is* our in-the-moment reality. Esoteric traditions have made much of this fundamental truth, the only truth there can be, while western science has totally ignored it until now. The only exception I have found was on a scientific delegation to China (in 1974), where a Chinese scientist defined science as "the summation of people's experience."

The task of a science accepting this fundamental truth is to sort and order reports of direct experience into an abstract public model of reality, using tools of reason, math, logic, experiment and narrative to construct it.

Consciousness as Axiomatic

In two of my books,[6,7] I introduced the idea of consciousness as fundamental to the cosmos without discussing human consciousness as fundamental to the construction of scientific models themselves. The fundamental assumptions of my model as listed above have to do with human experience of the universe and human conjecture about the universe based on, or derived from, human experience of it, because these are *all we have to go on* in creating models, scientific or other, of that universe. Human experience includes the perception of a tangible, substantive world, but this experience of a material world, even if coming through sense organs, lies entirely within human consciousness, or awareness.

The *Merriam Webster Dictionary* defines consciousness as "the quality or state of being aware" and awareness as "having or showing realization, perception, or knowledge." The *Cambridge International Dictionary of English* calls consciousness "aware, thinking, knowing" and awareness as "knowing that something exists, or having knowledge or experience of a particular thing."

Consciousness and awareness *are usually listed as synonyms of one another*, though awareness is more often linked to the concept of knowledge than is consciousness. The problem with this link to knowing is that knowledge is clearly culture bound. I shall therefore distinguish cosmic consciousness, a universal field of awareness, from human consciousness in its broadest, most fundamental, cross-cultural understanding as awareness of self-in-world and world-in-self.

This human awareness of having an internal and external life perceived in images, sounds, touch, smells, feelings, thoughts, stories, etc. can be shared with others to a certain extent through verbal and other forms of language, thus giving rise to a broader cultural, or public, shared awareness of many-in-world. Once humans acquire language, this awareness arises in large part as verbal thought, which is why Descartes' stated his bottom-line of knowing as: "*I think, therefore I am.*"

Taking Descartes' lead in seeking my most basic observations, they are:

· I experience myself and others as alive.

· I experience myself at the center of an apparently spatio-temporal "outer reality" or universe.

· I experience myself as an inner self of perceptions, feelings and thoughts.

· I/we have no experience of the apparently spatial "outer world" outside of our conscious awareness.

· I/we have no direct experience outside of an eternal present or Now, yet I perceive my experience as though it lies on a continuum from past through Now to future.

· We can share our experiences in stories that transcend direct experience because of this timeline and our ability to communicate.

Thus we clearly perceive ourselves as existing in a physical spacetime world, and are able to describe it, model it symbolically and create other sharable stories of past (memories, histories, evolutionary trajectories) and future (forecasts, projections, anticipations) experience within it. But we can only describe it from the perspective of human experience. If we believe other species, planets, etc. to exist in their own right, we must also believe in the possibility of alternative scientific descriptions of the cosmos from other perspectives. Therefore:

· Science can only order and model human experience within consciousness as communicated among humans;

· We cannot prove any "true" reality other than that composed of both uniquely personal and collectively shared experience;

· Recognizing our formalization of spacetime as a model of perception, rather than an objective reality, it becomes an important way of ordering shared experience. That human individuals *can and do* share considerable (though far from perfect) agreement on external reality and varying degrees of agreement on internal reality is of very significant interest as it both makes society possible and produces a larger reality than any one individual can experience independently.

The best argument we have for the existence of a "real" vast universe is the *limitlessness* of human conscious awareness, whether it is focused inward or outward. Every scientific or spiritual discovery can be contained within its expansive capacity. Inner focus, when sufficiently practiced through meditation and other spiritual practice gives rise to the experience of ultimate truth in a limitless Source, called I AM, Cosmic Consciousness or God by many names across all cultures and felt as loving bliss. Outer focus, when sufficiently practiced through scientific study and reasoning gives rise to the experience of a coherent, comprehensible, though limitless universe or cosmos and recognition of arrival at its truth also produces "breakthroughs" felt as bliss. Those who practice both disciplines come to recognize the unity of these end results as a non-dual cosmic reality.

Thus, building a scientific model on the fundamental assumption of consciousness as the source of reality does not shrink the cosmos one whit. But it keeps us within that cosmos as co-creators of it, as reflections of cosmic creation at all other levels. For reality co-created by humans through a private and public collaborative process suggests a greater holarchic universe of collaborative process. All Nature can thus be elegantly conceived as conscious collaborative process.

Note that as we have found no limits to human conscious awareness, our awareness is (necessarily) coextensive with any models we build of the entire universe. Anything we "discover" scientifically about the universe becomes part of our conscious awareness, and therefore of our experience.

Sophisticated ancient cultures such as Vedic, Taoist and Kotodama, along with many indigenous cultures, recognized the fundamental consciousness of all Nature, the entire Universe or Cosmos, and much in the findings and conceptualizations of physics and biology today leads us in that direction.

The Model and its Implications
We stand at a critical time in human history where the "self-evident"

axiomatic "truth" of a depressingly meaningless mechanical universe running down by entropy, magically giving rise to biological creatures doomed to endless competitive struggle to get what they can while they can, is no longer defensible. Most fundamentally, we see now that this model was built on the false concept of an objective universe independent of human observers. We are also in a position to see just how this western scientific model, which overrode previous religious models of "How Things Are," has led human society astray. Our mechanistic social organizations no longer serve us, nor does the competitive economy that destroys ecosystems and impoverishes vast numbers of humans and leads to the endless warfare so basic to its model.

In its place, happily, we can construct a new scientific model on the far more self-evident truths outlined above, one that takes into account the entire gamut of human experience and recognizes the cosmos as fundamentally conscious and alive. Much progress has already been made by myself and many other scientists to flesh it out.

The new model offers a holistic view of life in which biology, physics and consciousness studies are mutually compatible and consistent. The new axiomatic definitions and assumptions given here for this model of a living universe sees it not as a collection of accidental biological entities evolving on rare planets of a non-living universe through the mechanics of natural selection, but as a holarchic, evolving, intelligent, process intrinsic to the cosmos itself, in short, as *the* natural process of the cosmos itself, as self-organizing expressions of a cosmic field of consciousness.

Cosmic autopoiesis, the self-creation of a living universe, promises to become an elegant view of the whole, with essentially the same production *and* recycling processes at all scalar or fractal levels. The highly complex life forms familiar as "biological" are seen to emerge uniquely at a holarchic level halfway between microcosm and macrocosm.

Because this model offers a framework for understanding, and more consciously creating, our own human nature and trajectory within the greater cosmic process, it is consistent with the original Greek intent to develop scientific understanding of the Cosmos in order to find wise guidance for human affairs. A conscious, self-creating living cosmos is one in which life is sacred, ethics are inherent in evolutionary maturation processes and humanity itself can follow countless other species out of a juvenile mode of competitive aggression and into mature cooperation, a process I believe is apparent in our struggle to move beyond win/lose oil economics and into the establishment of true global family.

References

Ehrich, Thomas, "Defending Beliefs: Objectivity as Validation for Critiques of Health Care Resource Allocation," Gustavus Adolphus College, April, 1996. www.gustavus.edu/oncampus/academics/philosophy/ehrich.html

Sicher, F., Targ, E., Moore, D., Smith, H. (1998), "A Randomized Double-Blind Study of the Effect of Distant Healing in a Population With Advanced AIDS", *Western Journal of Medicine*, December 1998; 169 (6), 356-363.

Targ, E., Schlitz, M., and Irwin, H.J., "Psi-related experiences", In Cardeña, E., Lynn, S.J. & Krippner, S. (Eds.), *Varieties of anomalous experience: Examining the scientific evidence*, Washington, DC: American Psychological Association, 2000; pp. 219-252.

Wiseman, R. & Schlitz, M., "Experimenter effects and the Remote Detection of Staring", *Journal Of Parapsychology*, 1998; 61, 197-208.

Bateson, Gregory, *Mind and Nature*, New York: Bantam edition, 1980.

Harman, W. & Sahtouris, E., *Biology Revisioned*, Berkeley, CA: North Atlantic Books, 1998.

Sahtouris, E., *Earth Dance: Living Systems in Evolution*. New York: Universe.com: Ingram, 2000.

PHILOSOPHY

The present overarching materialist paradigm provides a reductionist-positivist science as the hard plank on which the Western worldview is built. A philosophy that becomes dominant affects how a whole culture views reality, and the essayists grouped together in this section (and in this book as a whole) are calling for a change to the dominant philosophy ruling our modern worldview. Philosophies are the products of human thought, with all the success and failings that entails. The philosophies of most of humanity throughout most of its history have said that there is a mind, a living spirit, in nature. Just because the paradigm that currently frames our worldview says matter is primary to consciousness does not mean that it is correct.

Indeed, it is crucially flawed.

The materialists fail to explain how the matter our brains and bodies are made of becomes aware, how collections of electrons and atoms manage to feel, to love, to sing. To think.

INTRODUCTION TO THE ESSAYS IN THIS SECTION

RICHARD TARNAS: *Two Suitors: A Parable*
Tarnas claims that everything we are learning from contemporary multidisciplinary inquiry tells us that our objective knowledge of the world has been largely shaped by a complex multitude of subjective factors. Yet we still live in a worldview structured by the European enlightenment of the seventeenth and eighteenth centuries. We are just beginning to realise that we have inherited a disenchanted worldview causing us to experience a spiritual and imaginative void where there is "no encompassing ground for transcendent values, moral, spiritual, aesthetic...". The void is filled by the values of the market and mass media. This in turn informs politics, economics and technology. He tests if this disenchanted worldview is, in the end, all that plausible by performing a thought experiment in which the reader is asked to imagine being an intelligent and ensouled universe.

NEAL GROSSMAN: *Individual Responsibility and the Wholeness of Consciousness*
Philosopher Grossman indulges in an imaginary (and often humorous) conversation with Plato and Socrates, discussing mind, matter, mysticism, and Wholeness. We are pleased to welcome these distinguished, if ancient, Greek philosophers to these pages...

DAVID C. KORTEN: *Two Stories – Conflicting Visions of the Human Possible*
Economist Korten contrasts two stories: one the standard Western model of a dead non-sentient universe, the other the story of a living universe in which consciousness is the primary reality. This latter is "a synthesis of ancient religious wisdom and the data of modern science", and is a story that would change everything. The story of the dead universe is

traced through its development from the beginning of the Age of Enlightenment in the seventeenth and eighteenth centuries; in the second story, he traces the implications of what new scientific thought is beginning to imply. For this new story to be told, he argues that there will be a need for the rift between science and religion to be healed. This can only be done if *both* science and religion allow their thinking to become broader and deeper than is currently the case. He tries to envisage the society that might emerge from this. He reminds us that the "stories by which we define ourselves play an important, often sub-conscious, role in shaping the evolutionary trajectory of the societies in which we live."

CORINNE McLAUGHLIN & GORDON DAVIDSON: *The Power of Consciousness to Transform Politics*
These essayists support the idea that "we are what we think". If we do not like the world we see, then we need to change our thinking. If we are to replace old thoughtforms, though, they point out that existing institutions, such as corporate management, will have to go with them, as will the ideas currently informing Western politics – defining politics as "the distribution and exercise of power in the collective sphere". Politics in a culture in which the primacy of consciousness was known to be a fact "would be almost the exact opposite of what we have today" – a vision they proceed to explore.

SEYYED HOSSEIN NASR: *In the Beginning Was Consciousness*
Nasr states that the great religions have always assumed that consciousness is primary, and that the act of denying it has fallen to the secular modern world. He notes the paradox that "human consciousness in modern times has produced a view of the cosmos which has no room for consciousness". It is a worldview that has left us feeling isolated and homeless in a dead cosmos. This has a harmful effect on our relationship with nature, and also weakens our "ethical norms and practices". He explores how an embracing of the primacy of consciousness could remedy this increasingly dangerous situation.

TWO SUITORS: A PARABLE
Richard Tarnas

The postmodern mind has come to recognize, with a sometimes disturbing acuity, the many ways in which our often hidden presuppositions play a critical role in constellating the reality we seek to know. If we have learned anything from the multidisciplinary wellsprings of postmodern thought, whether from psychology, anthropology, philosophy of science, sociology of knowledge, religious studies, linguistics, physics, or feminism, it is that what we believe to be our *objective* knowledge of the world is, to a crucial, even radical extent, shaped and forged by a complex multitude of *subjective* factors, most of which are altogether unconscious. Even this is not quite accurate, for we now recognize subject and object to be so deeply mutually implicated as to render problematic the very structure of a "subject, knowing, an object."

Such a recognition can engender humility or despair. Each of these responses has its place. But ultimately this recognition can also call forth in us a fortifying sense of joyful co-responsibility for the world we enact through the participatory, co-creative power of the worldview we commit ourselves to and evolve with.

But what is the current situation? The modern worldview that first emerged during the European Enlightenment of the seventeenth and eighteenth centuries still effectively structures the context for most of the world's activities and values. In this powerful vision, we live in a universe that is ultimately understood to be the random consequence of exclusively material evolutionary processes, a universe devoid of intrinsic meaning and purpose, soulless and unconscious, indifferent to humanity's spiritual and moral aspirations. From the time of Bacon and Descartes on, meaning and purpose, spiritual and moral values, are all seen as human qualities, and to perceive these in the universe apart from the human is regarded as a delusory projection.

In the course of our complex history, this vision has in certain respects been deeply emancipatory, freeing us from pregiven structures of cosmic meaning and purpose that in important respects had become existentially constraining, and were usually carried and enforced by traditional cultural authorities both political and religious. However, we are now coming to realize the loss as well. A disenchanted worldview essentially empowers the utilitarian mindset. The larger cosmological context within which all human activity takes place provides no encompassing ground for transcendent values, moral, spiritual, aesthetic, which are therefore seen as only human constructs. In the resulting void, the values of the market and mass media freely colonize the collective human imagination and drain it of all depth. Such a vision (or lack of vision) transforms what should be means into ends in themselves: political power, financial profit, technological prowess are the overriding values. The bottom line rules all. In turn, anxiety in the face of a meaningless cosmos creates a spiritual hunger and disorientation, an engulfing fear of death, and a major self-image problem, which lead to an addictive hunger for ever more material goods to fill the inner emptiness, producing a manic techno-consumerism that cannibalizes the planet in a kind of self-destructive frenzy. Highly pragmatic consequences ensue from the disenchanted modern worldview.

But, as we assimilate the deepening insights of our time into the nature of our knowledge of the world, must we not ask ourselves whether this disenchanted worldview is, in the end, all that plausible?

Let us consider a thought experiment. Imagine that you are the universe, a deep, beautiful, profoundly intelligent and ensouled universe. And imagine that you are being approached by two different epistemologies, two suitors, as it were, who seek to know you. To whom would you open your deepest secrets? Would you open most deeply to the suitor, the epistemology, the methodology, who approached you as though you were utterly lacking in intelligence or purpose, as though you had no inner dimension to speak of, no spiritual capacity or value; who thus saw you as radically inferior in being to himself (let us randomly give the suitor a masculine gender); who related to you as though your existence was valuable primarily to the extent that he could exploit your resources to satisfy his various needs; and whose motivation for knowing you was driven ultimately by a desire for increased mental mastery, prediction, and control over you for his own self-enhancement?

Or would you, the cosmos, open your deepest secrets to that suitor, to that epistemology, that approach to the nature of things, who viewed you as being *at least* as intelligent and valuable, as worthy a being, as permeated with mind and soul, as endowed with spiritual depths and mystery, as he; who sought to know you not to better exploit you, but rather to unite with you and thereby bring forth something new; whose ultimate goals of knowledge were not mental mastery, prediction, and control but rather a participatory co-creation, an honoring of your deepest being, bringing an intellectual fulfillment that was intimately linked with poetic and imaginative vision, moral transformation, aesthetic and sensuous pleasure, empathic understanding; whose act of knowledge was essentially an act of love and trust, and, as it were, mutual delight? To whom would you reveal your deepest interior glory?

This is not to say that you, the universe, would reveal nothing to the first suitor, under the duress of his objectifying, disenchanting approach. That suitor would undoubtedly elicit, filter, and constellate a certain "reality" which he would naturally regard as authentic knowledge of the true universe, *objective* knowledge as compared with the subjective delusions of everyone else's approach. But we might allow ourselves to doubt just how profound a truth, how genuinely reflective of the universe's deeper reality, this approach might be. And if this objectifying, disenchanted vision were elevated to the status of being the *only* legitimate vision of the nature of the cosmos upheld by an entire civilization, what a loss, an impoverishment, a grief, would ultimately be suffered, by both knower and known, with tragic, deforming and destructive consequences that would run their fateful course on every plane, intellectual, psychological, social, political, economic, ecological, spiritual.

To assume that purpose, meaning, conscious intelligence, and spiritual depth are solely attributes of the human being, and that the great cosmos itself is a soulless void within which our multidimensional consciousness is a random accident, reflects an invisible act of cosmic hubris on the part of the modern self. And hubris and fall are as indissolubly linked now as they were in ancient Greek tragedy. Our search for the true cannot be separated from our search for the good.

We need to radically expand our ways of knowing. We need a larger and truer empiricism and rationalism. We need to move beyond the relentlessly objectifying, unconsciously constructive epistemological strategies, the restrictive empiricism and rationalism that emerged appropriately during the Enlightenment, but that still dominate mainstream science and modern thought today, and that, in their narrowness and one-sidedness, now dangerously occlude our full vision. We need to build on those, while drawing as well on, to use a single encompassing term, the epistemologies of the heart. We need ways of knowing that integrate the imagination, the aesthetic sensibility, the moral faculty, revelatory or epiphanic experience, the spiritual intuition, the capacity for archetypal insight, for kinesthetic and sensuous knowing, for empathic understanding, the capacity to open to the other, to *listen*, to listen even to our *own* "other," our unconscious, in all its plenitude of forms. A developed sense of empathy, of loving, trusting, receptive observation and analysis, is critical if we are to overcome the great modern chasm between subject and object, psyche and cosmos. We need to be able to enter into that which we seek to know, and not keep it ultimately distanced as an object. We need, in the end, to transform our relationship to the universe from one of "I and It" to one of "I and Thou."

Our best philosophy of science has taught us the extent to which our epistemology co-creates our world. Not only reason and empiricism but faith, hope, and compassion play a major role in constellating the reality we seek to know. And this is perhaps the underlying message of our modern Enlightenment's unexpected darkening of the world: at the heart of cognition is a moral dimension. The "progress of knowledge" and the "evolution of consciousness" have too often been characterized as if our task were to ascend an immensely tall cognitive ladder, solving increasingly challenging mental riddles, like advanced problems in a graduate engineering exam. But our *hearts* must be transformed, not just our minds. We must go down and deep as well as high and far. Our world view and our cosmology, which define the context for everything else, are profoundly affected by the degree to which *all* our faculties, intellectual, emotional, somatic, imaginative, spiritual, enter the process of our knowing. How we approach the Other, and how we approach each other, will shape everything, including our own self.

We have a choice. There are many possible universes, many possible meanings, living within us *in potentia*, moving through us, awaiting enactment. We are not solitary separate subjects in a meaningless universe of objects upon which we can and must impose our egocentric will. Nor are we just empty vessels, as it were, on automatic, passively playing out the intentions of the universe, of God, of our social-linguistic community, of our class, our race, our gender, our unconscious, our stage in evolution. Rather, we are miraculously autonomous yet embedded participants, each a creative nexus of action and interpretation, microcosms of the creative and intelligent macrocosm, enacting a complexly and richly co-evolutionary unfolding of reality.

And critical to that participation is the capacity for radical openness to the other, an openness to mystery, an affirmation of the universe as Thou rather than It. With that insight, once again our knowledge of truth will be seen to be intimately connected with our moral and aesthetic aspirations for the good and the beautiful. Only then might we discover our deeper oneness with the whole. Only then might we finally trust death, in all its forms, as a threshold to the mystery of greater life. And only then might we discover just how thrillingly the True, the Good, and the Beautiful are all ultimately, intricately united.

[*This is a version of a chapter in Richard Tarnas's book,* Cosmos and Psyche: Intimations of a New World View.]

INDIVIDUAL RESPONSIBILITY AND THE WHOLENESS OF CONSCIOUSNESS (A CONVERSATION)

Neal Grossman

PLATO: It seems you are back sooner than you had expected.

NEAL: Yes, I've been asked to contribute an essay to an anthology, the basic premise of which is that consciousness is primary.

P: I know. That buzz of energy you felt around your head when you first got the request to write an essay – that was me. Well, let's get straight to business. Tell me more about this anthology.

N: The contributors to this anthology are to assume that consciousness is primary over matter, and to explore the consequences for society of that assumption, or rather, the consequences that might obtain if everybody believed that assumption. Specifically, we are not to argue the point – whether consciousness is more fundamental than matter – but rather, assume it and proceed from there. What do you think?

P: It's a good idea to "assume" what is in any case true, and it will free up the contributors' minds from having to constantly argue, justify, and so forth, any worldview that doesn't take matter to be primary. Now, there are two preliminary issues I wish to mention, one major, one minor.

N: OK, what are they?

P: The minor issue is to call attention to the difference between ontology and epistemology. Ontologically speaking, what follows from the fact that Pure Consciousness is primary is the entirety of Creation in all of its realms and manifestations. But this is not what we are asked to discuss.

N: Right. We are asked to discuss what might happen if everyone *actually believed* that this was the case.

P: And beliefs pertain to epistemology, not ontology. So we are asked to discuss, not what follows from the fact that consciousness is primary, but what might follow if everyone were to believe that this fact is in fact a fact. Now, there is a big difference between *knowing* that consciousness is primary based on one's own direct and immediate experience of a transcendent Reality, and *believing* that consciousness is primary, based on things other than one's own immediate experience.

N: Yes. Several months ago I read an interview with a psychiatrist, I think, who had just published the results of a study on the Near Death Experience. He was asked if he believed, based on his research, that he would survive the death of his body. He said yes, he believes it, but added that people who have had a near-death experience do not merely *believe* they will survive the death of their body, they *know* it as a fact.

P: Well said, indeed. This is such a simple and obvious distinction – between knowledge and true belief – and so fundamental to my philosophy. So, are we asked to imagine the consequences if (i) everyone came to know, based on direct experience of Reality, that consciousness is primary, eternal, etc., or (ii) everyone came to have true belief that consciousness is primary, based on things other than their own direct experience?

N: Or to put it in terms of the Near-Death Experience, under (i) we imagine that everyone has an NDE and experiences the Light directly, whereas under (ii) we imagine that, like the researcher mentioned, everyone comes to have the true belief that the NDE is real? I'm not sure which of these two should function as our major premise.

P: Perhaps it doesn't really matter too much.

N: Why not?

P: Because, as I once wrote, true belief is no less a guide to action than knowledge, as long as those who have true belief without knowledge have no doubt, and believe without any doubt that consciousness is primary.

N: But is that possible, psychologically speaking?

P: Of course it's possible. Do not your atheists and religious fundamentalists believe all kinds of absurdities without any doubt?

N: Yes, all the time.

P: So if it is possible to have an attitude of certainty with respect to false beliefs, it must certainly be possible to have an attitude of certainty with respect to true beliefs.

N: I agree. So our premise is that everyone has an attitude of complete certainty towards the fact that consciousness is primary, regardless of whether the certainty is arrived at through direct experience or through studying the direct experiences of others, or in some other way.

P: Good.

N: Now what is the other, more important, preliminary issue that you mentioned earlier?

P: The more serious preliminary issue is that, if everyone were to believe that conscious is primary, nothing much seems to follow.

N: What do you mean? How can you say such a thing?

P: Well, suppose everyone were to come to believe that there is a God. What would follow from that?

N: It would depend on the *kind* of God people believed in. For example some people use the concept of God to inspire them to do good; others use the concept of God to justify their hatred of those who do not believe as they do.

P: And doesn't your friend Huston Smith say that, on balance, it is difficult to say whether more harm than good has been done in the name of God.

N: Yes. So the mere belief in God, by itself, does not have any practical consequences for living one's life. We need to flesh out this belief by specifying something about the *nature* of God

P: And so it is with our premise that consciousness is primary. Before we can discuss what might follow if everyone believed this, we need to flesh out the *nature* of this primary consciousness. In particular, do we take consciousness to be singular or plural? Is it a One or a Many?

N: I believe it is a One which appears as a Many to Itself insofar as It has become embodied.

P: And do we also believe that this appearance as a Many is a kind of illusion generated by embodied existence?

N: OK, but embodied existence is itself brought about by consciousness, since it is the latter which is primary. But this "One and the Many" business is very abstract –

how in the world is it *useful*?

P: It's much more useful than you may think. Consider again the religious fundamentalists...

N: *You* consider them. I can't stand them myself.

P: Now, now, lighten up, my friend. Are they not embodied consciousness, just like you?

N: Yes, of course.

P: And do we not believe that anything less than unconditional love and acceptance is an inappropriate attitude for how one form of consciousness should regard another, whether embodied or not?

N: (groan)

P: And have you not heard the story that any animosity to another person or group of persons is a great disadvantage to the one who carries the animosity?

N: Yes, I have heard that hatred binds the individual to the object of his hatred and that...

P: ...a consequence of your animosity towards fundamentalists might be that you will have to reincarnate as one of "them" in your next life.

N: You're trying to frighten me. Yet this belief, or something like it, inspires me to strive to overcome my animosities, both towards individuals and groups. But it is most difficult to sustain a loving attitude to people who preach and practice hatred.

P: I understand. Yet they are the ones who are most in need of our love.

N: I agree. But now, you were going use the fundamentalists to make a point about the usefulness of regarding consciousness as a One which appears as a Many.

P: You have not been paying complete attention.

N: What do you mean?

P: I have already made my point, using *you* as an example, instead of the fundamentalists.

N: Could you spell that out for me?

P: Glad to oblige. If Consciousness is a One, or a Whole, then any individuated consciousness must be a part of that Whole, and hence, intrinsically connected both with the One and with all aspects of the One which appear to be individuated. Do you agree?

N: Yes.

P: And both you and the fundamentalist appear both to yourselves and to one another as individuated consciousnesses.

N: OK

P: Then you are both alike in this respect. Can it be otherwise?

N: No, of course not.

P: Then the fundamentalist's rejection of those who are different from them is an example of one form of individuated consciousness, or, one form of the Many, separating itself from and rejecting other forms of individuated consciousness. Do you agree?

N: Definitely. That is the problem with them. They reject everyone who is different from themselves.

P: And is not *your* rejection of the fundamentalists also an example of one form of individuated consciousness rejecting another form of individuated consciousness?

N: I suppose I am forced to agree.

P: So you are alike in this respect also. You are both examples of individuated consciousness rejecting, as something other than itself, other forms of individuated consciousness. But if all individual forms of consciousness constitute a One, an organic Whole, then this rejection is not in harmony with what we believe is true.

N: I see your point. It is as if the kidney were to reject the stomach, when in fact they are parts of the same organic Whole.

P: The true belief that consciousness is a Whole must function, then, as a guide for living. In a sense, you, my friend, have more responsibility than do the fundamentalists and other hate mongers for striving to align your emotional realty with this belief.

N: I think I understand what you mean. *Their* belief, that Consciousness is not a Whole, allows them to accept some forms of individuated consciousness while rejecting others. So when they feel hatred towards those who are different from themselves, they are at least feeling and behaving in accordance with what they believe, even though what they believe is false. But when I, who believe in the Unity of Consciousness, feel animosity towards the fundamentalists, my emotions are not in accord with my belief, even though my belief is true.

P: My point exactly. Now, you know better than to be too hard on yourself about this, since Spinoza has taught you that emotion and behavior do not automatically align themselves with true belief. It takes effort, vigilance, and much practice.

N: Yes. So when I find myself having less than loving thoughts and feelings towards the fundamentalists, or the republicans, or towards any other form of individuated consciousness, I should use my true belief that Consciousness is a One as a corrective for my feelings...

P: ...instead of wallowing in them. You have noticed, have you not, that there is a sort of deliciousness involved in feelings of self-right-eous anger and indignation, and hence a tendency to cling to such feelings.

N: Yes, the fundamentalists really enjoy these feelings. It makes them feel superior to everyone else, and it justifies their violence impulses.

P: But it is important to realize that it is not just the fundamentalists and Republicans who enjoy these feelings. All humans do. I felt the lure of such feelings myself, when I was embodied.

N: How so?

S: (*from afar*) He never quite got over it.

N: Who was that? What didn't you ever get over?

P: That was Socrates.

N: What did he mean?

P: We can go into that another time. Let's get back to…

S: {*nearer, addressed to P*} No, no, no you don't. If you can use our friend Neal as an example of an individuated consciousness who has less than loving feelings towards other forms of individuated consciousness, despite his belief in the Unity of Consciousness, then it is only fair that I be allowed to use you, dear Plato, as an example of the same thing.

P: {*to me, with great humor*} There is no escaping this fellow. He has been teasing me about this for the last 2400 years.

N: Will someone please tell me what this is all about. What is it that you never got over?

S: {*to me, playfully, with pretend seriousness*} He never got over the fact that the good citizens of Athens compelled me to leave my body a little sooner than I might otherwise have done. He was very angry at them, and felt very justified and self-righteous about his anger.

P {*to me*} You have to understand I was a mere youth at the time. My grief and anger were just what you call "youthful indiscretions".

S: {*to P, with pretend condescension*} No excuses now. Your emotions were not in harmony with what I taught you, or at least, with what I was trying to teach you. {*to me*} You see, he was so angry and upset at the time that he made himself sick. That's the real reason he wasn't present to see me off when I drank the hemlock. In the *UPhaedo*, he says only that he was sick; what he doesn't say is that he made himself sick with his anger and grief.

P: Well, I'm over it now.

S: I should hope so. {*to me*} But he was never able to fully release his anger towards the Athenians throughout his embodied life.

P: Well, that was then. Now let's move on.

S: Not so fast. I came here to make a point, and I'm not leaving until I make it.

N: I for one really want to hear what you have to say.

S: Good. {*to me, as an aside, mischievously*} And when you hear what my point is, you will understand why he is so eager to change the subject.

N: Proceed.

S: Very well. The discussion between you and Plato had reached the point where you were acknowledging the difficulty involved in aligning your emotions and behaviors with what you believe to be true.

N: Yes.

S: In particular, you were discussing feelings of anger and righteous indignation at those forms of individuated consciousness which falsely believe themselves to be different and better than other such forms, and which false beliefs allow them to be harmful and violent towards others.

N: Yes.

S: And Plato made three correct points, to which I will add a fourth.

N: What are they?

S: First, he observed that *your* feelings of righteous indignation towards them are akin to *their* feelings of righteous indignation towards those who disagree with them. Second, he said that such feelings have a certain "deliciousness" and "lure" to them, that makes the person who has them want to cling to them.

N: Yes, even though this "deliciousness" is unhealthy to the mind, just as the deliciousness of deep-fried food or excessive sweets is unhealthy to the body.

S: A good analogy. And the third point is that, because you have true belief (that Consciousness is a One) whereas the fundamentalists have a false belief (that consciousness is many), it is more your responsibility than theirs to resist the temptation to wallow in such emotions, and to strive to align your emotions with your true belief.

N: Yes. Now what is the fourth point?

S: It is this: the fundamentalists have ignorance, you have true belief, but Plato here had knowledge. He experienced directly the Unity of all forms of individuated Consciousness, and he still could not successfully eradicate the anger and indignation. He reduced their intensity to a large extent, but he did not eliminate them entirely.

N: {*to P*} Do you agree?

P: Yes. You see, what you call "enlightenment", "awakening" or the experience of Oneness, comes in degrees and in stages. The Eastern texts spell this out much more clearly than the Western texts. But without going into detail, I'll use my cave analogy to illustrate the relevant distinction. When I got out of the cave and saw the Light – the indivisible Wholeness of all souls – I could not sustain the vision. So when I re-entered the cave and returned to ordinary waking consciousness, all I brought back with me was the memory of the experience of the One.

N: Perhaps like people who have a profound Near-Death Experience.

P: Perhaps. But Socrates here, when he found himself outside of the cave, he didn't merely see the Light, he became the Light. So when he re-entered the cave, he brought the vision of Oneness back into the cave with him, and so for him, the cave was no longer a cave, but was transformed into the Light itself. That is, he never experienced what we have been calling individuated consciousness as individuated consciousness. He experienced all things as intrinsic and necessary aspects of the Whole.

S: And that is why I could never feel anger or indignation towards anyone. I experienced everyone as aspects of mySelf, or of the Whole, for these two had become One for me, even while still embodied. And so the fourth point is that, just as those who have right opinion have more responsibility than those who are ignorant to overcome the emotions that are predicated on a false belief that some forms of individuated consciousness are separate from the One, so also those who, like Plato, have the knowledge that only direct experience bestows, have even more responsibility than those who, like yourself, have only true belief.

P: Yes, and I have to add that it is considerably easier for those of us who have knowledge than for those who have only true belief. You see, the experience of being in the Light by itself burns away, so to speak, much of the lure of the emotions predicated on separateness.

N: Yes. People who have had a Near-Death Experience, and have experienced themselves as part of the Light, report that they no longer feel any need to compete with others, but they still feel difficulty integrating their knowledge into their lives.

S: Yes they do. And the difficulty is twofold. In the first place, they may still feel the lure of emotions based on separation. They may, for example, be tempted to feel superior to others because *they*, after all, wish to live in harmony with Love and Knowledge, whereas others are mired in the muck of greed and ambition. Because Plato never quite overcame his anger towards his fellow citizens for ejecting me out of my body, these feelings allowed him, ever so slightly, to feel superior to those who judged against me. *He*, after all, was too intelligent, too moral, too "evolved", too whatever, to do such a thing, and these feelings separated him from other forms of individuated consciousness.

P: So, to summarize our discussion on the path to Enlightenment, we might put it this way; first there is the stage of ignorance, represented by the fundamentalists and the atheists, second there is the stage of true belief or right opinion, third there is a stage of seeing the Light, fourth there is the stage of experiencing oneself as the Light, but only temporarily, and finally there is the stage of experiencing oneself as the Light permanently. It is only in the last stage that the Cave of physical existence ceases to be experienced as such, and in a sense, ceases even to exist.

S: And what Plato referred to as the lure of emotions predicated on the belief in separateness persists through the fourth stage, and dissolves completely only in the fifth.

N: I understand. I have noticed that the distinction between the third and fourth stages appears throughout the Near-Death Experience reports. Most NDEers who experience the Light report that they "see it", or feel Its presence and its Love. A minority report that they actually "became" the Light. But both kinds of experiencers – the ones who "see", and the ones who "become" – report difficulty adjusting to the darkness of physical embodiment, when they return to their bodies, just as Plato wrote in *The Republic*. Now, Socrates, you said the difficulty is two-fold. What is the second kind of difficulty.

S: It is this: every aspect of your culture, from personal relations to social and political and even religious institutions, is predicated on the false belief in separateness – that Consciousness is a Many, rather than a One. Those who have knowledge – who have seen or become the Light – automatically strive to live according to their knowledge. Even those who, like yourself, have only true belief, feel the tension between how you believe life ought to be lived, and how external conditions appear to compel you to live.

N: Perhaps it will be useful to say that only those who have attained to the fifth stage have knowledge; whereas those who have experienced the third or fourth stage have only the memory of having had knowledge?

P: I understand the motivation for making such a distinction. If we make the distinction the way you suggest, it would then follow that one who has either true belief or the memory of knowledge, but not continuous knowledge, are alike in that both will experience considerable incongruity while living in the Cave of physical embodiment. However, making the distinction in this way will conceal an important difference between the first two, as well as an important similarity between the second and third.

N: Please explain.

P: Consider this analogy: a person has read about some faraway place of great beauty. Assuming that what she read was true, then she has formed true beliefs about that place. A second person not only reads about the place, but also goes there and returns, perhaps many times. And a third person goes there and stays there. Now the first person, because she lacks direct experience of the place, cannot be absolutely certain that the place is as beautiful as described.

N: Especially if it is described as a place far beyond all earthly beauty.

P: But the second person, who has seen the place, however briefly, is not in a position to doubt. He will be as certain of its existence and beauty as the third person, who is living there.

N: OK, I get it. You prefer to use the distinction between true belief and knowledge to capture the difference between one who can still doubt and be uncertain of the existence of a transcendent realm, and one for whom it is impossible to doubt or to be in any way uncertain of the fact that Consciousness is primary and that it is a One, not a many.

P: Yes, both for a person who, like Socrates, is living there, so to speak, and for a person, like myself, who has only visited it, doubt about its actual existence is impossible. That's why I think we should call them both "knowledge".

S: If I might interject something here, it seems that this discussion has uncovered a subtle ambiguity in the statement of the first premise.

N: What is it?

S: When we state that consciousness is primary, it is reasonable to ask, what is it primary *over*?

N: Well, matter or physicality, presumably.

S: Yes, presumably. But what is the ontological status of matter? Is it real or unreal? The statement "consciousness is primary" seems to imply that there is a something over which Consciousness is primary. But what if …

N: …Consciousness is a One without a second, as the Eastern texts say. Then there would be nothing for Consciousness to be primary over.

P: And we would need to re-formulate our first premise as "only Consciousness exists", or something like that.

S: And from a subjective point of view, those who have not experienced the One, whether they have true belief or merely ignorance, experience physicality as real ....that is, they experience as real something other than Consciousness. Those who have what you earlier called the memory of knowledge still experience as real something other than Consciousness, but they know it to be unreal or much less real, than Consciousness, and that Consciousness is primary over them.

P: Yes, those were the shadows on the wall of my Cave. Even though I knew that they were in some sense insubstantial and unreal, I experienced them as places of relative darkness, places where the Light of Consciousness was not, and I occasionally had difficulty with them.

S: (*teasingly*) Only occasionally?

P: I'll let that pass.

S: All right. The point is that for one who has permanent knowledge, only Consciousness exists. It is not primary over anything because there isn't anything else. He experiences no difficulty adjusting to the darkness of the Cave, as Plato reports, because there is no Cave and no darkness. All is Light and is experienced as such. The Cave ceases to exist, and in a sense, is experienced as never having existed in the first place. There is no experience of separation. Everything is always experienced as it is and there is no incongruence between what is and ought to be.

N: And we should note, of course, that those who have only ignorance also experience no incongruence, since their personal false beliefs are completely aligned with and in harmony with the larger culture. In fact, those false beliefs have created the culture.

P: Well, I wonder...

N: What?

P: Whether those who are ignorant experience no incongruence. You see, we believe, do we not, that all souls, however forgetful, came from the One and originally experienced the Wholeness of all things.

N: Yes, we agree.

P: So ignorant souls, no less than knowledgeable souls, belong to the One. However, the memory of their connection with the One is buried deep inside the subconscious portion of their minds. And subconscious memories, as your psychologists correctly observe, can affect conscious feelings and emotions.

N: Yes. So when, through their ignorance and forgetfulness...

P: ...which is the same thing...

N: ...they behave in ways which are not in harmony with their connection with God and with all other individuated consciousnesses, they cannot feel totally congruent.

P: In fact, most of the illnesses in your culture can be traced to the fact that people are not living in accordance with what they subconsciously know to be true, even if they cannot recollect that knowledge. They live in accordance with the false belief that Consciousness is a many, not a One, and that parts of the One can be permanently separated from the Whole. From my perspective, this is insanity on a grand scale.

N: I agree. Earlier in our discussion, I think you were about to mention the fundamentalists as an example of an extreme form of this collective insanity...

P: ...until *you* presented yourself as a more convenient example. Well, we can still use them as an example. But they are not at all unique; in fact, it is to their credit that they articulate their false beliefs with greater clarity than most.

N: What do you mean?

P: They explicitly state that only some souls – namely theirs – will be "saved", will go to Heaven, and be with the Creator, whereas all other souls will be eternally separated from God.

N: Yes, this is what they say. And because they believe that those who are different from them are not worthy of God's love, they feel justified in behaving towards them as unlovingly and as punitively as they falsely believe God would behave.

P: But this is, in effect, what all Western religions teach, is it not?

N: I suppose so. Jews believe that God has chosen them to be special, in some way...

P: ...in a way that excludes other ethnic groups from being equally special to God, is that not so?

N: Yes. And Christians believe that one can be with God in the after-life only if one believes, as they do, in the divinity of a man who lived two thousand years ago.

P: A rather strange belief.

N: And Muslims believe that God last spoke to humans through a man who lived fifteen hundred years ago, and that there has been no connection between God and humans, between the transcendent and the embodied, since that time.

P: Very strange, indeed. All this nonsense reflects the false belief that individuated consciousness can be separated from the whole.

N: These religions would have a difficult time if everyone were to accept the truth of our two premises.

P: Yes, they would have a difficult time. Their only hope for surviving in a culture where everyone believed that Consciousness is a Unity would be to study the teachings of their own mystics, that is, people who have experienced directly the Oneness of Consciousness. All three religious traditions you mention above have produced many such individuals.

N: True, but the Western religions, unlike the Eastern religions, seem to be very threatened by their mystics, and many have been persecuted, even put to death, because what they Know about God contradicts the false beliefs of the religion.

S: Hey you guys, I know a little bit about being put to death. And in my case, it had nothing to do with contradicting religious beliefs.

N: What do you mean?

S: Well, I never really expressed beliefs that contradicted the religious beliefs of my time. I challenged people insofar as they expressed their belief in separation through how they were living, or desired to live, their lives.

N: I think I know what you mean, but could you elaborate?

S: Sure. I challenged people who believed that their happiness and well-being were to be found, not through experiencing the Oneness of

Consciousness, but rather, through having more wealth than others, or more reputation than others, or more worldly power than others. For these desires, for wealth, reputation, and power, are really desires to be separate from others, and involve very strongly the belief that such separation is both possible and desirable.

P: And this is the root cause of all the ills afflicting your society. Those who pursue such desires inflict much harm, both to themselves and to everyone else.

N: I agree. The greed and ambitions of a few are causing harm to the Earth itself.

P: But the problem is not just the "greed and ambitions of a few". For *everyone* in your culture, not just a few, believes that it is OK for some people to have more money than others, to have more fame than others, and to have more power than others. Your culture as a whole, through its institutions, believes that it is right that only children from well-to-do families should be well-educated, that it is right for a small minority of individuals to control the great majority of the planet's natural resources, that quality health care is a privilege for those who can afford it, that politicians have a right to be corrupt, that poor people do not have a right to quality legal counsel when needed, and that it is right for some people to be separated off from society and be put in prisons for the rest of their lives. All of this reflects a belief that Consciousness is a many, not a One.

N: I have sometimes thought that the poor person who buys a lottery ticket is just as greedy as corporate CEOs. His only complaint against the system is that it is someone else, not himself, who is wealthy.

P: Whereas *our* complaint against the system is that it is based on the false belief that Consciousness is a many... that some forms of individuated consciousness can and should be separated off from the rest.

S: Now, now, it does no good to complain about the "system", since any system merely reflects the level of thinking of the individuals that constitute it. It would be more fruitful, I think, to focus on the individual, and his effort to live in accordance with the true belief that Consciousness a Unity. This effort, so to speak, requires constant vigilance against desires that run contrary to the belief.

N: What are these desires?

S: Any desire to "have" more or to "be" more than another, to measure his or her self-worth against other people, so that by having more (more money, more reputation, more status, more influence) he judges himself to be better than others. These are the kinds of desires which are incompatible with the belief that consciousness is a whole.

N: And we should add any desire that involves harming others.

P: Of course. But we must interpret this broadly.

N: What do you mean?

P: A person can harm another bodily, through physical violence. A person can harm another psychologically, through verbal abuse and other ways. But other, indirect ways of causing harm are more serious in your society. For example, a company that pollutes the environment causes great harm to people who live in that environment. A company that makes products that are harmful to children, such as tobacco and fast-foods, seeks to gain advantage by harming others.

S: And of course, an immediate consequence of the true belief that Consciousness is a Unity is that it is never possible to gain an advantage through harming others, whether that harm is done directly, or indirectly, by harming the environment.

P: Hence, the first, and most important, responsibility of any individual who has arrived at the true belief that Consciousness is a One must be to examine herself, as Socrates is fond of saying, and to root out all desires which are inconsistent with this belief.

N: I agree.

P: And furthermore, the very desires which are most admired in your present society – greed, ambition, competitiveness – would rightly be regarded as forms of mental unbalance, and would be treated as such.

N: Spinoza calls them "species of madness".

P: And madness indeed it is, when seen from the perspective of Wholeness. For it is quite insane to believe that Wholeness can be separated into distinct parts, and that some parts are more important than others.

N: And this form of insanity is involved whenever anyone desires to have more than others, or to be thought better than others, or to gain advantage by harming another.

P: Or even to compare herself in U*any* way with others. The examples we have been giving are examples of those who judge themselves to be better than others by comparing themselves – their money, their reputation, their achievements – with others. But we should remember that the general principle also applies to the opposite sort of case. People who feel despondent because they are not wealthy, or who suffer from low self-esteem because they are not famous, and so forth, are people who have judged themselves to be a failure by comparing themselves negatively with others.

N: So both the person who believes "I am better than others because I have more money, reputation, etc. than others" and the person who believes "I am not as good as others because I have less money, reputation, etc., than others" have made the same mistake. What they both believe, together with the emotions those beliefs generate, is contrary to the true belief that Consciousness is a One. Actually I think many more people suffer through negative comparison with others than vice versa.

P: Well of course. In most competitive games, there are many more losers than winners. So if everyone is competing, say, for fame and reputation, many more people will fail than will succeed.

N: So in a society where everyone believes that Consciousness is a Unity, a person's sense of value, of self-worth, of meaning, will not depend on either positive or negative comparisons with others. Perhaps people will be taught that everyone – every individuated consciousness – has value simply by being an intrinsic part of the Whole.

P: There is, as you say, intrinsic value simply in being. But there is also value added, so to speak, by living a life that is in conscious harmony with the Wholeness of all Consciousness.

S: And this is something you can strive for right now.

N: What do you mean?

S: Just what I said. It is all well and good to think about what things might be like if everyone came to believe that Consciousness is a Whole. But there is a danger that this could be used as an excuse.

N: An excuse for what?

S: Well haven't you heard people say things like "if everyone *else* cared about the environment, the poor, their soul, etc., then so would I"?

N: Oh yes. We humans often use the fact that others behave in less than exemplary ways to excuse our own less than exemplary behaviors.

S: So a possible danger in raising the question "what if everyone believed, etc?" is that some people might think that they cannot live in accordance with the belief in Wholeness until everybody else does.

N: But it is very difficult to live this way, given that so very few people are, or even think they should.

S: Difficult yes, impossible no. I did it.

N: But you were an exception.

S: To call me an exception is to separate me off from the Whole of Consciousness.

N: OK, not an exception. Unusual?

S: But everyone can be "unusual" in this way. Everyone who has come to the true belief that Consciousness is a Whole is responsible for trying to live his or her life in accordance with that belief, and this is so regardless of whether or not everyone else, or anyone else for that matter, is doing the same. Do you agree?

N: Yes.

P: And this responsibility involves the effort to become aware of and root out all emotions and behaviors that are contrary to the Wholeness of Consciousness.

N: I agree.

P: Good. So, do you feel we have discussed the issues, as charged?

N: Well yes, we have certainly discussed the issues. But there is a lot more to discuss. Our discussion, it seems, has focused mostly on the responsibility incumbent upon individuals who have come to believe in the primacy and Wholeness of Consciousness. We have not discussed how the institutions of society, indeed, society itself, would be changed as a result.

P: It would certainly be interesting to discuss the large scale social, cultural, economic, and political ramifications that would necessarily occur were everyone to believe in the Wholeness of Consciousness. Indeed, considerable social change would occur right now if those who actually believe that Consciousness is a Whole were to apply, with diligence, their true belief to their personal lives. Individual responsibility is the key to social change. Social change can come about only through the personal effort of individuals who have come to see the falsity of the myth of separation, and who strive to live their lives accordingly. This is why we have stressed individual responsibility. So perhaps this is a good time to bring our discussion to a close. (*to S:*) Do you have anything else to say, old man?

S: I always have something else to say. But it can wait until another time.

TWO STORIES – CONFLICTING VISIONS OF THE HUMAN POSSIBLE

David C. Korten

Through the stories we share, we humans define what it means to be human, our place in Creation, our responsibilities to one another and Earth, and the possibilities it is within our means to actualize. Rarely, however, do we step back to examine the underlying assumptions implicit in these stories and how those assumptions shape the cultures and institutions by which we live.

The issues are revealed with particular clarity by playing out the implications of two sharply contrasting stories. One is the story of a dead universe that assumes matter is the sole reality and consciousness but an illusion. This is the standard story of contemporary Western science. The other is the story of a living universe that takes consciousness to be the primary reality. This is a new story emerging as a synthesis of ancient religious wisdom and the data of the scientific leading edge — and it potentially changes everything.

The Dead Universe Story

The story of a dead universe traces back to the sixteenth and seventeenth century scientists and philosophers who gave birth to the age of science and reason. In 1543, Polish astronomer and mathematician Nicholas Copernicus (1473-1543) published *On the Revolution of the Heavenly Spheres* setting forth his thesis that the earth makes one rotation on its axis each day and makes one rotation around the sun each year —challenging the prevailing faith that the earth is the stationary center of the universe. Compelling support from the astronomical observations of Italian scientist, Galileo Galilei (1546-1642) ultimately convinced the majority of scientists that Copernicus' main conclusions were true.

Building from these findings, French philosopher René Descartes

(1596-1650), an influential advocate of rationalism, taught that the various bodies that comprise the universe move in predictable mechanical relationship to one another as they play out forces originally set in motion by God. Sir Isaac Newton's (1642-1727) mathematical description of the law of gravity and the extension of its application to the bodies of the solar system provided confirmation of Descartes' teaching and led to broad acceptance of the view that universal laws that can be described in mathematical notation govern every event in nature.

Backed by the teaching of English philosopher John Locke (1632-1704) that the human mind is at birth a blank slate with nothing written on it, science came to accept the idea that all knowledge originates from sense perception and that observation and reason are the only valid sources of truth. Together these ideas freed science from the obligation to pay homage to religious revelation and the authority of the church.

Gone was the medieval conception of a universe guided by a benevolent purpose; men now dwelt in a world in which the procession of events was as automatic as the ticking of a watch. Newton's philosophy did not rule out the idea of a God, but it deprived Him of His power to guide the stars in their courses or to command the sun to stand still.[1]

In the earlier stages of the scientific revolution many scientists made an accommodation to religious teaching in their effort to explain how this extraordinary machinery came into being. Lacking any better explanation, many accepted Descartes' basic position that it was all created and set into motion by a master inventor – God. In the eyes of science, if there ever was a God, however, he had long ago departed the scene – leaving only mechanism behind.

Thus, it was that science came over time to see the universe as a gigantic clockwork driven by a spring that is gradually running down to a state of exhaustion – a mere collection of material parts that interact according to fixed physical laws knowable through observation, measurement, and mathematical calculation. That which cannot be observed and measured – such as spirit and consciousness – came to be excluded from consideration by science – and therefore do not exist within the scientist's worldview.

Although science could scarcely deny life, it worked from the premise that life is purely the accidental result of mechanical, chemical, and electrical processes and can ultimately be understood solely in terms of its component physical parts. Given its centrality to the human experience, the reality of consciousness is also difficult to deny, but science concluded that it is nothing more than an illusory artifact of material complexity. As astronomer Carl Sagan put it, "My fundamental premise about the brain is that its workings – what we sometimes call 'mind' – are a consequence of its anatomy and physiology, and nothing more."[2]

Throughout the scientific-industrial era, this mechanistic view of reality served effectively to focus our collective human attention on understanding and mastering our material world. We unlocked countless secrets of matter, traveled beyond our own world, dramatically extended the average human life span, created vast organizations able to function simultaneously throughout the world, and installed a global system of communication that – if we choose to do so – could link every person on the planet in instantaneous communication with every other.

However, these accomplishments came at a heavy price. The scientific premise that life is an accident and consciousness an illusion stripped our lives of purpose and meaning. Seventeenth-century philosopher Thomas Hobbes (1588-1679) extended this premise to its logical conclusion in the articulation of a moral philosophy of competitive self-interest and materialistic hedonism subsequently embraced by modernist culture, current mainstream economic thought, and contemporary capitalism.

Much like his modern counterpart Carl Sagan, Hobbes maintained that absolutely nothing exists except body, matter, and motion: "Every part of the Universe, is Body; and that which is not Body, is no part of the Universe: and because the Universe is All, that which is no part of it is Nothing."[3] Therefore, Hobbes maintained, mind is nothing more than motion in the brain. Even God, if he exists, must have a physical body.

Hobbes also argued that what we humans do is determined by our appetites (primarily a desire for power) and our aversions (primarily a fear of others). Without rule by an all-powerful king to restrain and channel these animalistic impulses, our lives would be "poor, nasty, brutish, and short." This Hobbesian theory of governance is now known as Hobbism, defined by *Webster's New Collegiate Dictionary*, as "the Hobbesian theory that absolutism in government is necessary to prevent the war of each against all to which natural selfishness inevitably leads mankind."[4] The Hobbesian logic leads from material primacy to a belief in a world without moral purpose in which the pursuit of material gratification is life's only source of meaning and the brutish impulses of man must be restrained by authoritarian rulers

Modern economics turned the Hobbesian ideology of rational materialism into an applied science of human behavior and social organization that embraces hedonism as the goal and measure of human progress, assumes human behavior is motivated solely by material self-interest, and absolves the individual of responsibility for moral choice. Indeed, one might argue that Hobbes, not Adam Smith, properly bears the title of intellectual father of neoliberal economic theory and the rapacious excesses of corporate capitalism. Adam Smith was, by contrast, a man of deep ethical conviction engaged in an intellectual crusade against the concentration of unaccountable power and a search for the foundation of moral behavior.

Recognizing that the corporate global economy is grounded in the intellectual and moral philosophy of Hobbes helps to explain an otherwise puzzling anomaly. As an institution for serving the needs of people and nature, i.e., for serving life, the corporate global economy is failing nearly everywhere. An explosion of human knowledge and technology has greatly expanded the possibility of creating human societies that serve the whole of life. Yet those possibilities go unrealized. Indeed, even as the economy grows, productivity increases, and stock indices climb we work longer hours to make ends meet, our lives seem to have less meaning, we feel less secure, and we can no longer afford things we once took for granted like leisure time, family life, education, health care, retirement, parks, clean water, and secure jobs that pay a family wage with benefits. Citing indicators of economic growth and increasing stock values, the institutions we entrust with the power to set priorities and make the rules assure us that we are enjoying the fruits of economic success, even as our lives become ever more impoverished.

The apparent anomaly is readily explained as soon as we recognize that what the corporate global economy serves with ruthless efficiency is the Hobbesian drive for power – concentrating ever more power in the hands of a small ruling elite and indulging their insatiable appetites for material gratification. Ruled by global financial markets and organized by mega-scale global corporations that operate beyond the reach of public accountability, the system mobilizes the world's people, resources, markets, and governments behind a dual purpose – maximizing returns to financial capital, i.e., to the already powerful, and providing the winners in a relentless global drive for power with material indulgences in proportion to their financial wealth. Rebellious tendencies of the excluded masses whose needs and wellbeing are denied are dismissed as brutish impulses that must be restrained by use of the state's police and military powers in the name of "maintaining essential order" – which is a code phrase for protecting the property rights of power holders. By the moral logic of a Hobbesian view grounded in a story of material primacy, this is as it should be.

This brutal and amoral philosophy lends legitimacy to an economic system in which power is delinked from moral accountability, instrumental and financial values override life values, and the expedient and profitable take precedence over the nurturing and responsible. As Hobbes aptly demonstrated, it all follows logically from the premise that the material is primary and that life is therefore accidental and meaningless. A story that denies life of meaning and respect absolves us of responsibility for the harm we do, and has led to a suicidal global economy that is wantonly destroying life to serve the drive for power and material hedonism of a small ruling elite with an underdeveloped moral consciousness. The result is a deepening global crisis of accelerating social and environmental breakdown that increasingly threatens human survival. Grounded in a belief that life is an accident, consciousness an illusion, and corrective action might require a redistribution of power and some restraint on material indulgence, the Hobbesian response to a crisis born of unmitigated greed is a shrug and a scowl, saying in effect, "What's mine is mine. When it's over it's over; last one out turn off the lights." Stories have real consequences.

The Living Universe Story

What if the assumption of material primacy is wrong? What if consciousness is real and life is more than an accident? Indeed, what if consciousness is the primary reality? What if the universe is best described not as a clock works running down, but rather as a great intelligence seeking to know itself through an unfolding journey of discovery toward ever-greater complexity and potential? How might that change the human story and our sense of human responsibility and possibility?

Consider the creation story as science itself now tells it. It all began some 15 billion years ago when in a sudden flash the energy and mass of our known universe burst forth as dispersed energy particles across the vastness of space. With the passing of time these particles, self-organized into atoms, swirled into great clouds that eventually formed into galaxies, then coalesced into stars that grew, died, and were reborn as new stars, star systems, and planets. The cataclysmic energies unleashed by the births and deaths of billions of suns converted simple atoms into ever more complex atoms and molecules – at each step opening new possibilities for the growth and evolution of the whole.

More than 11 billion years later, at least one among the countless planets of the cosmos gave birth to tiny but enterprising living organisms that launched the planet's first great age of invention. They discovered the processes of fermentation, photosynthesis, and respiration – building blocks for what was to follow. Learning to share their discoveries with one another through the exchange of genetic material, they created the planet's first global communication system. With time, they discovered how to join in cooperative unions to create complex multi-celled organisms with capacities far beyond those of the individual cells of which they were composed. Continuously experimenting, creating, building, life transformed the planet's material substance into a web of living beings of astonishing variety, beauty, awareness, and capacity for intelligent choice.

The species called human is one of the more extraordinary products of this enterprise and an awe-inspiring demonstration of life's capacity for cooperation. Each human body is comprised of some 30 to 70 trillion individual living cells, plus an even larger number of assorted beneficial bacteria and fungi, all cooperating to create a being of extraordinary ability and potential. Many scientists hold firmly to a belief in material primacy, even though science itself now tells a creation story that reveals at every turn the working of a grand creative intelligence engaged in bringing forth a great thought unfolding.

Our task here is not to debate the scientific merits of the premise that consciousness is primary, although this premise surely fits the data of science far more convincingly than the premise that Creation is nothing more than the outcome of mechanism and chance. Rather the task is to examine what might be the social and political implications of embracing the story of a living universe in which the cosmic metaphor is not the machine, but the organism; the irreducible building block is not a particle, but a thought; and far from being illusion, consciousness and the capacity for choice are the defining reality of the cosmos.

In the living universe story, the spiritual intelligence we call God no longer resides apart, a distant king with a physical body occupied in making rules, rewarding the obedient, and punishing the disobedient as a stern father, but rather becomes recognized as the ground from which all being flows – the vital source of the illusion we perceive as matter. In a cosmos in which we recognize every particle and being as a manifestation of what we call God, the Hobbesian logic of "war of each against all" disintegrates in favor of the logic of "all for one and one for all".

As the wonder of life's extraordinary capacity for creative self-organization is revealed, our hearts are opened to experience the awesome grandeur of Creation with love and reverence for the whole of life, the miracle of our living planet, and the creative potentials of each person. We awaken to the reality that we are neither the end products of Creation nor the abandoned children of a forgetful God, but rather instruments of Creation's continued unfolding with a responsibility to act as mindful stewards of its treasures and to find our role in fulfilling its great cosmic purpose. By the logic of a living universe in which consciousness is primary, meaning and purpose are found not in an escapist pursuit of material gratification, but through engaging in the cooperative, creative exploration of Creation's vast possibilities.

Perhaps we might even heal the centuries-old breech between science and religion that has left us with an artificial and often schizophrenic separation of our intellectual and spiritual lives – torn between a theology that denies the evidence of logic and observation and a science that denies our experience of consciousness and spirit.

In the story of a living universe, the demeaning and limiting self-image of the Hobbesian world view gives way to a faith in our ability to create truly free and democratic societies grounded in principles of justice, freedom, and compassion that unleash the full potential of human creativity and capacity for responsible choice. The organizational model of the all powerful king who imposes his will by fear and physical force gives way to the model of deeply democratic societies in which responsible citizens work in cooperative partnership toward the creation of healthy families, communities, nations, and a global society that works for all.

Liberated from the moral arguments of a dead universe logic, we might withdraw our support from an economic system that destroys life to feed the drive for power and material indulgence of a small ruling elite and redirect it to creating self-organizing, life-serving, living economies that share power and resources equitably to secure the well-being of all. Liberated from the quest for power and material indulgence we could devote ourselves to the pursuit of life in all its possibilities. Conspicuous consumption would naturally give way to voluntary simplicity. We would turn off television sets and cut back our work hours in favor of turning to one another for conversation, artistic expression, sports, and community service.

A life seeking society would end the practice of subsidizing the conversion of life into the financial assets of ruling elites. This would mean introducing a regime of full-cost pricing of energy, materials, and land use that would quickly expose the real inefficiencies of global outsourcing, factory farming, conventional construction, and urban sprawl and make life-serving alternatives comparatively cost-effective. This would motivate a major economic restructuring in favor of local production, economic justice, and sustainability. We would grow most of our food fresh on local family farms without toxic chemicals, and process it nearby. We would compost our organic wastes and recycle them back into the soil. We would design environmentally efficient buildings for their specific microenvironment, and construct them of local materials to radically reduce energy consumption, improve health, and increase comfort. Much of our remaining energy needs would be supplied locally from wind and solar sources. Local wastes would be recycled to provide materials and energy for other local businesses. The environment would be cleaner. We would be more secure and enjoy a higher quality of living.

The elimination of energy and transportation subsidies would create an incentive to bring work, shopping, and recreation nearer to our residences – thus saving energy and commuting time, reducing CO_2 emissions and dependence on imported oil, and reducing commuting to free more time for family and community. Land now devoted to roads and parking could be converted to bike lanes, trails, and parks.

By reducing waste and unnecessary use of energy and other resources, those of us who live in high consumption countries, like the United States and many European countries, could reduce our need to expropriate the resources of other countries. This means we would no longer need to allocate a major portion of our national treasure to the large military required to secure our access to those resources. The world's poor would regain access to the resources that are rightfully theirs to improve their own lives – and the threat of terrorism would be greatly reduced. The elimination of power seeking global corporations with their massive overhead, inflated executive compensation packages, and myopic focus on short-term profits would free still more resources. Together these savings could provide workers with family wages and finance first-rate education, health care, and community services for all.

We would expect to see the effects of living economy institutions ripple out across the social landscape. With ample living wage jobs, educational opportunities, and essential services, crime rates would drop, and we could spend less on police, courts, and prisons.

An economy that responds to rather than creates demand diverts fewer resources to advertising. Fewer ads mean less visual pollution and wasteful consumerism, an improved sense of self-worth, and still more resources freed up to be converted into shorter workweeks and more leisure time. We would work less and live more. Our lives would be freer and richer. Our environment would be cleaner and healthier. A world no longer divided between the obscenely rich and the desperately poor would know more peace and less violence, more love and less hate, more hope and less fear. The Earth could heal and provide a home for our children for generations to come.

The stories by which we define ourselves play an important, often sub-conscious, role in shaping the evolutionary trajectory of the societies in which we live. We have a great need to change our defining stories. Perhaps a first step is to become more conscious of the influence of our stories and their underlying assumptions on the individual and collective choices that shape the direction of our development as persons and societies.

* * *

Our species, far beyond any other, has been engaged in a continuing process of intellectual, social, and technological evolution toward ever-greater species abilities. It is one of the great and mysterious wonders of the cosmos that as each of humanity's developmental stages has exhausted itself it has left behind both the means and the imperative to break free from the familiar and take an uncertain step into the unknown. We now stand at the threshold of a new era.

Life and intelligent consciousness are defining qualities of the human experience. To deny them, as the predominant creation story of Western science has done, is to deny our most important and exciting possibilities. On the positive side, denying the place of a cosmic intelligence helped science master the secrets of the physical world and build the extraordinary technical capabilities now in our hands. At the same time, this denial has led us to misuse these abilities in terrible ways that now threaten our survival. We must now use our powers of choice to turn the capabilities now in our hands to the service of life as we create environmentally and socially healthy societies free of physical want and deprivation and supportive of the social, intellectual, and spiritual growth of all.

The story that brought us to this threshold of opportunity now prevents us from crossing that threshold, because it prevents us from seeing the reality of our unrealized social, spiritual, and intellectual potentials. It is time for a new story that embraces the reality of consciousness as a creative force and directs our attention to mastering the arts of living.

References and Notes

1. McNall Burns, Edward, *Western Civilizations: Their History and Their Culture*, 5th ed., New York: W. W. Norton, 1958; pp. 522-523.

2. Sagan, C., *The Dragons of Eden*, New York: Random House, 1977; p. 7.

3. As quoted by Laurence Berns, "Thomas Hobbes," in Strauss. L. & Cropsey, J. (eds.), *History of Politics Philosophy,* Third Edition, Chicago: The University of Chicago Press, 1987; p. 397.

4. 1973 edition, p. 544.

THE POWER OF CONSCIOUSNESS TO TRANSFORM POLITICS

Corinne McLaughlin and Gordon Davidson

"Nothing is as powerful as an idea whose time has come," Victor Hugo wrote centuries ago. Ideas have changed the world – great ideas such as "love your neighbor as yourself" or "all men are created equal." Why are ideas so powerful? Because consciousness – not physical form – is primal. Consciousness is the causal factor. Consciousness refers here to the mind, the emotions, the intuition and the soul (or higher self, monad, Buddha mind, etc.) As Buddha said, "With our thoughts we create the world." Christ said, "As a man thinketh in his heart, so he is."

According to the new science of psychoneuroimmunology and the study of neuropeptides, our negative thoughts and emotions weaken our immune system and harm our personal health and well-being. Our positive thoughts strengthen us. But what about the effects of our collective thoughts on our collective political health as a society? The world we see around us is what our past thoughts have created. If we don't like what we see, we need to change our thinking. To create a healthy world, we need healthy minds. Energy follows thought. Whatever we think about, we direct energy towards, and this focused energy, combined with our emotional desire and vital energy, gives thought the power to manifest physically. Thought is the basic building block of the universe. With each new thought we help create the world anew. This is the incredible power we as humans have – for good or evil.

If the physical forms we have created with our thoughts become too limiting or dysfunctional, they need to be destroyed. The ancients taught that "in the shattering of form lies hid the secret of all evolution." As we shatter old thoughtforms, such as limiting ideas about what women are capable of, then we begin the process of shattering old institutions, such as corporate management or sports that exclude women.

Politics is essentially about the distribution and exercise of power in the collective sphere. How would our politics be different if citizens personally understood that consciousness is primal and thoughts are the cause of everything in our lives and in the physical world? Politics would be almost the exact opposite of what we have today, as we would focus more on the inner, subjective side of life, and less on personalities, money and power. Citizens would take more responsibility for what their consciousness had created, both personally and collectively, and they'd stop blaming others for problems. Politicians would serve the greatest good of the greatest number of people – the opposite of today.

Politics is affected by the values held in people's consciousness. The values of the market place (e.g. competition, money, and so forth) currently dominate our consciousness, and thus control politics. If spiritual values (e.g. compassion, sharing) ascend in our consciousness, they will guide and direct our politics. Real, transformational political power begins with inner consciousness, not with outer, material forms such as government agencies.

If consciousness is seen as primary, then the key to real progress would be helping people expand their consciousness and identify with ever more inclusive groups – from family to community to nation to the world and all life on earth. With each expansion of identity, there would be a new focus on finding a sense of unity amidst diversity and developing a shared purpose. Identifying ourselves as world citizens and aligning with the higher purpose of the United Nations would be recognized as a more advanced stage of consciousness.

Despite appearances, life is constantly moving forward, and human consciousness is constantly changing and evolving into greater wisdom, compassion and sense of purpose. The responsibility of the political sphere is to establish the conditions for this evolution of consciousness to occur most easily and clearly. When most effective, politics is responsive and adaptive to positive changes in consciousness, rather than manipulating people's consciousness through fear or hatred to maintain control.

A Nation's Evolutionary Purpose

There is an evolutionary purpose or higher plan unfolding through all human activity which is developing both greater individuation and a greater sense of oneness and unity. If consciousness is seen as primal, political leaders would seek to discern, and then implement, the higher purpose and intention for their nation. Understanding a nation's evolutionary purpose would then be the goal of all political leaders and political activity. The higher purpose of the United States, for example, is to demonstrate human equality and show how true freedom and democracy can benefit an individual's growth and development.

Once a nation's higher purpose is known, political leaders who are purely motivated can shape this into a clear, effective thoughtform, energize it with passion, and widely broadcast it. The purpose then becomes highly attractive and draws the people, energy and resources to help it express in the world through specific strategies. The purpose then becomes unstoppable. This was the process, for example, that unfolded with the Marshall Plan after World War II, as an effort to express something of the higher purpose of the United States. Rather than punishing them, the US helped the defeated Axis nations rebuild along democratic lines. This approach was far more effective and beneficial to people than punitive action. Today, however, America's "democracy-building" in many places around the world seems to be failing due to questionable motivations and bad planning. Each nation has a higher destiny. Each has an historical experience, a unique cultural and racial makeup, and karma (or debts) to be fulfilled. When consciousness is seen as primary, each nation will become aware of its destiny and the contribution it can make to the whole. A measure of the maturity of nations is how consciously they accept their world responsibilities and help other nations. For example, the Scandanavian nations model support for social and humanitarian action at home and abroad, as well as at the UN.

Consciousness Training and Visioning

If our national politicians knew that consciousness was primary, our government would provide consciousness training for all so that more people could become empowered, wise leaders. We'd be called "citizens" again – not just "consumers." Education would be far more important than today, and would be a key funding priority for government tax dollars. Educators would be hired who have a more refined and advanced consciousness, and we'd prioritize raising salaries for them. In addition to rational, left brain education, the curriculum would include right brain, affective education, such as training in character development and in right relationship with all life. Educators would teach people how to align with a higher purpose, hold a positive intention, and develop their will so they could accomplish constructive goals effectively. They'd teach them how to think clearly and compassionately and serve others and the larger whole.

If we knew how powerful our thoughts are, we would learn how to think positively and focus collectively on solutions rather than problems. We would learn how to control our negative thoughts and emotions and create harmonious, compassionate ones. We'd learn how to avoid projecting our unowned shadow or negative patterns on our political adversaries, accusing them of what we ourselves are guilty of. We'd no longer see political ads with one candidate accusing the other of being dishonest or aggressive, as people would realize that candidate may be in fact describing his/her own behavior.

If we focused on consciousness and addressed the root causes in both individual and collective *thinking*, we'd be more effective in eliminating social ills such as poverty and drug abuse. We'd find, for example, that the root causes of these problems are dysfunctional thinking about resources and society. We'd see clearly the illusion that a small percentage of greedy people can somehow isolate themselves from the effects of their selfish economic decisions on the majority. We'd see that a lack of self-esteem is the root cause of self-destructive, addictive behavior like drug abuse to numb personal pain. People would realize that true happiness and fulfillment comes not from how much they accumulate, but rather from what they give to others.

Knowing the primacy of consciousness, we'd also focus more on prevention of social problems, and would be proactive, rather than reactive, to crisis and change. We'd have visioning and dreaming sessions engaging a wide cross section of citizens in determining our political priorities, as we'd recognize this was how to best prevent crises and create the future we choose. Trained facilitators would lead policy makers or groups of citizens in guided imagery sessions on key issues, such as healthcare. For example, they'd have people imagine they had traveled ten years in the future, to see what our healthcare system looks like.

Consciousness and Public Policy

If we knew consciousness was primary, we would prioritize the need to think together as citizens about our problems, using public dialogues and whole systems approaches, where all ideas are heard and included in decisions. The more perspectives on a problem that are aired, the closer we would get to the full truth and to the root causes of a problem. The solution would thus be more effective and long lasting. Just as diversity strengthens an ecological system, so different political points of view give more information and a wider perspective on an issue. We could then find the underlying unity in the apparent diversity and conflicting opinions, and work towards a new political synthesis. If we knew the primacy of consciousness, our main focus would be to synthesize as many points of view as possible and build a consensus on our shared political priorities.

Citizens would attend these dialogues with an open attitude and a willingness to change their thinking and be transformed. They would refuse to become entrenched in a polarizing position on a controversial issue. Violent demonstrations would then no longer be needed to get the attention of those in power, because all relevant concerns would have been aired and included in the final decisions. We'd avoid the usual political strategies of winning at all costs and we would be far more sensitive to relationships.

Citizens would be trained in conflict resolution, in how to transform conflicts among families, communities and nations, by searching for common ground and win/win solutions. A political conflict such as that around the issue of abortion, for example, would be resolved by finding what both sides can agree on, rather than focusing on what they disagree about. Instead of fighting about when exactly is a fetus life and whether removing it is murder, they would instead search for common ground. They might find, for example, that both sides want to prevent unwanted pregnancies, so they could then collaborate on a campaign to prevent teen pregnancy.

If citizens could agree on a preferred future in a specific area such as transportation or energy use, we could all then visualize very clearly and with much detail this desired future and so help it manifest in the present. For example, we might want to solve the problem of smog, crowded freeways and depleting oil reserves by visualizing and desiring the creation of low cost, totally energy efficient cars that run on solar or other alternative energy. If millions of people did this type of detailed, regular visualization, we could precipitate into human consciousness the solution to any problem.

If we knew consciousness was primary, we would also be more aware of the battle of ideas and the impact of evolutionary, spiritual thinking that serves the good of the whole versus involutionary, materialistic thinking that is dysfunctional and benefits the few at the expense of the many. We would be aware of the need for equal access to the means of projecting ideas, especially the media. Our media would not be controlled by monied interests as it is now or by a particular political agenda – it would be more accessible to all legitimate ideas and points of view.

The Power of Meditation

If we knew that consciousness was primary, we would all learn how to meditate and still our minds, so we could contact the wisdom of our higher self or soul and be more fully present in the moment. We'd learn to listen to our intuition and the inner guidance of our soul, rather than relying on the rational mind or the opinion of so-called "experts". We'd realize that help is always available from higher levels and from the wisdom of our soul. The soul would be our guide in both our personal lives and also in our collective political life, providing solutions to larger social problems.

To create a powerful thoughtform of a solution to a social problem, we would meditate collectively to receive an inspirational vision or an idea. Then we would think out the idea clearly and concretely, seeing the practical details. We would then energize the thoughtform with our desire, our passion and enthusiasm to give it the power to manifest physically. Finally, we'd have to detach ourselves from the thoughtform, letting go of it emotionally, in order that it may be free to do its work and precipitate onto the physical plane. If the idea is held onto too tightly and possessively, it can't be free to manifest.

The practice of meditation would also help us become more detached observers of the political scene, able to see things clearly, rather than seeing through the distorted lens of our own limited beliefs, fears or desires. This would make it very difficult for politicians to manipulate our fears and hatreds for their own ends, or to promise endless government services without raising taxes. We'd then have balanced federal budgets and no national debt.

We'd also have trained meditators in the room whenever important negotiations or political decisions were being made. They could maintain a positive, intuitive energy field of goodwill that would lead to greater insights and wiser decisions. We'd train people in how to use group meditation and a consensus process for making political decisions. People would learn how to meet together and begin by sharing all the known facts and opinions about an issue. Then they'd work on releasing their opinions and enter a meditative silence together. They'd ask to be inwardly guided to find the wisest decision that would serve the highest good of all stakeholders. After a time of silence, each participant would share what they'd received in the meditation, and then they'd all work to build a consensus on the wisest course of action.

If all citizens were trained meditators, we'd be more detached from outcomes, knowing that politics, like everything in the world, is impermanent and ever changing. We'd then have the patience to work for the future, for long-term change and so wait out short-term difficulties, knowing that things will change again. If more citizens would meditate regularly, we'd have a more peaceful society with fewer violent crimes and fewer wars, as inner peace leads to outer peace.

Moral Lessons Learned

If we knew that consciousness was causal, we'd focus more on the moral lessons being learned through each crisis in this schoolhouse called Earth. We'd more closely examine all opportunities for both personal and collective growth. For example, in corporate scandals and subsequent bankruptcies, we'd recognize the moral lesson that honesty and fairness are needed for the long-term business success of all. Or when floods cause major property damage, we might ask whether we ignored ecological concerns in our impatience to build.

Interconnection and Oneness

If we knew consciousness was primary, we'd recognize that separateness is an illusion and that everyone and everything is interconnected. We would all feel the suffering of the poor and the sick as our own and would naturally make sure they are taken care of. We would feel our essential oneness with all of the human family and so would treat the peoples of other nations as we treat our own citizens. We would feel our interconnection with nature and all of life and so would prioritize environmental protection and sustainable agricultural and forestry policies.

If we experientially knew the reality of oneness, we could also avoid the "tragedy of the commons" problem, where each individual acting in rational self-interest creates a catastrophe for the community as a whole. Everything is related to everything else, so we cannot solve a problem in isolation from its context. We'd realize, for example, that an unfair socio-economic system breeds poverty (as liberals argue), but also that an individual's personal choices contribute to poverty (as conservatives maintain). We'd train people in how to transcend dualistic thinking and find a true third way in politics beyond left and right. In ancient Greece, initiates to the Mysteries were trained in paradoxical thinking, in understanding how something could be "both/and" rather than "either/or." This type of thinking would transform all our political debates and help us find more effective, long term policy solutions to every problem.

Reading the Book of Life

If we knew consciousness was primary, we'd understand the law of karma: as we sow, so shall we reap. Whatever causes we set into motion through our thinking (as well as through our actions) come back to affect us – not as punishment, but to educate us. Karma is a learning opportunity – so we can change our thinking and experience a different outcome next time. Karma is a cosmic recycling system creating equal opportunities for us all to learn. We would all learn, for example, that violent thoughts (and actions) are ultimately dysfunctional because there is always some "blowback," or negative karma, that comes back to the perpetrator. Ultimately, we never get away with anything.

Native Americans say the world is a mirror where we can observe reflections of our past thoughts, and thus see what we might want to change. They call this "reading the book of life." If we would apply this approach to the current terrorist crisis, we might explore how the collective thought field of fear about terrorists might have attracted random sniper attacks a few years back in Washington DC, as they occurred at the exact time that politicians and the media were debating whether to attack Iraq. Civilians could be randomly (though accidentally) killed in a war against Iraq, just as civilians were being attacked in the streets of Washington DC.

We might be courageous to ask if there was some message in the fact that both the sniping (and the earlier anthrax attacks) were not perpetrated by foreign terrorists, but rather by some of our fellow citizens, trained at our military facilities? Isn't it obvious when two lone snipers shooting a few people at random can completely terrorize a whole city, that we can't possibly protect ourselves in the usual form-oriented, material way? Wouldn't a "Fortress America" mentality actually lock us in – rather than lock others out?

When people are acting out of deep paranoia, any solutions to the terrorist crisis are bound to only create more of the same, and not really make anyone more secure. What's needed is to break through the cloud of fear and think more clearly about the deeper causes of the anger and hopelessness that leads desperate people to terrorism. The solution to true security has to be on a consciousness level – becoming internally strong and spiritually aligned as individuals and as a nation.

Franklin Roosevelt's wise reminder about the power of consciousness – that "the only thing we have to fear is fear itself," is as important today as it was during the earlier crisis of World War II.

Invoking Enlightened Leaders

And lastly, if we knew that consciousness was causal, we'd elect those truly enlightened thinkers and leaders whose consciousness was more advanced – rather than those with TV personalities and lots of money. We would elect politicians who are wiser and more compassionate, and who embody honesty, integrity and courage. Our leaders would be truly concerned about the common good, rather than about their own personal ego. We'd have fewer power-hungry, self-serving politicians, and more leaders like Mohatmas Gandhi, Martin Luther King and Robert Kennedy serving long term in elected office – rather than getting killed striving for justice.

In order to create the right conditions that invoke more leaders of this quality and truly transform politics, there is work we each need to do now. We can adopt a leader who has high potential, and support him or her inwardly by sending our prayers and positive energy in meditation so she/he might align with his/her highest self. We can align meditatively with the soul of our nation and visualize its higher qualities coming into greater expression, to create a more just and peaceful world for all people. And most importantly, we can each realize the power of our own consciousness on others, and so take more responsibility for refining and transforming it. Only thus can we collectively create a better world that works for all and be truly happy and secure.

IN THE BEGINNING WAS CONSCIOUSNESS
Seyyed Hossein Nasr

One alone is the Dawn beaming over all this.
It is the One that severally becomes all this.

      Rg-Veda, VIII, 58:2

The nameless [Tao] is the beginning of Heaven and Earth,
The named [Tao] is the mother of ten thousand things.

      Tao Te Ching, One

In the beginning was the Word, and the Word was with God,
and the Word was God.

      Gospel of John, 1:1

But His command, when He intendeth a thing, is only that He saith
unto it:
'Be!' and it is.

      Quran, 36:81

When we turn to the sacred scriptures of various religions, we discover that in every case the origin of the cosmos and of man is identified as a Reality which is conscious and in fact constitutes consciousness understood on the highest level as Absolute Consciousness, which is transcendent and yet the source of all consciousness in the cosmic realm including our own. Furthermore the "in the beginning" is understood not only as belonging to the past but also to the present moment which is the eternal now. That is why "in the beginning" must also be understood as "in principle" as the Latin translation of the opening verse of the Gospel of John asserts, "*in principia erat verbum.*"

    Whether we speak of Allah who commands things to be and they are, or the Tao, or the Word by which all things were made, or Brahman, we are speaking of Consciousness as ever-living and present. This truth is made especially explicit in Hinduism where the principal Reality which is the source of all things is described as at once Being, Consciousness and Ecstasy. Nor is this unanimity of vision of the Origin of all things as identified with consciousness confined to sacred scriptures. Both Oriental and traditional Western philosophers speak of the same truth. The *tò Agathon* of Plato is not only the Supreme Good but also supreme awareness of the Good, and *nous* or intellect, so central to Greek philosophy, is of course inseparable from consciousness. Islamic philosophers consider being to be inseparable from knowledge and therefore awareness, and consider cosmic levels of existence also to be levels of knowledge and awareness. As for Hinduism, in its worldview the existence of a thing, even a rock, is also a state of consciousness.

One can then assert safely that in the traditional world there was unanimity concerning the priority of consciousness in relation to what we call "matter" today. The Reality which is seen by all these traditional religions and philosophies to be the origin of things both temporally and in principle is also Supreme Consciousness and can only be reached when human beings are able to elevate their own level of consciousness. Even in Buddhism, which does not speak of an objective Supreme Reality and of cosmogenesis as understood in the Abrahamic and Iranian religions as well as Hinduism, *nirvana* is the supreme state of consciousness and Buddhahood is also inseparable from consciousness. The only exception to this unanimous traditional view in the old days was to be found in certain anti-metaphysical philosophies of the late Antiquity accompanying the death throes of Hellenistic and Roman civilizations and in certain marginal schools of ancient India which were thoroughly rejected by the mainstream orthodox schools of Hindu thought.

The privilege of denying the primacy of consciousness wholesale remained for the modern world, especially with the advent of the materialistic and scientistic philosophies which came to the fore after the Scientific Revolution in the seventeenth century. Furthermore, this transformation did not take place until the modern idea of matter, not to be confused with its understanding in Greek philosophy and science, was developed with Descartes and Galileo. By taking away from corporeal existence all its qualitative aspects and reducing it to pure quantity, these men, followed by many others, created a world-view in which there was such a thing as pure inert matter divorced totally from life and consciousness but somehow mysteriously known by the knowing subject or the mind. Cartesian bifurcation created a dualism between mind and matter which has dominated Western thought since the seventeenth century, a dualism which has led many to choose the primacy of matter over mind and the establishment of the view that in the beginning was matter and not consciousness, even if some still hold to a deistic conception of a Creator God.

The prevalence of this supposedly scientific materialism gained momentum in the nineteenth century with the evolutionary theory of Darwin which itself is an ideology in support of this so-called materialism and also based on it. The penetration of the view that all things begin with matter which then evolves into life and later consciousness into the worldview of the general public in the West has been such that despite the total rejection of the classical view of matter in modern quantum mechanics, there still lingers in the public arena reliance upon a materialistic perspective which reduces ultimately all things to "matter". This reductionism has become part and parcel of the modern and even postmodern mindset. People believe that it is possible to understand a thing only through analysis and the breaking up of that thing to its "fundamental" parts which are material. They are led to believe that the whole is nothing more than the sum of its parts and physicists continue to search for the ultimate particles or building blocks of the universe which the less sophisticated public envisages as minute billiard balls which are then accumulated together to create all the beings of the universe. In such a perspective based on materialistic reductionism both life and consciousness are seen as epiphenomena of material factors whether they be matter or energy. The whole rapport between consciousness and corporeal existence is thus reversed.

In traditional cosmologies Pure Consciousness, that is also Pure Being, descends, while remaining Itself transcendent vis-à-vis Its manifestations, through various levels of the cosmic hierarchy to reach the physical world whereas in the modern reductionist view things ascend from the primordial cosmic soup. Even if certain individual scientists believe that a conscious and intelligent Being brought about the Big Bang and originated the cosmos, consciousness plays no role in the so-called evolution of the cosmos from the early aggregate of molecules to the appearance of human beings on the planet. In the traditional worldview, human beings have descended from a higher realm of being and consciousness, whereas according to the modernist perspective so prevalent in present day society, they have ascended from below. These are two diametrically opposed points of view, one based on the primacy of consciousness and the other on the primacy of unconscious and blind material agents, forces, and processes.

How we view the nature of reality has a direct bearing upon how we live as human beings. For millennia human beings lived in a universe dominated by the idea of the primacy of consciousness over all that is corporeal and material. They fought wars and there was disease but they lived in a world of meaning and beauty. They created traditional arts of surpassing beauty and lived, to a large extent, in harmony and peace with their natural environment. They knew who they were, where they came from and where they were going. The denial of the supremacy and primacy of consciousness and the substitution of a materialistic reductionism in its place, has given human beings greater domination over nature and certain earthly comforts while, needless to say, creating new discomforts. It has cured many diseases while opening the door to diseases unknown before. And it has been defended as being a way to peace while making possible wars with a degree of violence and lethal effects not imagined in days of old. But most of all it has destroyed the harmonious relation not only between man and God and the spiritual world but also between man and nature by permitting the creation of a science based not on wisdom but on power and its applications as a new technology which has the capability of destroying the very order of life on Earth. On the individual level, it has taken away from human beings the ultimate meaning of life and destroyed the home which they considered the universe to be, making human beings aliens within a worldview constructed by human minds.

Let us examine further the consequences of substituting for the primacy of consciousness, the primal reality of matter or matter/energy according to the modern scientistic perspective. By positing matter as the ground of all cosmic reality, and for many the only reality, a reductionism has developed which reduces the spirit to the psyche, the psyche to biological processes, life to the activity of chemical agents and chemical elements to the particles of physics. People continue to speak of finding the "fundamental" building blocks of the universe from which one could build up step by step to the greatest prophets, saints, sages, thinkers, and artists. The reality of higher levels of being is thereby seen as nothing more than phenomena resulting from purely material and quantitative entities and processes. Life is seen as an accident and consciousness an epiphenomenon of life. The universe is depicted as a "dead", one devoid of any life, meaning, soul or consciousness. Consequently, human beings are made to feel like an island amidst a vast, threatening ocean of blind and dead matter. They have no home in the cosmos as did their ancestors and feel alienated from all that is not human. Furthermore, this alienation has nothing to do with the alienation of the spiritual human being from the world as understood religiously. Nor is it in any way related to the saying of Christ, "My kingdom is not of this world." The new alienation from the world resulting from scientistic reductionism is of a very different order. Traditional men and women found their home ultimately in the Divine but they also saw in this world a domain dominated by God and full of souls and spirits which corresponded to different aspects of their nature. They never felt as if they were alone in a universe totally blind to their deepest hopes and aspirations. The modern forms of human alienation whether psychological or social, issue from the cosmic isolation created by a worldview which denies the primacy of consciousness.

Human beings are in need of meaning as much as they are in need of air to breathe and food to eat. Modern materialistic reductionism has not only resulted in chemically infested food and polluted air, but also the loss of meaning in its ultimate sense. There can in fact be no ultimate meaning without the acceptance of the Ultimate in the metaphysical sense. It is indeed a great paradox that human consciousness in modern times has produced a view of the cosmos which has no room for consciousness. And when human beings do seek to find consciousness in the objective world, or experience what they consider to be encounters with conscious beings outside of the human realm, they are marginalized and condemned to the category of hallucinating men and women in need of psychiatric care. When our ancestors could encounter angels and even lesser beings in nature, and when such encounters were acceptable within the *Weltanschauung* in which they lived, they did not encounter "aliens" in the modern sense nor did they feel the need to do so. Nor were they marginalized as abnormal in the societies in which they lived. And the conscious beings they did encounter were not alien to them.

The denial of the primacy of consciousness also resulted both directly and indirectly in the desacralization of nature and the reduction of nature to a pure "it", to a commodity to be used by human beings as they deemed necessary. The care for nature was turned into its rape as the prevalent view of nature became ever more impervious to its spiritual qualities, its mystery, its innate harmony and beauty. All those aspects of nature, celebrated over the centuries by sages, saints, poets and artists, became subjectivized and made to appear as being objectively unreal. Turned into a commodity to be used by the ever growing avaricious appetite of modern humanity as consumer, the natural environment soon began to suffer leading to the environmental crisis which now threatens the web of life on Earth. Even today few want to accept the direct relation between the materialistic view of nature and the destruction of nature on the unprecedented scale that we observe everywhere on the globe today.

The materialistic worldview and the denying of the primacy of consciousness have also had a direct bearing on the weakening of ethical norms and practices. In all civilizations morality was related to religion and a philosophical worldview in which good and evil, right and wrong had a cosmic as well as human dimension. We can see clear examples of this rapport not only in the Abrahamic religions, but also in Hinduism, Confucianism, Buddhism and Zoroastrianism. Ethics is always related in one way or another to metaphysics. In denying the primacy of consciousness in favor of the material, the modern paradigm has weakened the objective cadre for human ethics not only by marginalizing and weakening religion, but also by reducing the cosmos to a purely "material" reality in which good and evil have no meaning any more than does beauty. *À la* Galileo and Descartes, all such categories are relegated to the subjective realm and banished from objective reality. Ethics is thereby weakened wherever this worldview has flourished and secularized ethics based on such a truncated view of reality has never been able to gain widespread acceptance. Moreover, all this has occurred at a time when human beings are in the greatest need of an environmental ethics which would appeal to the vast majority of the human family, most of whom still closely identify ethics with God, with sacred laws and teachings of various religions. Nor is the need for ethics confined to the environment. It is also of the utmost importance to emphasize ethics in the dealing of human beings with each other when, thanks to modern technology, weapons of war and conflict have become lethal to a degree beyond imagination.

If in the beginning was only the soup of molecules, then our deepest yearnings and aspirations, our deepest feelings, our sense of love, beauty, justice and goodness are all ephemeral subjective states caused by blind evolutionary forces and truth has meaning only when operationally defined. What we call our humanity is only an illusion. What is real is what we experience of the outside world seen only as a domain of material entities and forces in various interactions and processes which are totally indifferent to our humanity. To deny the

primacy of consciousness is in fact to confirm knowingly or unknow-
ingly our own inhumanity and to admit that all that we consider to be
the deepest elements of our thoughts, emotions, and even spiritual
states are ultimately illusory and unreal, being reducible to material
agents and forces. It is to surrender ourselves to the sub-human, which
in fact we see manifesting itself, by no means accidentally, to an ever
greater degree in the human order as it pulls humanity with ever greater
speed downwards toward the abyss.

If consciousness in its highest sense is not the alpha of cosmic and
human existence, it cannot, metaphysically speaking, be its omega
either. By denying the primacy of consciousness, modern materialism
has also cast doubt on the reality of the immortality of the human soul
and the afterlife. Today in the West even many religious people do not
take eschatological realities seriously. Besides the most tragic consequences for the human soul who denies such realities, the weakening
of belief in eternal life also has a direct consequence on how we live in
this world and more particularly, upon the destruction of the natural
environment. If life on this Earth is the only life we have, then we
should do everything possible to live a worldly life as fully as possible.
For most people such a life means hedonism and consumerism to the
fullest extent possible. A few agnostics might be satisfied with "the life
of the mind", but for most people loss of fear of the infernal states and
hope for paradise results in giving full vent to their sensual passions
and their gratification which result in ever greater expectation of material "benefits" from their environment with catastrophic consequences
for the natural world as well as for the human agent within that world.

The consequences of the loss of the vision of the Sacred Origin of
the cosmos and denial of the primacy of consciousness are so many and
so multifarious that they cannot all be mentioned here. And yet, opposition to this view is so strong within the citadel of the modern scientistic paradigm, that even scientific arguments for intelligent design of
the universe, which implies of course the primacy of intelligence or
consciousness, are brushed aside in dogmatic fashion by many high

priests of the pseudo-religion of scientism. Despite this negative situation, the truth of the primacy of consciousness must be asserted whenever and wherever possible. And there are signs that more and more perspicacious people are awakening from their "dogmatic slumber" and realizing this truth.

If the truth of the primacy of consciousness cosmically and ontologically as well as microcosmically were to be reasserted and accepted on a wide scale again in the contemporary world, human life would become different qualitatively and many of the obstacles facing humanity today would be removed. Human life would have meaning beyond transient psychological states and evanescent sensuous experiences. Human life would also regain the aspect of ultimacy which all religions believe it possesses. The reason for the sacredness of human life would become clear and the quality of sacredness would have an ontological basis rather being mere sentimentality as it is today when seen in the context of a strictly scientistic point of view. And the intimations of immortality would be seen as a blinding reality rather than sentimental wishful thinking combined often with doubt.

Were we to accept the truth that "in the beginning was consciousness" and that "it is now as it was at the beginning," we would no longer feel as aliens in a dead and forbidding cosmos, as accidents in a lifeless universe. Far from being aliens, we would feel once again at home in the cosmos as did traditional men and women over the ages. Our rapport with animals, plants and even the inanimate world would change from one of strife and need for control and domination to one of harmony and equilibrium with a much greater possibility of intimacy with more human beings than the current mind-set makes possible.

Finally, we would regain the cosmic dimension of our existence. Our deepest values, our attraction to and yearning for beauty, peace and justice, and the experience of love itself on all levels would not be seen as being simply subjective states devoid of any objective reality but on the contrary as corresponding to cosmic and ultimately metacosmic realities. And our ethical actions and norms, far from being simply based on standards set by merely human decisions and agreements, would be seen as having a divine origin and cosmic correspondences and as being much more real than simply convenient accommodations created by human societies for their survival or selfish interests.

If human beings were not to live below the human level, but were to realize the full possibility of being human, they would grasp intuitively the truth of the assertion of the primacy of consciousness. Their own consciousness would be raised to a level where they would know through direct intellection that the alpha and omega of cosmic reality cannot but be the Supreme Consciousness which is also Pure Being and that all beings in the universe possess a degree of consciousness in accord with their existential state. They would realize that as human beings we are given the intelligence to know the One Who is the Origin and End of all things, who is *Sat* (Being), *Chit* (Consciousness), and *Ananda* (Bliss), and to realize that this knowledge itself is the ultimate goal of human life, the crown of human existence, and what ultimately makes us human beings who can discourse with the trees and the birds as well as with the angels and who are on the highest level the interlocutors of that Supreme Reality who has allowed us to say "I" but who is ultimately the I of all I's.

PSI

If we are to proceed from reductionist-materialist science to a worldview embracing the primacy of consciousness, the issue of psi phenomena (telepathy, precognition, remote viewing, apparitions and so forth) is going to have to be tackled. As things currently stand, the status of psi research (which goes under various terms ranging from "parapsychology" to the study of "anomalous psychological processes") is a rather mixed picture. In some countries it has found a place within universities – in Britain, for instance, there are around sixty Ph.D.s in the subject plus three or four professors. In the United States, by contrast, much psi research has tended to be funded by interested individuals or foundations; as that support has waned or become diverted, research has been severely dampened. In general cultural terms, the attitude to psi phenomena is highly polarised: the media sensationalize it on the one hand, while mainstream science dismisses it on the other. Consequently, there has been precious little balanced (we might say "grown-up") debate about psi, even though surveys indicate that large percentages of Western populations claim to have experienced paranormal events. Properly resourced psi research could not only help heal this rift between people's experience and the "official storyline", but could also extend our knowledge of human nature.

In the process it would provide the portal through which our culture could pass from operating under a wholly reductionist paradigm to one recognising consciousness as being integral to the fabric of the universe.

TO THE ESSAYS IN
THIS SECTION

DEAN RADIN: *A Brief History of the Potential Future*
This is indeed a brief history, a fragment in fact, unearthed by future
archaeologists. It seems some of the same problems we have now will
still exist in the distant future, even if in a different ontological context!
Radin uses a fictional approach to make his points about the status of
the psi-mainstream tension currently existing. We always thought we
hadn't grasped the significance of all that dark energy in the universe...

MICHAEL GROSSO: *Consciousness and Parapsychology: A
Thought Experiment*
Grosso parades the "gaggle of interpretations" regarding the nature of
consciousness, showing there to be no consensus. He attempts "an evocation of the extraordinary potential of human consciousness" and tries
to imagine how the world would look if we exploited it in full. He basis
his model on "a body of anomalous psychological [psi or paranormal]
data that has been neglected by mainstream science", noting that parapsychology is "an embattled enterprise".

PAUL DEVEREUX: *The Moveable Feast*
Devereux argues that cultures are effectively hallucinations and that
even "matter" is a mental construct in terms of our experience of it.
Each cultural hallucination has its own idiosyncrasies, and some tribal,
non-Western societies, even today, see mind as preceding matter, of it
existing within the non-human world. He gives examples of accounts
from anthropologists in the field who have experienced what we call
"paranormal" or psi phenomena, and describes how those other, older
societies embrace and structure such experiences. By contrast, Western
societies have no structure to cope with them, but he sketches out two
visions, one negative and one positive, of how Western societies might
adapt themselves if they had.

HANK WESSELMAN: *The Transformational Perspective: An Emerging Worldview*

Citing his own transformative psi experiences when in the field as an anthropologist and his learning from tribal societies who see what we call reality as part of a system of dreamworlds that are "minded", Wesselman thinks he perceives what in his discipline would be called a "cultural revitalization movement" beginning to take hold in the West. He sees "contemporary spiritual seekers" *ipso facto* forming a "transformational movement", an as yet unnamed "new spiritual complex", as the old ideas that have been driving our culture are increasingly seen as being inadequate and obsolete, leading to growing ecological, political, religous and social ills. These people are not religious extremists, cultists, or ascetics and tend to be distrustful of any organized religious hierarchy. Wesselman feels that this potentially emergent spirituality is predicated on a "cluster of principles that were embraced at one time by all the world's indigenous peoples". As the entranced shaman could penetrate the dreamworlds in his mind-altered state, so too will non-ordinary states of consciousness need to be a part of this growing spiritual complex in which the "transformative experience of the sacred" is directly accessed.

A BRIEF HISTORY OF THE POTENTIAL FUTURE

Dean Radin

Portions of an antique written document, retrieved from archaic silicon memory chips, was recently discovered during an archeological dig in the land mass formerly known as North America. Precise dating of the book has been difficult to achieve due to its degraded condition, but best estimates place it at about the beginning of the 23rd century AD. Scholars who have examined the book agree that it was probably an early progenitor of today's Encyclopedia Galactica. *Only a small portion of the recovered text is readable:*

It is difficult for us today to fully grasp what it must have been like to live at the dawn of the 21st century. The climatic and geophysical environments were spiraling out of control, inter and intra-governmental tensions had created chronic states of emergency, armed conflicts were common, youth violence and suicide had dramatically increased, the food distribution system was faltering, and the world's economy was rupturing under all the uncertainties. Many turned helplessly to superstitions and religions, but faith alone was powerless to stem these global forces. And the confused state of hundreds of scientific specialties made it impossible to devise a rational solution to the bewildering series of problems faced by humanity.

It was not until the mid-21st century, with the crisis in extremis, that a new synthesis began to appear among the sciences. Pressure to devise solutions to the global calamity had finally cracked through entrenched dogmas and allowed radically new concepts to flourish. The resulting consilience hinted that the problems threatening to extinguish humanity were actually reflections of a single, underlying dilemma – a dilemma that new technology alone could not solve. The problem, and its ultimate solution, had been rooted in humanity's common sense, but faulty, understanding of the fabric of reality. It took decades to adequately define how those ontological assumptions had contributed towards a near-extinction event, but once the limitations of common sense were understood, the solution was clear.

Historians continue to debate precisely when the new era began, but most agree it was around 2090 AD, when Prof. Hu Lee Bernstein of Hunan State University first convincingly demonstrated the plasticity of reality. His proof that the speed of light and gravitational "constants" were actually contingent on subjective factors provided the clue required to shift the world from catastrophe. By the turn of the 22rd century, after Marie Smernov-Chavez's theory of spectrum relativity placed consciousness within the same continuum as energy and matter, specialized human intention teams had already begun to regulate the global climate. Equilibrium was not wholly achieved until after it had been verified that the unconscious mind was identical to what physicists had previously called "dark energy." By 2155 federal regulatory intention squads were fully engaged in their duties and were well along in calming the global system.

Those early efforts offered a striking example of how necessity could force humanity to overcome threats which were regarded at the time as inconceivably complicated. What they did not know then were the unintended consequences of awakening the global mind. Today we appreciate that humanity faces a new problem, one far more serious than our ancestors could have imagined. In their time, rebellious youth would express their burbling adolescent angst by surreptitiously hosting spontaneous art exhibits in public places. Such displays, known as wall scribblings or *graffiti*, have appeared throughout history, found even in the ruins of Pompeii many millennia ago. In ancient times, graffiti was considered a mere nuisance because minds had not yet coalesced in spectrum relativistic ways, so those displays of youth torment were not powerful enough to seriously influence space or time. But today, with our modern understanding of consciousness dynamics, unruly youth are beginning to threaten the very stability of spacetime. For our own sake, we must enforce restrictions prohibiting placement of graffiti on the fabric of reality. If we fail, the consequences are too ....

At this point the remaining text is unreadable, but the writer's distress is already palpable. We sympathize with our ancestor's apprehension, but we also know that the fabric of reality is far more robust than they knew at the time, and that while intentional graffiti may indeed wrinkle spacetime, the effects can usually be mopped up with modest effort. But today we face a genuinely serious problem – the problem of seditious youth who so carelessly litter the mindscape with rebellious thought forms. We must devise a sustainable means of dealing with growing mounds of spacetime rubbish, or our future will be bleak indeed.

CONSCIOUSNESS AND PARAPSYCHOLOGY: A THOUGHT EXPERIMENT

Michael Grosso

Consciousness is a recent phenomenon in the history of planet Earth; we know nothing of it beyond or prior to terrestrial history. What we do know is part of the story – the unfinished story – of human evolution. The true function of consciousness is quite puzzling, and its relationship to the central nervous system is riddled with hard questions. Some regard consciousness as eluding rational explanation, as does the mysterian philosopher, Colin McGinn, while some like William James contend that consciousness does not exist, at least not in any substantive sense. As to its causal powers, there is a spectrum of opinions, ranging from epiphenomenalism (consciousness as impotent brain off-shoot) to hypophenomenalism (brain as somehow derivative from consciousness). Some say it is an emergent property, the result of a critical measure of brain complexity; others think it something implicit in being or nature, waiting to be teased into manifestation. Some call it a glorious excresence of chance, others see in its purity God throwing off sparks of soul life. Dostoysevsky thought consciousness was a disease, a freakish pain, an impediment to life.

Obviously, there is no consensus here. This may be a clue to something important, a kind of wink daring us to push boldly onward. I will therefore take up the gauntlet – and in the spirit of this anthology – attempt an evocation of the extraordinary potential of human consciousness. Now the question we are asking: What might the world look like – what would it be like? – if we used human consciousness at full throttle?

Views have varied. The eighteenth-century *philosophes* seemed confident that rational consciousness would dominate human development leading in time to an "age of light". By the nineteenth century, Darwinian evolution prompted some to believe that human consciousness was still nascent; so we find different models of its possible manner of ascent. Nietzsche's Zarathustra said that man is a "rope tied between beast and overman" and believed the key to the ascent for the few was by means of creative voluntarism. Richard Bucke wrote about the future of cosmic or mystical consciousness, drawing his models selectively from experience, using his friend Walt Whitman as an example. Teihard de Chardin conceived of the advance in accord with a Christian model of evolution, a struggle to enter into the noosphere. There are all sorts of attempts to imagine the future of consciousness.

Here I will sketch a model based on psychological data usually avoided if not repressed by mainstream science. My thought-experiment will draw on parapsychology, or psychical research, the study of certain unexplained or "paranormal" phenomena that clearly have dramatic implications for the primacy of consciousness. Since this is an exercise of the hypothetical imagination, we will not review the evidence for the phenomena.[1] Our job is to imagine their implications for human life and ask how they may contain the seeds of human transformation.

Parapsychology is an embattled enterprise, generally unwelcomed by mainstream science or religion. True, great names in science and philosophy may be invoked who were sympathetic to the cause – Wallace (co-founder with Darwin of the theory of natural selection), Myers, Freud, Jung, William James, and many others – but the majority of mainstream scientists keep their distance. With few exceptions, theologians are aloof, whereas religious fundamentalists tend to be hostile and somewhat paranoid about the claims of parapsychology. The latter often identify psychic phenomena as probably of diabolic origin.

Why do some people resist the paranormal with religious zeal? Perhaps they sense that if psychic potential were a fact of nature, it would challenge many of our basic assumptions and institutions. Imagine, for example, that we could all effectively read each other's minds. Many might bridle at the prospect of such an unmasking and loss of privacy. Hostility to the idea of possessing such powers implies recognition of their disturbing implications.

What then are the implications for human function of paranormal phenomena? We just mentioned telepathy, a word invented by F.W.H. Myers, literally meaning "feeling at a distance," or, more precisely, "the communication of impressions of any kind from one mind to another, independently of the recognized channels of sense." Telepathy, if it exists, names a huge extension of human consciousness (and indeed subconsciousness); in human relations it enables us to transcend the limits of sense life, suggesting that the boundaries separating our personalities may be more porous than we think.

Telepathy seems to occur infrequently and not to everyone, although some think it is taking place all the time only below the threshold of awareness. Suppose that some psychoactive agent, inner discipline, or genetic mutation raised the level of telepathic performance to a general human capacity. Of course, some might recoil from too much openness and transparency. On the positive side, the greater the mutual openness and transparency the more likely intimacy, empathy, sympathy; it would be hard, for example, to witness the sufferings of others with indifference and detachment; it might also help us penetrate the interior worlds of nonhumans, thus intuitively supporting the notion of animal liberation. It would be more natural to acknowledge that nonhumans suffer and enjoy and we would more readily share their pathos and enjoyments.

The ancient philosophers insisted on frankness and outspokenness as virtues in social life. In a telepathically open world, frankness and outspokenness would naturally be more common. This widening of sympathies would lead to a Whitmanesque enlargement of the individual "I" or ego sense. I would more readily feel and share the inner reality of other sentient beings; the golden rule would be less a moral command than an effortless extension of the sense of my identity. My individual pains and joys would in a sense belong to everyone, and as John

Donne said, everyone's death would "diminish me" as everyone's life would augment me.

Frederic Myers saw a link between love and telepathy. "Love," he wrote, "is a kind of exalted and unspecialized telepathy." It would be hard to ignore the misery of the other just as I find it hard to ignore the misery inflicted on me, my friends, or my loved ones. Compassionate social activism would cease being a rarity but part of our normal response to the world. Generosity of spirit would be commonplace not exceptional, love a byproduct of the ordinary pathos of perception. Greed and other vicious psychic dispositions would shrivel in direct proportion to the new scope of pathos consciousness. Thus, in the flitting epiphanies of what today we call telepathy, we may be seeing signs of a new order of love.

Let us now ask what would happen if our *clairvoyant* capacity were dramatically enlarged. Genius, Myers thought, represented the true normality of future humanity: a state in which the waking self is in continuous vital relationship with the subliminal self. That deepened interaction is what he meant by genius. Clairvoyance implies a supernormal consciousness of distant scenes, objects, and in Myers' usage – planes, modes, as well as symbols of existence. As Myers linked love with telepathy, he linked genius with clairvoyance. Among other things, genius for Myers implied clairvoyant access to the subliminal mind, which in its totality contains the repository of world history, world-soul, and whatever timeless wisdom and inspiration is available to the mind of man.

Myers' theory of genius has profoundly democratic leanings. Ordinary people harbor extraordinary creative ability. All that is lacking is the requisite stimulus: a dream, an illness or close brush with death, or even some deficit or trauma in organic function as in cases of savant-syndrome. The oddest things are apt to jolt people into wider awareness. No rule predicts what may serve as the requisite stimulus. We all live on the threshold and near the springs of great creative powers. Lautreamont, one of the saints of surrealism, said, "Poetry should be made by all," and Rimbaud in a famous letter described how he taught himself to become clairvoyant by exploring his *autre* (other) self, i.e., his subliminal mind. There are, in fact, many cases on record of psychotic patients, mediums, or ordinary uneducated persons suddenly becoming possessed by creative inspiration. Cesar Lombroso was one of the first to collect the art of mental patients and Jean Dubuffet and Andre Breton were artists who testified to the value of the automatisms of the untutored psyche, confirming Myers' intuition of the implicit normality of genius. With telepathy and clairvoyance enhanced, the quality of human relationships and the range of creativity would be powerfully enhanced.

Paranormal investigation suggests that our consciousness of time is latently more flexible and certainly more puzzling than commonly supposed. Time is one of the shapers of conscious existence, critical to novelty and creative advance but also an entropic shadow on our lives, a philosophical curse, a force as relentless in destruction as it is in creation. But time has some cracks in its mighty façade. Psychical researchers flummox us with reports of precognition and retrocognition; people occasionally seem to catch unmediated glimpses of past and future. Glimpses of the future especially raise questions about our conventional ideas of time. The obvious objection is that true precognition would reverse the customary causal sequence, creating the awkward idea of backward causation. But more to the point: What concrete life-difference would it make if we could expand our consciousness of time?

The 1986 Francis Coppola movie, *Peggy Sue Got Married*, takes up a theme from Charles Dickens' *A Christmas Carol*. Scrooge and Peggy Sue travel around, back and forward, in time and get a chance to review some of the highlights of their lives; they see, feel and understand things they missed, or couldn't have seen, the first trip around. Scrooge, hitching a ride on the spirit of Christmas future, also gets to see his own probable future, and what he sees horrifies him. Thanks to their enlarged consciousness of time, Scrooge and Peggy Sue are inwardly changed and return to the present with a more refined set of values and gained something of the wisdom of the heart.

It's an interesting question: What would it be like if we could experience the full presence of the present; in short, see ourselves more clearly, the impact of our words and deeds on the world around us, all the effects radiating outwardly? This idea of a more comprehensive vision, of experiencing the fullness and diversity of life, the fusion of past, present, and future, is how I construe the idea of eternity, which differs from the everlasting. Time, Plato said, is the moving picture of eternity. What we mostly know in normal consciousness is the restless, scurrying picture of things under the shadow of the clock racing; if we could widen our consciousness sufficiently, we might learn something about "eternity", the "world" in Blake's "grain of sand." The eyelids of eternal vision flicker; we are enfolded in something greater than piecemeal time. Hints of this may come to us in forgetful moments, in the peace of love, art or nature, or in study, work, struggle. They turn up in accounts of mystics, saints and yogis: people who have fasted, practiced breath control, and meditated.

We find flickers of enlarged time sense in the anomalies of memory: reports of children who remember past lives, and of people who nearly die and see "panoramic" visions of their whole lives before them. Surely we would dramatically change if we learned to see in one glance the pattern of our life, its shape and direction and dominant motifs?

So far we've looked at some possibilities of perceptual transformation. There is also the question of bodily transformation. ESP is receptive, but PK or psychokinesis is expressive, intentional, directed. Here consciousness performs what must seem like a miracle to our mainstream materialists: it seems to leap beyond its physical integument and exert influence on states of matter. That of course will seem retrograde to people of a certain cast of mind for whom it will imply an authentication of *magic*! For what is magic but an exaltation of the will? An example are the famous dice-throwing experiments of J.B.

Rhine, in which subjects "will" a particular die face to come out. Consciousness here expresses itself by directly transforming states of physical reality. If one is not astonished by the thought of this, one is not thinking of the implications.

However, conscious volition is only one way that consciousness may express itself psychokinetically. There may be *involuntary* forms of psychic influence on living bodies or physical objects, for example, as in the metaphysically charged antics of poltergeists. Here, a living agent, often a youngster undergoing emotional turmoil, involuntarily causes objects to move, break, or otherwise behave anomalously. Sometimes the poltergeist agent learns to control the initially involuntary effects. The implications of this could be seen as frightening. These and other documentable cases suggest we may one day learn consciously to direct the matter-molding powers of the subliminal psyche. If and when that time comes, a new stage of the human adventure will have been launched.

The extreme forms of psychokinesis tell us something about the powers of the human mind. In a few cases evidence for levitation is very strong indeed – for example, St. Joseph of Copertino and St. Teresa of Avila. What seems theoretically most intriguing is that the levitation seems a byproduct of the saint's ecstatic state of mind. The records show that prayer or ecstatic visionary experience were the triggers of the levitations. A peculiar psychophysical state generates the "miracle." Another example are the stigmata produced by saints known to have been focusing their attention on paintings or statues of the crucified Christ. Finally, there are cases of inedia where a saintly individual lives without eating or drinking for months or even years, sustained apparently solely by the Eucharistic host. We can call this psychokinesis by symbolic action. These examples (there are other well documented cases) illustrate the potential of consciousness to directly influence physical reality: ecstasy suspending gravity; fixation on an image causing wounds with strange properties; belief in the value of a symbol altering the physiology of nutrition, and so on. All these suggest the power of mind for enhancing or, of course, damaging health and life itself.

One final conception our experiment compels us to contemplate: the psychokinetic powers of saints, yogis, physical mediums, and aboriginal "people of high degree" suggest the possibility of some kind of afterlife body and afterlife environment. Ecstasy or anxiety, love or enmity may shape the kinds of mental body and the kinds of environment, in traditional talk, hellish or heavenly, we are said to experience in the postmortem world.

So to the last part of our thought-experiment.

The early psychical researchers sought to determine if there were empirical grounds for the belief in a life after death. So far, well over a hundred years of research has harvested much interesting (and various sorts) of data suggesting we may (at least some of us for some time) survive bodily death. Now suppose survival were a fact of nature, what difference would it make? That of course will vary from individual to individual, but a few remarks might stimulate some thinking.

From Plato to the Founding Fathers of America, the fear of hell and the promise of heavenly reward served a useful purpose. Fear of hell served as a lid on our criminal propensities while the promise of heaven alleviated the dangerous resentment of the discontented masses. One might with reason say that the unprecedented criminality of the twentieth century was due to having lifted that lid of myth-fostered repression, unleashing the destructive pandemonium of the subconscious; free of the old fear of hell and the old hope for heaven, men proceeded to create hell on earth. Nowadays there is little evidence that fear of hell is a major factor driving people's conscience (except perhaps among disposed fundamentalists). From surveys I have read, Americans, at any rate, are sanguine about going to heaven; practically everyone seems to think they're going to heaven, unlike the old Puritans who were more afraid of going to hell.

We need to imagine a better use of a twenty-first century, science-based afterlife mythology. In my view, if we survive death, it would mean entering fully into the surreal world of lucid dreaming, for which some measure of self-knowledge might be useful in what Plato called "the journey of a thousand years." For example, if we saw our passage to the next world as one of ever-deepening self-revelation, a kind of sudden and imposed openness and transparency, as a scene where the unconscious becomes conscious and the inner becomes the outer, I would think we might feel motivated to know ourselves in preparation for what is to come. All experience here on Earth would be charged with new significance, for we would know we are creating the future, planting seeds for unpredictable growths in possibly unknown environments. The idea of another round of existence on another plane of existence would force us to revise our attitude toward life, provided we viscerally believed it. Whatever we did and whatever we thought would gain an intensity of meaning, becoming part of the myth of each of our personal world-lines as they drive and cut their tangled way through the jungle of space and time.

Consciousness is often said to be intentional; it is always *about* something. It always points to a world of one or another type or dimension. Consciousness, in short, is always a transparency, an opening. Now, its power to extend to a "next" world is also the power that can open us to *this* world. Here, in my opinion, is the greatest gift of consciousness – its freedom to choose, select, emphasize, reject, affirm, praise, and love. It is this power to highlight what is essential, what is vitally important to *any* world, that is the greatest thing about consciousness.

The prospect of death concentrates the mind, Samuel Johnson once said; the prospect of an afterlife would concentrate our minds no less. For if this strange story, this uncanny adventure goes on, even after the body is reduced to lifeless atoms, then we have to be incredibly alert and totally alive to the dangers and wondrous possibilities that await us along the way. Add the provocative evidence of psychical research, and we are entitled to imagine continuous adventure as definitive of the human condition. In contrast, the view that death is flat out the end is, frankly, depressing.

To sum up: taking inventory of the paranormal potentials of human consciousness, we find grounds for undreamed of possibilities for enhancing life. Our telepathic potencies herald a new order of love based on the natural empathy between sentient beings. The unfolding of clairvoyant capacity points to a new democracy of genius, to deeper access to the many layers of self, and rapport with the natural world. Our enlarged consciousness of time will enrich the quality of life experience, adding depth, perspective, complexity. The unfolding of our psychokinetic potential foreshadows radical changes in the manner of our embodiment on Earth. Emancipation from physical constraints will free us for the supreme pursuits of our lives as each of us sees them. Finally, we will learn to experience the timeless core of our consciousness. The old terror of death will be lifted – an albatross from our backs – and we will become citizens of the evolving universe, free to enjoy the gift and adventure of life.

Note

1. But see: Kelly, E., Kelly, E.W., *Irreducible Mind: Toward A Psychology For the 21st Century,* Rowman & Littlefield, 2006.

THE MOVEABLE FEAST

Paul Devereux

The contributors to this book have been asked for their vision as to how our lives, thinking and society might change if it were to be culturally accepted that consciousness is primary, that it is bound up in the very fabric of the universe rather than being the epiphenomenon of a relatively recently evolved biological organism, the brain. Even if one accepts that consciousness is primary, as I do, it is a deceptively complex proposition to deal with.

Prior to the now globally-embracing materialistic culture created by the modern Western mind, most cultures did believe to some extent that material reality was only part of the picture, and some societies were deeply embedded in the view that the physical world was secondary to a non-material, spiritual otherworld – meaning in our language and concepts that to them consciousness was primary. So dreams, for instance, were viewed in such societies as having greater reality than everyday existence. It is worth reminding ourselves that there are still a few surviving tribal societies that adhere to this kind of worldview. What do we find when we look at them?

Transpersonal Anthropology[1]
It is primarily the testimony of anthropologists that can best advise us, and I am currently in the process of assembling the accounts of transpersonal anthropologists in order to investigate the nature of societies in which consciousness is deemed to be primary. There is space here for just a few brief examples from this work-in-progress,[2] and they are given simply to provide glimpses of the sort of effects one might expect in such a society, allowing for specific cultural conditioning and local circumstances.

The Barok, New Ireland Province, Papua New Guinea

Anthropologist Marianne George lived and worked among these people for a total of twenty months between 1979-85.[3] Early during her first stay she was visited by the elderly "big woman" or shaman of the village she was staying in, and who seemed to be checking the anthropologist out. A short while later, George had a dream in which the big woman spoke to her. Before George spoke to anyone or had even left her hut the next morning, the big woman's sons came to her hut to enquire if she had understood what their mother had been telling her in the dream. On subsequent occasions, George had similar dreams in which the big woman provided information that the anthropologist was seeking. Not only was such information later born out objectively, but the sons always knew the content of the dream George had experienced without her saying anything. George discovered that this phenomenon of transpersonal dreaming, *griman*, was common knowledge among the Barok. During George's period of visits, the big woman died, but she *continued to speak to the anthropologist in dreams* and the sons still knew such communications had taken place. It seems that one does not have to dream alone among the Barok.

The Mazatec, Oaxaca, Mexico

Allan Richardson was the photographer and travelling companion of Gordon Wasson during his 1955 trip to Oaxaca where they became the first white people to take part in an ancient ritual using mind-altering mushrooms. While Wasson was undergoing out-of-body experiences Richardson was experiencing visions of palaces and oriental designs. Then he beheld the vivid mental image of a "beautiful mantelpiece with the portrait of a Spanish caballero over it". Later, the two men were in Mexico City where they were invited to a hacienda they had never visited before. "When we walked into the drawing room, there was the portrait I had seen in my vision," Richardson recalled.[4] Even decades later, he still didn't know "what to make" of the coincidence.

The Cashinahua, Peruvian Amazon

While living with this Amazonian tribe, anthropologist Kenneth Kensinger noted the fairly common occurrence of apparent remote perception by many of those who took part in ritual sessions using the mind-altering brew, ayahuasca. He observed that participants "have described hallucinations about places far removed both geographically and from their own experience".[5] Several of his informants who had never been to or seen pictures of the distant Amazon town of Pucallpa "were able to describe their visits under the influence of ayahuasca to the town with sufficient detail for me to be able to recognize specific shops and sights". On one notable occasion, six out of nine men who had taken part in an ayahuasca session told Kensinger that his *chai* (his maternal grandfather) had just died. It was not until two days later that the anthropologist was informed by radio of the death.

The Sisala, Ghana, Africa

In 1967, Bruce Grindal was invited to participate in a Sisala funeral.[6] He underwent the same preparations as his Sisala companions, and this involved fasting, sleep deprivation, and suffering physical ordeal. At the funeral, the anthropologist saw the corpse apparently become re-animated; it danced and played drums. He perceived a glow radiating from the corpse and from certain people attending the funeral. Some of the Sisala witnessed the same events, and recognised that Grindal had done so too.

Gilbert Islanders, Gilbert Islands, West Pacific

Arthur Grimble was a District Officer of the British Colonial Administrative Service in the Gilbert Islands archipelago. It was the native belief that when a person died the spirit moved northwards through the island chain along special routes to finally arrive at a promontory known as the Place of Dread on the northernmost island, Makin-Meang. From here, if it had successfully escaped ambuscades by evil spirits, the person's soul sped across the ocean to a heaven-world beyond the horizon. To aid the deceased in this process the Gilbert Islanders performed a funeral ritual known as *Te Kaetikawai* (The Straightening of the Way). Grimble insisted on visiting the Place of Dread, and after some local resistance was taken there by a native policeman. After viewing the spot, Grimble started his return to the nearest village, walking back down the funeral or spirit path, a taboo act, and was followed most unwillingly by the policeman. En route, the British official passed a Gilbert Islander coming the other way. "He walked with a strong limp," Grimble observed. "He was a stocky, grizzled man of about 50, clad rather ceremonially ... As he came up on my left, I noticed that his left cheek was scored by a scar from jawbone to temple ... He totally ignored the greeting I gave him. He did not even turn his eyes towards me ... It was so grossly unlike the infallible courtesy of the islanders."[7] On arriving at the village, Grimble witnessed a Straightening of the Way ritual taking place around a corpse – it was the man he had passed on the pathway. The islander had died during the time Grimble had been walking back to the village.

The Ndembu, Zambia, Africa

In 1985, anthropologist Edith Turner (wife of the celebrated anthropologist, Victor Turner) was invited by the Ndembu to participate in a long and complex healing ritual under the leadership of an experienced native healer known as Singleton. After carefully collecting a variety of plant medicines from the wild in a prescribed manner, Singleton led Turner and others who were to participate to the village home of the sick person, a middle-aged woman called Meru, where an altar was erected and a series of ritual actions including chanting, drumming and clapping were conducted around the patient. Eventually, the healing procedure reached a climax, and Turner "felt a spiritual motion ... a tangible feeling of breakthrough encompassing the entire group".[8] Meru collapsed on the ground, and Singleton knelt beside her pressing and scrabbling at her back as if trying to work some object out of her body. "I saw with my own eyes a giant thing emerging out of the flesh of her back," Turner testified. "It was a large gray blob about six inches across, opaque and something between solid and smoke." At the same moment "there was a huge flash of lightning and a clap of thunder that exploded overhead". Everyone watching the procedure shouted and jumped with excitement as it became clear Meru was healed. Singleton then placed an object in a specialised container and this was subjected to further ritual attention later. It was a physical object, an old tooth, and not what Turner had actually seen emerge from Meru's body. It seems that the physical object was magically symbolic of the actual phenomenon.

The Lacandon Maya, Southern Mexico

German anthropologist Christian Rätsch walked into a Lacandon Indian community in the rainforest of southern Mexico having already learned the Mayan language. Both these factors helped the Indians to warm to him. He was "adopted" by the head man and spent many months living with the Lacandon, during which time his own European conditioning was softened to some extent and he was able to take to heart the Lacandon worldview. Consequently, things happened to him that back home would have been considered impossible or paranormal. For example, one early morning he was guarding an almost-ripe corn patch some distance from the village against animal intruders. Several yards away from Rätsch's position there was a dead tree – basically just a trunk and a branch. After a while he saw a bird land on the branch. Thinking this would provide some welcome protein, he shot the bird which exploded in a flurry of feathers as the bullet struck home. The anthropologist went over to the dead tree but was unable to find the bird's body or any sign of feathers. Then, turning his attention to the dead tree, Rätsch discovered that the branch did not exist either! His Indian hosts told him later that this was typical of the forest spirits who liked to play tricks. "That was the explanation, and I had to be satisfied with that," Rätsch concluded.[9] On another occasion, Rätsch learned how to perform a Lacandon healing spell. This involved voicing a long and complex incantation, which he had to learn by heart, while applying saliva to the wound. A few days after this training, Rätsch was a distance from the Indian village, accompanied by a few children. He was hacking his way through the jungle when his machete slipped and he gashed himself on the leg. It was a deep, life-threatening wound, for blood was gushing copiously from it. Realising the seriousness of his situation, the anthropologist sent the children back to the village for help. Left to his own devices, all he could think of doing was to perform the healing spell he had recently learned. By the time he was halfway through the second attempt at this, the bleeding had ceased and healing had commenced. When the village elders reached him they explained that anyone who learns that spell always suffers a serious accident shortly afterwards. It was the ultimate test. "I got inside of a magical universe I never expected to be there," Rätsch later admitted. "That was the most dramatic experience, because to get involved with magical spells meant that I had to leave my German, scientific background totally."

All the above indigenous peoples are societies in which what we would call consciousness is considered primary. If we want to gain a hint of what living in such a culture would be like, then we had better strain to hear what these societies have to say before they fade from our earshot, for they are rapidly disappearing.

The Magic Theatre

Of course, similar experiences also occur to some people in our own Westernised societies, if not usually in such extravagant or dramatic ways. The distinction is that in tribal societies such experiences are an accepted and vital part of the collective cultural worldview whereas in our mainstream culture they are dismissed as superstition or charlatanism. In short, they are *repressed*; they do not officially exist, and are the interest only of marginalized groups.

It is clear that the cultural environment determines to a large extent the reality one experiences – as was particularly noticeable in the

Rätsch case. Why should this be so? The truth is that all our experience of even the most concrete of material realities is in fact a function of consciousness. Culturally, we never appreciate or recognise this fact; indeed, it seems so anti-intuitive to our experience that even those of us aware of it intellectually do not think or act as if it were so. But just ponder on it for a moment – it is self-evident. We are immersed in something-or-other – "an n-dimensional energy soup" as someone once described it. Energies impinge on our sense organs and are then translated into electro-chemical signals that are whisked along the hard-wiring of nerve fibres and through synaptic connections into various parts of our brain where by some unknown and miraculous process they are coalesced into a three-dimensional, sense-surround experience that we take to be outer reality. So, for instance, sunlight doesn't actually shine its beams through our eyes to lighten the interior darkness of skulls; no, light energy (whatever that is) hurtles into the rods and cones of our retinas and is there transduced into electro-chemical signals that pass through various parts of the cortex on their way to a point in the brain towards the back of the head. We never see the sun as-it-is. No one ever has. The same with sound: vibrations beat against the eardrum like waves against the shore and are then transformed into neuronal signals. We have never heard the true is-ness of a Beethoven symphony or a lover's voice. We only know the neuronal representations of them. The same with touch and smell and taste. And it is not simply a matter of the transduction of exogenous energies: associations, memories and feelings colour the raw signals within the brain. So I see a tree, recognise it as an oak, and recall that as a child I sat beneath it listening to my grandfather telling me stories. I hear the wind soughing through its leaves and remember the tree in rain and snow as well as sunshine. The tree makes me feel both happy and a little sad, thinking about how I miss my grandfather and how transient life it. This spurs me on to ponder the meaning of life, and…

We inhabit a magic theatre in which external signals are transformed into what we are persuaded we see, hear, touch, taste and smell

– and there are perhaps other, subtler signals as well which are usually "drowned out" in a culture like our own that does not recognise them. All that we take to be reality is a production of the mind-brain, of consciousness. Even our bodies (and that means our brains too) are a construct of the "outer" world.

The nature of the production put on within the magic theatre is coloured by various factors, both individual and cultural. In a culture that allows there to be spirits and magical phenomena then they will appear in the production; in cultures that censor such things then they will tend to be absent – if they do occur due to some transient glitch they are said to be "paranormal" and ignored, marginalised or denied.

Cultures are themselves essentially hallucinations. If one is born into an Amazonian tribal hallucination then one's perceptions will relate to that, if one is born into a Western society hallucination, then that will largely determine what one perceives. So in a culture that considers matters of the spirit or mind to be more real than the material world, one will expect to visit the dreams and thoughts of others, to see spirits, to talk with the ancestors, to clairvoyantly perceive physically distant places and events, to fly out of the body, to heal by magical means, and to transcend the physical laws of nature as we know them (for such laws relate only to any given production of the magic theatre).

Reality is a moveable feast that has a fixed menu only when we are a captive audience.

Towards Utopia?

If the mainstream of the Westernised cultural hallucination we inhabit was to accept the primacy of consciousness over matter it would very much depend on how that came about as to whether or not it would lead to some form of utopia. As I see it, there are only two ways in which such culture-wide acceptance could occur in the West – inescapable proof though science, or via mass direct awareness.

Taking the scientific possibility first, as things currently stand the most likely breakthrough will be the unambiguous demonstration that the human brain taps directly into quantum-level reality through specialised neurophysiological structures, with the possible corollary that raw, unstructured consciousness exists at those deep, sub-atomic levels of potential, at the roots of both mind and matter. Of course, it may come entirely unexpectedly through some other scientific doorway. Whatever, it will have to be scientific proof that convinces the establishment forces that control and direct our Westernised cultural bloc. But this will be fraught with danger, for acceptance that consciousness is primary *will not necessarily be accompanied by moral enhancement*. Knowledge of the primacy of consciousness confirmed through scientific channels could potentially open up just another way for the powers-that-be in our culture to control people and to wage war. Psychic surveillance would make today's electronic methods of spying and monitoring seem trivial; advertisers could get directly into your head, into your thoughts, into your dreams. Magical wars would be fought, with even the spirits of those who died being marshalled into Guantanamo Bays of the hereafter – man-made hells and purgatories. (Don't think we wouldn't do it; if it proved possible, we would.) Awareness of the primacy of consciousness does not necessarily equate with spiritual development, and this is especially so if the advanced technologies of consciousness that would soon develop fell into the hands of the power-brokers of our culture. None of this is necessarily a dark fantasy, for once more we can learn from those societies where acceptance of the primacy of consciousness already exists: their technicians of consciousness, the shamans and sorcerers, are engaged in perpetual war with one another. As one Amazonian tribal teacher chillingly put it to the anthropologist Françoise Barbira Freedman, "there is no respite ever".[10]

The other (and, in my view, better, safer) way the acceptance of the primacy of consciousness could become established in mainstream Westernised culture is for so many people to have direct experience of non-mundane, heightened mind states that it would become a *fait accompli.* How could this come about? It is unlikely that sufficiently large numbers of Westernised people will ever become mystics, or engage in meditational, yogic pursuits that the required scale of cultural change could take place. Even though many people take part in workshops and lessons in all kinds of mind-change practices in the New Age and Human Potential movements, this is still far too marginal to seriously affect the mainstream. The only answer seems to me to be the use of mind-altering substances, and again we have the example provided by ancient traditional societies concerning the ritual, sacramental use of vision-inducing "medicine" plants. The trouble is that so many Westernised societies have set their faces against such substances, and even where they are used it is all too often in a hedonistic and undirected context – anything but sacramental. Although there *is* knowledgeable usage of such substances in the West directed towards spiritual goals and heightened consciousness, it is again on too small a scale to catalyse the culture as a whole. It remains marginal.

If this present unsatisfactory situation with mind-altering substances could be changed and made mainstream, resulting in safer, more controlled and ever better-designed substances, then I can to some extent envisage a society along the lines of Aldous Huxley's utopia as described in his final novel, *Island.* There would be places like the mystery temple of Eleusis in ancient Greece, where at a given point in their development young people would be initiated into enhanced mental states by skilled, qualified guides using mind-altering substances. A teenage rite of passage ensuring that within a couple of generations all members of society had direct knowledge of such levels of consciousness without priesthoods and other intermediaries. In such a utopian culture, academics and scientists would use specially-designed mind-changing substances to aid their pursuits[11] – biologists and doctors would see how organic forms grow and develop, learning the secrets of DNA and disease, physicists would surf the quantum sea (indeed, they should now, already, be using psychedelic compounds to probe their mathematical universes), historians and archaeologists would go back down the DNA change of cellular memory, astrophysicists and cosmologists would return to the first moments of the universe (as shamans still do to this day), and fly beyond time to distant galaxies. Society would concern itself with unravelling the mysteries of death rather than the manufacture of armaments, ecological right behaviour would become self-evident to a culture able to see through the cleansed windows of the senses, and we might even learn to walk with spirits and communicate with other beings, whether of this time-space continuum or other dimensions.[12] And so on. The controlled, carefully-applied, culture-wide usage of such (often specially synthesised) substances could allow human beings to break through to a new level. The moveable feast of reality would take on enhanced aspects as we entered a higher, more refined, cultural hallucination, and because it would be happening at a mass level it would be less easy for the cultural power-brokers to hi-jack the process.

As wishful and slightly deranged as this utopian vision might seem to the uninitiated, it could actually happen, for I know personally that it almost commenced one brief, shining moment in the 1960s, when a large percentage of a whole generation in the West was taking powerful psychedelic substances. I remember seeing – in normal consciousness – extraordinary, almost biblical signs in the sky in the company of other witnesses in 1967, as if another level of reality was about to break through.[13] But, as with Camelot, the shining moment passed, and we fell from grace. Perhaps another turning of the cosmic tide will find us more ready, more worthy.

Notes and References

1. This strand of anthropology became a formal academic discipline in the mid-1970s, about a decade after the founding of transpersonal psychology. Transpersonal anthropology is simply the cross-cultural study of transpersonal – anomalous, paranormal – experiences.

2. The working title is *Cultures Collide*. An interesting if minor observation is that after publishing 26 books over the years, I have yet

to find a publisher to take this title on. Perhaps it's a comment on our times. No matter, the book will be completed.

3. George, M., "Dreams, Reality, and the Desire and Intent of Dreamers as Experienced by a Fieldworker", *Anthropology of Consciousness*, 1995; 6 (3), 17-24.

4. Richardson, A., "Recollections of R. Gordon Wasson's 'Friend and Photographer'", in *The Sacred Mushroom Seeker*, Riedlinger, T.J. (ed.), Portland, Dioscorides Press, 1990.

5. Kensinger, K., "Banisteriopsis Usage among the Peruvian Cashinahua", in *Hallucinogens and Shamanism*, Harner, M.J. (ed.), New York: Oxford University Press, 1973.

6. Grindal, B.T., "Into the Heart of Sisala Experience: Witnessing Death Divination", *Journal of Anthropological Research*, 1983; 9 (1), 60-80.

7. Grimble, A., *A Pattern of Islands*, London: John Murray, 1952.

8. Turner, E., "A Visible Spirit Form in Zambia", in *Being Changed*, Young, D.E. and Goulet, J.-G. (eds.), Peterborough, Ontario: Broadview Press, 1994.

9. Rätsch, C., "A Conversation with Christian Rätsch", *The Ley Hunter*, 1990; no. 112, 1-9.

10. Freedman, F. B., "The Jaguar Who Would Not Say Her Prayers: Changing Polarities in Upper Amazonian Shamanism", in *Ayahuasca Reader*, Luna, L.E. and White, S.F. (eds.), Santa Fe: Synergetic Press, 2000.

11. That mind-altering compounds can be synthesised to produce specific mental effects and last for varying durations has been amply demonstrated by that scientific hero of altered mind states, Alexander Shulgin. Psychedelic substances *can* be designed for specific purposes, and this technology would only become more sophisticated and exact in a culture where it was encouraged and valued. Even with this there are precedents in ancient, traditional cultures. The technologists, shamans, of the Amazonian Tukano tribe, for example, can distinguish between six types of ayahuasca brew, each having its own characteris-

tic visionary effects, while the Harakmbet Indians distinguish between
twenty-two varieties. Again, various ancient tribes in South America
use Brugmansia ("tree datura") as a visionary plant, employing less-
powerful strains for divinatory purposes and stronger ones for deeper
entry into the spirit otherworld. Though these various strains give different visionary effects some of them cannot be distinguished botani-
cally one from another by Western eyes.

12. Indigenous users of psychoactive plants claim that they can
speak with the spirits of those plants – Mazatec Indians, for instance,
refer to their hallucinogenic mushrooms as sentient entities, and in the
same way Siberian shamans refer to the "mushroom spirits" belonging
to the hallucinogenic Fly Agaric. There is a deeply ancient tradition of
communicating with such supposed beings. While we may dismiss the
idea of plants having – or being – spirits, expert Western "psycho-
nauts" like the late Terence McKenna have stubbornly insisted that
encountering visionary entities during DMT (dimethyltriptamine) sessions is truly like interacting with non-human intelligences. When
undergoing an ayahuasca session under the guidance of a Secoya
Indian shaman, the writer Daniel Pinchbeck found himself entering
mental spaces he did not understand in which he encountered strange,
protean beings that the shaman and the elders in the session seemed to
be communicating with by their special chanting and whistling songs.
"I had no doubts that the Secoya engaged in extradimensional exploration," Pinchbeck stated (*Breaking Open the Head*, London,
Flamingo, 2003).

13. In May, 1967, I saw a glowing upright rectangle in the skies
over Kent, England. Up to two dozen other people also witnessed it
from varying locations. Over a period of minutes the perfect, glowing
geometric form (for the technically minded, it was a　5 rectangle, pro-
portionally related to the human form) collapsed and then restructured
itself into the glowing outline of a human figure. Had other people not
witnessed it I would have thought I was going mad. (I give a much
more detailed account in my *Earth Lights*, Wellingborough, Turnstone

Press, 1982, pp.11-18.) I saw other odd aerial phenomena later that year, as did a great many other people around the world and from all walks of life. In fact, the numbers of reported sightings of strange things seen in the skies crept steadily higher from 1965, and far more were reported in 1967 than in the previous six years combined. Unfortunately, this intriguing phenomenon of human testimony was subsumed within "ufology", and became subjected to mechanistic, twentieth-century notions of extra-terrestrial spacecraft – "flying saucers" or UFOs – and so was marginalized and lost from mainstream discourse. To me, the salient fact is that 1967 was the culmination of the "psychedelic revolution" in which hundreds of thousands of people were experiencing mystical and visionary states on a scale of intensity never known before in human history.

THE TRANSFORMATIONAL PERSPECTIVE: AN EMERGING WORLDVIEW

Hank Wesselman

The Invitation

On a bright autumn day in New Mexico, in October of 2002, I crossed trails with Dr. John Mack at an international conference on altered states of consciousness at which both he and I were offering keynote presentations. John had read several of my unusual books and over dinner one evening, he asked me if I would consider contributing an essay to the Primacy of Consciousness Project that he was co-chairing with Trish Pfeiffer. When I responded with interest, John began to talk about the project's epicenter – how the world might be transfigured as the public at large becomes increasingly aware that consciousness, not matter, is the ultimate reality and thus the ground of all being.

As I listened, my thoughts turned toward those parts of my life spent working as an anthropologist among the tribal peoples of Africa, for it was out there, among the indigenous traditionals, that I had first stumbled upon this perspective more than thirty-five years before. It was expressed differently, of course, but it was always there, right at the core of their worldview – the perception that the multi-leveled field of the dream is the real world; that we human beings are actually dreaming twenty-fours hours a day; and that the everyday physical world came into being in response to the dream, not vice-versa. These assertions were always accompanied by a conviction, strongly-held, that the dream world is minded, that it is consciousness itself, alive, intelligent, and power-filled, infusing everything that emanates from it with awareness, vitality, and life force.

In the Western world, this perspective is often referred to as panpsychism, a view that has found notable supporters among such mainstream philosophers as Schopenhauer and Goethe, Leibnitz and Rudolf Steiner and Alfred North Whitehead. Among the indigenous peoples with whom I had lived and worked, this was not a philosophical theory, nor was it a concept. It was a percept, an absolute known based upon direct experience. But it wasn't until I became aware of the "Mind-Within-Nature" focused upon me one starry night in 1972 while I was out on the savannas of southwestern Ethiopia that I began to understand what they were talking about.

I was thirty years old then, a member of the Omo Research Expedition, spending my days with an international team of scientists involved in the search of answers to the mystery of human origins. One evening a group of us drove north from our safari camp, out across the grassy plains to a place we all knew. I turned off the engine, then we all climbed up to sit on top of the Land Rover in the light of the full moon. In retrospect, this was one of the most magnificent moments of my life, my friends and I inhaling the sweet winds of eternity into our lungs in deep draughts, our blood sparkling with the light of the twinkling stars and the simple joy of being alive. Far and away, jackals offered their high keening song to the moon followed by the hoarse, churring calls of nightjars that drifted on the warm wind. And then I felt the Presence. The sense of being watched surged within me like boiling water as I looked slowly around in the ghostly light, staring out in all directions across this empty dry land, but nothing out of the ordinary presented itself. It was just there, at the edge of my awareness, that sense of being observed by something, or someone. It was very, very close. And then it was gone.

This spooked me, and spooked me good. I was certain that it had been *right here*, whatever it was. Raymonde Bonnefille, a French palynologist picked up on the shift in my mood. "What is it?" she asked. "I dunno," I hedged. " I felt like there was something here... something that was watching us..."

"*Ah oui*," she breathed with an intake. "We all feel this from time to time, I am sure, although we don't talk about it." A sudden sweet scent swept over us from some unseen night-flowering plant. The air was thick with this wonderful smell and then it was gone, as quickly as it had come.

"What do you think it is?" I had asked her. "I do not know but sometimes I feel it too…" she offered. We all continued to sit thoughtfully, in silence, for the best part of an hour, then in the end, we climbed down and drove slowly back to camp, the nightjars rising like ghostly spirits from the dusty track in front of the car.

This brief anomalous experience marked the inception of an ongoing continuum of spontaneous epiphanies involving abrupt, transient altered states of consciousness – unsought experiences that completely changed my understanding of the nature of the self as well as the nature of reality. Profoundly challenging psychologically, these episodes took me far beyond the carefully patrolled borders of science, and not surprisingly, my personal worldview shifted in response.[1]

As I continued to listen to John talk about his project with rising enthusiasm, my thoughts rotated again, this time toward the experiential workshops that I had been leading for almost a decade at various retreat centers like the Esalen Institute in California and the Omega Institute near New York. Motivated by the need to more fully understand what had happened to me, I had designed these gatherings to draw in other visionaries so that together we might explore aspects of an ancient technology pioneered tens of thousands of years ago by the shamans of the Paleolithic Period – a technology of transcendence. Utilizing techniques such as monotonous, rhythmic percussion combined with focused intentionality, the participants in these gatherings were encouraged to search for an inner doorway through which they might journey into the dream worlds while very much awake. Surprisingly, most were able to do this on first attempt, and once "there" most were able to establish connection with those inner sources of wisdom and power that the traditional peoples call "spirits". Through my ongoing participation in these groups, I came to conclude that the different levels of reality on which the shaman operates are simultaneously levels of consciousness as well as levels of experience. By intentionally expanding their conscious awareness, shamans are able to transcend the physical world and change their level of experience, effectively shifting from one level of reality to another.

My years of facilitating such groups had left my inner scientist deeply impressed by the internal consistency of these experiences and by the transformative effect that they obviously conferred upon the experiencer. I had watched, fascinated, as these inner explorers were led toward an inescapable conclusion – that the fabric of reality is composed of a multi-leveled vibrational field that is alive, conscious, and intelligent.

So allow me to take up John's invitation and share some thoughts about what I have come to think of as the Transformational Community, an important subculture that is coming into being in the Western world. Perhaps through consideration of their closely held values and beliefs, we shall gain glimpses of what our world may become once the certainty that consciousness is primary takes hold on an increasingly wider and potentially societal scale.

The Foundation

It is no news to anyone that a widespread spiritual reawakening is currently taking place – one that has two distinct aspects. On one side, we find a resurgence of religious fundamentalism that embraces an historic view derived from the Middle Ages – a literalist belief system that proclaims this world to be the kingdom of a remote, transcendent authoritarian father-God, alternately wrathful or beneficent. This narrow perspective has been embraced in our time by misguided religious zealots who have the capacity to ensure that this world will be their God's kingdom – or nothing. On the other side and in opposition to this view, we have the spiritually awakened and expanded perspective of the secular humanists who perceive an omnipresent, immanent Divine Presence or Creative Force existing within all of creation, one that is benevolent, life enhancing and life sustaining.[2]

It is significant that this latter view is quietly, yet definitively, being embraced by increasing numbers of well-educated, well-informed, and well-connected individuals, many of who are in professional and social positions from which they may influence the larger society's ideas and trends. Their secular yet spiritual perspective is intensely democratic, cutting across socio-economic levels of achievement and status, transcending cultural, political, and ethnic boundaries as well. In response, a broad social movement is taking form, one made up of people who hold a set of beliefs and values that differ considerably from those of the fundamentalists as well as those of the public at large. The number of people who hold the new view is not known with certainty, but fourteen years of sociological research conducted in the United States by demographer Paul H. Ray and his wife Sherry Ruth Anderson, has revealed that more than fifty million Americans fell into this group as of the year 2000, representing more than twenty-six percent of the adult population. This is not a small number, and it appears to be growing.[3]

Ray's analysis suggests that we Westerners have arrived at a point in our history in which our prevailing mythologies are not working any more. The fifty-plus million among us know, without being told, that the time has come to create a new cultural mythos in which we synthesize a new set of ways of viewing ourselves and our society, our problems and our strengths, our communities and our world – a concern shared by another ninety-or-so million in Western Europe.[4]

Ray and Anderson have observed that a shift of this magnitude in a dominant cultural worldview happens only once or twice in a thousand years, and this one is occurring during a period of ever-accelerating social change, enabled by a high technology and a communication system unlike any seen before. Their survey reveals these citizens who hold the new view to be socially concerned, environmentally aware, and spiritually focused, creative people who are carriers of more positive ideas and values than in any previous period in history. These awakened souls know with absolute certainty that if we continue to do business as usual and fail to produce a new story, Western Civilization may well collapse, taking the rest of the world with it.

As the awareness of this percolates into the public psyche, it is being reinforced by the specter of catastrophic environmental change, producing a sense of urgency, accompanied by a growing insistence on social, political, and economic reform that will benefit everyone, not just the powerful and the privileged. Anthropologists might call this a new kind of cultural revitalization movement, one that is oriented toward the future rather than retreating into the past, and a recent analysis of Western history reveals that this one is happening right on schedule.

Recurring Phases in Western History

Historian Richard Sellin has suggested that our Western preoccupation with the linear development of human civilization is, in fact, a misconception, and that the *zeitgeist*, the spirit of the times embodied within the intellectual trends and moral values characteristic of any age or epoch, has tended to express itself in cycles that repeat themselves every several thousand years.[5]

From my perspective as an anthropologist, the Neolithic Period could be considered as the first of these cycles, a long one that began with the closure of the last ice age and the end of hunting-gathering as the predominant lifeway. This cycle lasted for perhaps four thousand years and was defined by animal and plant domestication and by the establishment of settled communities. Spiritual awareness during this period was animist, a view that affirms everything, both animate and inanimate, to be invested with its own personal supernatural essence or soul. For the cultures of the Neolithic, everything in Nature was ensouled and the religious practitioner was the shaman.

This cycle came to an end with the emergence of the first city-states in the Middle East, and it was among them that a new religion took form – polytheism, a stratified, hierarchical view of the supernatural world that reflected an entirely new perception of ourselves.

The cycle that followed lasted about three thousand years and included such cultures as the Sumerians and the Akkadians, the

Babylonians and the Persians, the Assyrians and the Egyptians, the Mycenaeans, the classical Greeks and the Romans among others. All of these cultures expressed polytheistic religions featuring various high gods and goddesses situated above and beyond Nature – a new perspective that resulted in the creation of the first organized hierarchical religions run by full-time priesthoods. With the collapse of the Roman Empire, this second cycle came to an end, and as before, a new religion emerged: monotheism.

This new belief system, originating in the deserts of the Middle East, could really be considered a form of polytheism with an omnipotent creator deity variously known as YHWH, Jehovah, Allah or simply "God" as the divine CEO, the heavenly father, king or president on top of the supernatural stack, with all the reified saints and prophets, angels and demons ranked below it. Monotheism's three major expressions – Judaism, Christianity, and Islam – have been the dominant religions in the Western world for our current two-thousand-year cycle.

Sellin has proposed that our cycle began with a comparatively long Theocratic Phase in which society relied heavily on religious doctrine and truth was determined by divine direction from the father God operating through a bureaucratized and politically motivated priesthood. Any informed overview of Western History reveals that such has indeed been the case from the emergence of Christianity at the end of the Roman Era until the Renaissance, a period that lasted roughly fourteen hundred years. The spirit of the times changed considerably at this point. The rise of science, as well as the infrastructure of the current corporate world-state through the guilds, initiated the second stage of our cycle, a Secular Phase, in which an expansion of our geographical and intellectual horizons, as well as economic power, occurred on an unprecedented scale. In response, truth was redefined within a new mythology – science – and religion was generally discredited. This relatively shorter phase, dominated by rationalism, has lasted for about three hundred years.

The current spiritual reawakening suggests that it has now drawn to a close. With the dawning of the astrological age of Aquarius, Sellin asserts that we are moving into the third and final stage of our two-thousand-year cycle, a Spiritual Phase, in which science and spirituality are being synthesized and integrated in an attempt to transcend both previous stages. The plethora of recent conferences that have featured mystics and scientists, shamans and quantum physicists as plenary speakers are a testament to this impulse. It is also significant that this revitalizing impulse appears to be associated with the appearance of a new spiritual complex, emerging much in the same manner that Christianity took form at the end of the last cycle.

The New Spiritual Complex

It is not surprising that the "new spirituality" is integral in nature, drawing on all the world's wisdom traditions, from the East to the West, from Animism to Zen. What is surprising is that right at its core can be found a cluster of principles that were embraced at one time by all the world's indigenous peoples. (It must be acknowledged here that the religions of the traditional peoples were as diverse and varied as they themselves once were, with each region of the world encompassing hundreds of cultural groups and subgroups, some large, some small, each devoted to their own unique spiritual ways that could differ markedly from those of their neighbors.)

In approaching the idea that principles of indigenous wisdom are involved in the genesis of a new spiritual complex in the West, it is not necessary to compile yet one more academic stockpile of esoteric minutia of interest only to scholars and theologians. Rather, I am broadly concerned with the general mystical insights that were once held in common by virtually all of the traditionals and are thus the birthright of all people everywhere. I should add that modern spiritual seekers do not seem to be retreating into archaic belief systems, nor, with rare exceptions, are they interested in "playing Indian" or becoming born-again Aboriginals. To the contrary, members of the Transformational Community are beginning to reconsider the core beliefs and values once held by the traditionals, and in the process, something entirely new is taking form.

This new religious complex has no name as yet, nor is it focused on the teachings of some charismatic prophet, guru, or holy person. Its singular, distinguishing feature involves the realization that each of us can acquire spiritual knowledge and power ourselves, making the direct, transpersonal contact with the sacred realms that defines the shaman/mystic, without the need for any priest or religious organization to do it for us. In this manner, each person acquires the freedom to become their own teacher, their own priest, their own prophet, receiving their spiritual revelations directly from the highest sources themselves. As they engage in this ancient human experience, each inevitably discovers that their personal consciousness is part of a greater field of consciousness at large, a deep insight currently being illuminated and confirmed by quantum physics. This is the direct path of the mystic at its absolute best, one that leads the spiritual seeker into the experience of self-realization and spiritual empowerment.

At its inception, this quest is usually intensely personal. Yet as it progresses, it leads inevitably toward a universal and ultimately altruistic perspective, one that takes the seeker straight into the irreversible vortex of personal transformation. This advance, once begun, changes us profoundly and forever because it conveys to each of us the experience of authentic initiation. This is the great game that has been played by the shamans and mystics, saints and sages across time – one that some authors have called the Master Game.[6] But at this point, the beginning of the Third Millennium, just how might we categorize these contemporary spiritual seekers, these players of the great game?

A Spiritual Revolution

It has been my experience that modern mystics tend to develop in isolation, becoming deeply immersed in personal, spiritual studies that are often triggered by paranormal experiences that society at large has taught them to conceal. An oft-cited Gallup Poll revealed more than a decade ago that as many as forty-three percent of the general population in the United States has had such experiences, revealing that this pool may be even deeper than Paul Ray has suggested. Modern mystics tend to be individualists, people with very full lives who like to gather in local meetings or spend their vacation time attending conferences and workshops in which they can acquire direct experience of such practically useful subjects as qigong and reiki, psychic healing and shamanism, meditation and yoga to name only a few. They then tend to disperse back into the wider society where they utilize what they have learned to benefit themselves, their networks of family and friends, and their communities at large.[7]

Beyond these general contours, it is easier to describe what modern mystics are not, rather than to accurately define what they are, and perhaps this is just as it should be because it is much in keeping with the nature of transitional, evolutionary events. For example, most of these individualist seekers are not religious ascetics, shutting themselves away in monasteries, ashrams, or remote mountain caves. They are not involved in practicing austerities and enduring endless periods of deep meditation. They are not religious extremists, invoking fundamentalist belief systems in search of their own exclusive connection with the godhead. Nor are they outright religious wackos, embracing recently uncovered secret doctrines, hidden away for ages and proclaimed as divine revelation by some smooth-talking New Age charismatic. Modern mystics are not involved in cults, nor are they the least bit interested in turning their power over to some holy so-and-so who claims to have the inside corner on the market of spiritual truth. The time of the guru is over.

It has been my experience that contemporary spiritual seekers are interested in spiritual liberation, not repressive or rigid dogma, and they tend to be deeply distrustful of any organized religious hierarchy. Because of this, steadily increasing numbers are leaving our mainstream religions in droves. In their search for authenticity, they are quietly, yet definitively, gaining a level of spiritual freedom that has not been experienced in the West for almost two thousand years.

Ray and Anderson's research reveals that these transformationals are evenly distributed throughout the general population, suggesting that they are everywhere, in every community, and at every level of society. In short, this quietly and steadily escalating social phenomenon has all the appearances of a spiritual revolution.

Let us now have a closer look at these transformationals, examining their beliefs and values in particular. And as we do, we must keep in mind that these individuals are the seed people who may well determine the shape and orientation of spiritual practice in the Western world for much of the next two thousand years.

Values of the Transformationals

When I started leading workshops a decade ago, I perceived that members of my circles tend to express a distinct character profile that I find deeply reassuring – one that the media finds puzzling at best or unworthy of serious news coverage at worst. Our newspapers, magazines, and television news programs inundate us with negative information on a daily basis, creating the impression that violent crime and genocide, economic catastrophes and political mendacity are reaching unprecedented proportions. While this may be true to some extent, it must also be remembered that all the murder and mayhem, political corruption and corporate fiascos are being generated by only about two percent of the world's population. Despite this, the media seems to believe that this is what makes news, a supposition reinforced by polls and surveys created by the demographers who serve the media. The same could be said of the film industry, of course. There is no question that Hollywood knows the big money is to be made by appealing to the dark side of the human psyche.

Given this understanding, I was surprised to discover that most of the participants in my seminars and workshops lack the blade-runner mentality, as well as the cynicism it tends to generate. Instead, they express a strong sense of social justice and seem to be deeply concerned about the quality of human life at all levels of society. They feel strong support for women's issues as well as those of minorities. They are concerned for the safety and well being of both children and the elderly, and human relationships are clearly seen as more important than material gain. Social tolerance, personal individualism, and spiritual freedom are highly valued ideals. The reweaving of the social fabric through the rebuilding of families, neighborhoods, and communities are major areas of concern. This is what I mean by deeply reassuring.

In looking at these values, it quickly becomes apparent that they have little to do with being a liberal or a conservative, a Christian, Jew, or Muslim, or even a patriot. Yet they have everything to do with being a humanist in the evolved sense of the word. Although the Western world continues to be driven by greed and fueled by denial, motivated by fear and dominated by competition, members of the transformational community are oriented toward democratic, humanistic ideals, and they tend to favor cooperative endeavors that benefit the many.

The importance of balance and harmony lies right at the core of their values, and in this respect, they, like the indigenous peoples, have grasped that humans must strive to live their lives in ways that contribute to the greater good rather than following lifestyles and pursuing goals that create its opposite. Accordingly, the value of simple, natural living is seen as a high ideal, and the monumental waste being generated at every level of the world capitalist system is regarded with grave concern.

Another area of consideration involves healthcare. Ever increasing numbers of the transformationals feel a growing distance from Western allopathic medicine. While all are very much aware of Western medicine's miraculous achievements, more and more feel that it is failing on many levels. Elders who are terminally ill, for example, are often kept alive by a medical system that is trying to do the right thing, but in the process the physical suffering of the dying may be needlessly prolonged while the escalating costs of treatment can wipe out their family's financial resources. In addition, all see quite clearly how the business-oriented and profit-motivated Health Maintenance Organizations (HMOs) are affecting the quality of health care in an increasingly negative way while inflating costs beyond the imaginable. The need for healthcare reform in the United States, for instance, is overwhelming. The majority within the transformational community express strong interest in preventative and alternative health care strategies, perceived as adjuncts to rather than as replacements for allopathic medicine.

The transformationals are environmentally savvy, and like the indigenous peoples, they feel an active, almost ritual respect for Nature. They express a deep concern for the environment and, by association, the survival of the human species. All are seriously committed to stopping corporate polluters, reversing greenhouse warming, and discovering the limits to short-term growth so that we can achieve the long-term ecological sustainability upon which the future of humanity, as well as Western Civilization, depends. Unlike many of the hardcore environmental activists of the last several decades, however, members of this emerging social movement are deeply committed to achieving the direct, transformative experience of the sacred, and it is really this that defines them as mystics.

Modern Mystic Beliefs

These direct transpersonal experiences leads the transfomationals to an inescapable conclusion: that everything, everywhere is interconnected, and that consciousness is the "etheric field" through which this linkage is achieved. This is a core belief that is clearly articulated by the indigenous tribal peoples at one end of the human continuum and by the quantum physicists and Zen Buddhists at the other.

Another core belief concerns the existence of more than one reality. In addition to the everyday, objective physical level in which we all live and have families, friends, and careers in an ongoing basis, there are the nonordinary, subjective levels of the dream worlds or spirit worlds outside the time-space continuum, where the laws of physics and cause and effect do not work in the same way. This belief leads directly into another: the ability of some individuals to expand their conscious awareness and enter into these alternate realities – a conviction that reveals why the rediscovery of shamanism has become a major thrust within the movement. The relative ease with which the shaman's time-tested methods for achieving mystical states can be learned and practiced, even by non-tribal Westerners, stands in stark contrast to the years of rigorous training often required in many of the contemplative disciplines like meditation and yoga before significant consciousness shifts are achieved.

Another belief: by utilizing the shamanic method to journey into these inner worlds, the same levels that C.G. Jung called the archetypal realms of the psyche, the seeker may enter into relationship with spirit "allies" – inner helpers and teachers who may provide them with access to power and knowledge, protection and support. Among these beings can be found the personal Higher Self, variously known as the Transpersonal Self, the Angelic Self, the God Self, the Over Self, or simply the Oversoul.

Interestingly, despite their disaffection for and lack of affiliation with organized religions, most transformationals profess belief in some form of universal god-like consciousness, and Jesus of Nazareth is regarded as an important spiritual teacher, whether or not the seeker is psychologically Christian.

Another related belief concerns the existence of a field of mystical power, perceived by virtually all as an invisible essence or vital force that is widely dispersed throughout the universe and highly concentrated in certain objects, places, and living beings. It is becoming generally understood within the movement that everyone can learn how to access, accumulate, and focus this power, and that one's health, well-being, and success in life are ultimately dependent on being able to maintain, and even increase, one's personal supply.

This awareness gives rise to the belief in the existence of a personal energy body – a subjective self-aspect that carries this power as life force and provides the "etheric pattern" around and within which the physical body is formed and maintained. The ability of some transpersonal healers to manipulate the energy body in restoring and repairing the physical is a skill that many in the transformational community have personally experienced. It is believed that this energetic matrix can be perceived as an aura by those who have psychic awareness and that it can be enhanced utilizing the energy centers within it called *chakras* in Eastern systems of thought.

Taken together, these beliefs and values constitute an emerging worldview that is being embraced by an ever-growing population of well-informed souls. Those who hold the new view perceive quite clearly that it offers an unprecedented promise of hope for all human beings everywhere as well as a firm guarantee of sweeping changes to come.

The Global Consequence

In summation, the perception of the primacy of consciousness is embedded within a larger complex of beliefs and values being held by an ever-growing sector of the general public in the West. In the United States for example, their numbers currently match and will shortly surpass those of the fundamentalists. It is also significant that this heightened awareness within our citizenry is emerging in a time in which humanity's problems appear to be reaching critical mass – a time in which our leadership seems to be failing us at all levels, political, corporate, military, and even religious.

Whether the solutions to our issues can be achieved by our current political leadership or by the increasingly questionable machinations of our military-industrial complex is in doubt. In response, increasing numbers of concerned citizens are coming to consider the possibility that our problems may not have political, military, or economic solutions, but rather that they may actually be spiritual in nature, in alignment with the beliefs and values outlined above – a conviction that may, in turn, enhance the growth of the new spiritual complex. In addition, if our children are acquiring these altruistic, spiritually based values and beliefs within the fabric of their families, they are already spreading rapidly throughout the larger society, accelerating the shift.

Although the current spiritual reawakening is most visible in North America and Western Europe, the invasive influence of Western Culture upon the rest of the world suggests that it may, in fact, extend deeply into the international community. In Paul Ray's words "we should take heart, for we are traveling in the company of an enormous number of allies."

His Holiness the Dalai Lama has put it this way:

Nowadays, whatever happens in one part of the world will eventually affect, through a chain reaction, people and places far away. Therefore, it is essential to treat each major problem (and social movement), right from (their) inception, as a global concern. It is no longer possible to emphasize, without destructive repercussions, the national, racial, or ideological barriers that differentiate us. Within the context of our new interdependence, self-interest clearly lies in considering the interest of others.[8]

This insight confirms that the transformational community taking form in the West is of enormous import, for the emergence of the new spiritual complex within it, as well as the awareness that the complex is engendering on an increasingly societal scale, has the power to alter the directions of history in much the same way that the emergence of Christianity utterly changed the Roman world, as well as the Western mind, almost two thousand years ago.

While the time frame for this shift may vary with the ebb and flow of current events, there are no maybes here. The proverbial handwriting is on the wall. The history of the world's peoples will be profoundly and inescapably changed by the spiritual awakening going on in the West. The results will be felt at every level of society, in every country, and will, by association, determine much of the politics and individual lifeways of the twenty-first century and beyond.

References and Notes

1. These anomalous experiences are fully documented in my auto-biographical trilogy *Spiritwalker: Messages from the Future,* New York: Bantam Books, 1995; *Medicinemaker: Mystic Encounters on the Shaman's Path,* New York: Bantam Books, 1998; and *Visionseeker: Shared Wisdom from the Place of Refuge,* Carlsbad, California: Hay House, 2001.

2. See Sankara Saranam's *God Without Religion: Questioning Centuries of Accepted Truths,* East Ellijay, Georgia: The Pranayama Institute, 2005.

3. Ray, P.H., and Anderson, S.R., *The Cultural Creatives: How 50 Million People Are Changing the World,* New York: Harmony Books, 2000. Ray now estimates that the number of people involved exceeds 60 million in the United States alone.

4. Ray, P.H., personal communication, March 2002.

5. Sellin, R., *The Spiritual Gyre: Recurring Phases of Western History,* Fort Bragg, California: Lost Coast Press, 1997.

6. De Ropp, R.S., *The Master Game: Pathways to Higher Consciousness Beyond the Drug Experience,* New York: Delta Press, 1968. See also my *Visionseeker,* chapter 1, and Walsh, R., *The Spirit of Shamanism,* Los Angeles: Jeremy Tarcher Press, 1990; chapter 3.

7. See Townsend, Joan B., Neoshamanism and the Modern Mystical Movement, in Doore, G. ed., *Shaman's Path: Healing, Personal Growth and Empowerment,* Boston: Shambhala Press, 1988; pp. 73-85.

8. The Dalai Lama, The Global Community and Universal Responsibility, in Shapiro, E., and Shapiro, D. eds., *The Way Ahead: A Visionary Perspective for the New Millennium,* Rockport, Maine: Element Books, 1992.

COMMUNION

Contributor Christopher Bache uses the term "communion" to refer to a profound interaction with the living universe. We cannot yet properly envisage what such an interaction would be like because we have not made the paradigm shift that would enable it to occur, so we can only offer visionary descriptions at this stage. But these final essays at least allow us to glimpse from this side of the paradigm portal what our consciousness would have to take on board if it was operating in a society in which knowledge of the primacy of consciousness was fully absorbed.

All this may sound like wishful thinking, but, using Bohmian language in the manner of Will Keepin in this section, in order to generate effects in the explicate order we have to initiate powerful intention within the implicate order. In simpler language, even our popular songs (unpretentious messages from the collective unconscious, perhaps) tell us that we have to have a dream for a dream to come true, that we must reach for the unreachable star.

It is dark here on this side of the paradigm portal, so hopefully the essays in this final section can allow a glimmer of visionary light to shine through from a more profound way of knowing beyond.

INTRODUCTION TO THE ESSAYS IN
THIS SECTION

WILL KEEPIN: *The Inner Net of the Heart: The Fractal Nature of Consciousness*
Basing his thinking on the work of David Bohm (of which he provides an elegant summary), Keepin "cruises aloft through the heights of consciousness and spirit and lands, eventually, in love." In doing so, he travels "beyond scholarly formulations". He concludes that in a world where the primacy of consciousness was an obvious fact, then "our primary work would be with consciousness", and talks of a universe that is not a collection of objects, but "a communion of subjects".

ANNE BARING: *A Metaphysical Revolution? Reflections on the Idea of the Primacy of Consciousness*
Baring suggests that we may be approaching the point in cosmic time where "more than a handful of individuals could awaken to this understanding [of a conscious, living universe]." Baring sees the rise of the feminine principle and the mythological consciousness that belongs to it as being a necessary factor in such a transformation of understanding. She foresees us reaching through non-ordinary states of consciousness to a "deeper field of reality" on which the universe is created – perhaps what the quantum physicists refer to as the electromagnetic vacuum, or the zero-point field. She observes that there is a yearning for a broader science and a new sense of spirituality beyond the old religions, the old "images of God". A critical mass may be achieved, and matter would be seen as alive, not dead. If we fully realised we were all connected we could "abandon the need to kill others" and lose the fear of death. The culture would resound with the sure knowledge of being in an ensouled world.

ROSE VON THATER-BRAAN: *Thoughts on a World in Which Consciousness is Reality*

This educational officer in astrophysics refers to her essay as "a collage of thoughts" rather than a linear narrative. This is so she can more accurately offer the perspectives of her own Native American roots, a worldview in which the universe is most certainly "consciousness, animate and interactive", in which time is a series of rhythms rather than a linear progression. "Living practically within a world that is conscious calls for a different understanding of time," she explains. Another important factor is the understanding of "relationship", which is at "the core and focus of consciousness". A crucial aspect of relationship is the "restoration of the masculine and feminine principles to their place of symmetry and cohesion". Thater-Braan further states: "To live in relationship with a conscious world is to live a practice of the art of listening." Listening is more important than speaking, she avers, and it is important to know where to listen from. A close ally of listening is waiting, but to prevent that from becoming paralysis requires "a knowledge of self and of the languages consciousness uses". The "cognitive imperialism" of Eurocentric education divorces us from many other forms of learning, and isolates us from the living nature of the universe. "Part of the human journey is learning the geography, voices and languages of consciousness," she observes.

CHRISTOPHER BACHE: *Communion*

Bache calls for a deep communion with a sentient universe, in which what is currently fickle inspiration is turned into a constant stream. A communion that would enable ancient wise conversations to be renewed and fresh dialogues to commence that would push us towards new science, new medicine. Such "communion" is predicated on "nonordinary states of consciousness" he states. And adds: "The answers [from the living universe] will be as sophisticated as the questions each of us is holding."

THE INNER NET OF THE HEART: THE FRACTAL NATURE OF CONSCIOUSNESS

Will Keepin

At the cutting edge of science today there is a cross-disciplinary theme that is emerging in field after field: in biology, physics, nonlinear dynamics, artificial life, brain physiology, complexity theory, and so on. This new idea is that beyond the physical realm, there exist invisible patterns and principles that somehow organize what we observe and experience. This development is highly auspicious, because it points Western science in an unprecedented direction toward the existence of a realm beyond the observable, material, empirical world. Science is discovering that something transpires behind that which appears.

This "something" is explored below in a narrative style that takes off from science, cruises aloft through heights of consciousness and spirit, and lands, eventually, in love. I took seriously the encouragement for this anthology to step beyond scholarly formulations and their attendant justifications, and instead to give free reign to the intuition in weaving the threads of this vision. The story begins at the cutting edge of physics, moves through its cosmological and consciousness implications, and then formulates a simple, integral model of the cosmos. Finally we bring it all together in the "inner net" of the heart, which links all beings in love through the vast, invisible doorway of our own hearts. We conclude with a few reflections on how science and Western society might be different if consciousness were viewed as fundamental to reality, rather than an epiphenomenon of physical existence.

Toward a Science of Consciousness: Beyond $E = mc^2$

We begin on the solid ground of science, by summarizing the work of physicist David Bohm (1917-1992). Bohm was a colleague of Einstein's at Princeton University, where the two of them began a promising collaboration on the theoretical foundations of quantum theory, on which they shared similar views. But then Bohm suddenly lost his job at Princeton and had to leave the United States because he refused to testify in the McCarthy hearings against Robert Oppenheimer, with whom he had gotten his doctorate at Berkeley. Despite being born and raised an American citizen, Bohm was effectively exiled. He went to Brazil and later Israel, and ended up at the University of London for the last 35 years of his life.

Bohm was driven by a deep passion to understand the nature of the Universe. He felt this was the true purpose and spirit of science, a quest for truth. He was disturbed by the fact that many scientists regarded science primarily as a pragmatic discipline for prediction and control of natural systems. In contrast, Bohm, like Einstein, felt the true purpose of science was a kind of spiritual quest, a form of jnana yoga that seeks to know the true nature of existence.

In Bohm's own work, he not only delved deeply into modern physics, where he made major contributions, but he also carried his quest into other disciplines, quite beyond science itself. He explored art, for example, to try to understand the nature of order in art. He also had extensive dialogues with leading spiritual masters, including a twenty-year dialogue with Krishnamurti, the Indian sage. He had many conversations with the Dalai Lama and other masters, and eagerly explored their epistemologies of inner inquiry – their other ways of knowing. In addition to applying the scientific method, Bohm wanted to explore these other epistemologies so that he could "triangulate," so to speak, on the nature of reality, taking into account the broadest possible range of data and methods of inquiry.

Bohm had noticed a fundamental contradiction in modern physics and was puzzled that it didn't seem to trouble most physicists: The twin pillars of modern physics, Quantum Theory and Relativity Theory, were contradictory at their foundation. Quantum Theory required the nature of reality to be discontinuous, nonlocal, and noncausal. In contrast, Relativity Theory required reality to be continuous, local, and causal. So here were these two foundational theories whose implications for the nature of reality were in utter contradiction. Pondering this, Bohm asked "What do these two branches of modern physics have in common? What is unifying here?" And the answer emerged: wholeness. Both theories proposed that the universe is an integral whole, and that the laws of physics apply everywhere, from the microscopic to the macrocosm. So, he surmised, let's start with wholeness itself, and build a theory from that foundation which is consistent with the data of both Quantum Theory and Relativity Theory.

What he came up with after decades of rigorous scientific work was the proposal that the essence of the universe is what he called the holomovement. "Movement" meant that the nature of existence is a process of continual change, and "holo" meant that it has a kind of holographic structure, in which each part contains the whole. To quote Bohm precisely, "The cosmos is a single, unbroken wholeness in flowing movement."

The holomovement is in effect similar to a synthesis of two ancient spiritual principles: (1) the Buddhist teaching of impermanence – the notion (also from Heraclitus) that the nature of manifest existence is perpetual change, and (2) the microcosm is the macrocosm, as characterized for example in the Hindu mythological image of Indra's Net, where reality is represented as an infinite lattice of glistening jewels, each of which reflects all the others in its own facets. So for Bohm, the nature of the cosmos is a single, unitive process, an unbroken, flowing wholeness in which each part of the flow contains the entire flow. Each part of the flow replicates the totality of the flow – a structure analogous to "holons" as Aldous Huxley dubbed them, utilized extensively in the work of Ken Wilber and others.

The Implicate Order
Bohm proposed that there are two fundamental aspects to the holomovement: the *explicate order* and the *Uimplicate order*. Now why, after we've just said it's a single unbroken wholeness, are we breaking

it into two aspects? Does this mean we are creating a duality from what is actually a oneness? No, because the explicate and implicate order only *appear* as distinct, although convincingly so, because of our perceptual limitations. Human beings have five fundamental senses plus the thinking mind, and the subset of the wholeness that is directly perceived by these human faculties constitutes what Bohm calls the explicate order. *Everything* else, that which we don't directly see, hear, taste, feel, touch, or think, constitutes the implicate order. Human perception is limited and so there needs to be this distinction between what is directly perceptible and what isn't.

To illustrate the relationship between the implicate and the explicate order, consider the following example that Bohm himself articulated. Take two concentric cylinders, one larger than the other, and fill the annular column between them with a thick transparent liquid like glycerin. Now place a small droplet of ink on the top surface of the glycerine, and begin rotating the inner cylinder (while the outer cylinder remains fixed). As the rotation continues, the ink droplet gets stretched out and becomes longer and thinner, and ever fainter. Eventually, it disappears altogether. At this point, the natural conclusion to draw is that the *order,* or organization, of the original ink drop has been lost, rendered chaotic, and the ink appears to be randomly distributed throughout the glycerin in microscopically small particles. However, if you now rotate the inner cylinder in the opposite direction, the ink structure will begin to reappear very faintly, and as you keep rotating, it gets stronger and thicker and eventually comes all the way back; the ink droplet reconstructs itself completely.

Bohm used this example to illustrate the relationship between the explicate and implicate order. Before rotation begins, the ink drop is plainly visible, its order is *explicate*, or "unfolded." After sufficient rotation, the ink drop disappears, yet its order is still preserved, albeit hidden. The order is now "enfolded" in the glycerine, or *Uimplicate*. The key point is that the order may not be visible, but it is there nonetheless.

In an analogous fashion, Bohm posits a vast realm called the "implicate order" that lies beyond what we directly perceive in the physical universe. Indeed, throughout science, often times we see certain processes that we don't understand, or in which we don't see any order, or where we observe what we call "random" behavior. But this is no guarantee that what we're observing actually is random. There may be an underlying hidden order, which may (or may not) by some means become an explicate order perceptible to our scientific instruments. In Bohm's eloquent words, the key lesson is that "a hidden order may be present in what appears to be random."

At first blush, it's natural to suppose that the implicate order is some kind of secondary, ethereal reality floating around somewhere in space, whereas the primary reality is the physical universe as our senses perceive it and science describes it. However, for Bohm, precisely the opposite is the case. The implicate order is the *fundamental* reality, and the explicate order is secondary. The explicate order is akin to the foam on the waves of the ocean, and the implicate order is the ocean itself. This is reminiscent of what God (Krishna) tells the warrior Arjuna in the *Bhagavad Gita*: "I support this entire cosmos with a tiny part of my Being." The implicate order is a profoundly vast, kind of interpenetrating field of conscious information and presence that far transcends the known physical universe.

The implicate order thus extends throughout space and time, but also way beyond space and time. This is very important. Space is not some giant vacuum through which matter moves. For Bohm, matter and empty space are intimately interconnected, and they are both part of the explicate order. The implicate order is beyond space and time altogether, although it's accessible at every point in space-time. It is present everywhere, but visible nowhere. You can think of the implicate order as a synonym for the Unseen, for that which is neither manifest nor accessible to our mind and five senses, in short, a synonym for the spiritual realm. We don't directly perceive it, except through inner intuitions and contemplative forms of spiritual practice.

Of course, Bohm underpinned his theory with a mathematical foundation, which is beyond the scope of this paper. But it's important to know that he showed how these ideas are consistent with the data of modern quantum and relativistic physics, and various remarkable corollaries like Bell's Theorem and quantum nonlocality. Bohm and his colleagues analyzed the Schrödinger equation, the central equation of quantum theory, in a remarkable yet natural way, which revealed a mathematical formulation for an unmanifest realm that Bohm originally called the "quantum potential," which later evolved into his concept of the implicate order. Bohm called his theory an ontological interpretation of quantum theory.

Matter, Energy, and Consciousness

Another vital aspect of Bohm's thinking is that the nature of reality has three fundamental components. Science has generally dealt with only two of them: matter and energy. These two are equated in the famous equation from Einstein: $E = mc^2$. This equation essentially affirms that energy and matter are different forms of the same thing. Bohm insists there is a third element, which he called "meaning," which is a synonym for consciousness. For Bohm, meaning is as significant as matter and energy, and he proposed a tripartite structure to reality: matter, energy, and meaning. Moreover, each of these basic notions enfolds the other two. Thus, "energy" consists not only of explicate energy, but also includes implicate matter and implicate meaning. Put another way, energy "enfolds" both matter and meaning. Similarly, matter enfolds energy and meaning. And finally, meaning enfolds both matter and energy. Bohm reaches a powerful conclusion: "This implies, in contrast to the usual view, that meaning is an inherent and essential part of our overall reality, and is not merely a purely abstract and ethereal quality having its existence only in the mind." What we call the evolution of consciousness is basically the unfolding of meaning as it becomes manifest in the explicate order. Thus meaning,or consciousness, includes all the invisibles of life's purpose, yearning, intention, love, despair, all of the intangibles of life, which are no less real for being intangible. They are just as real as matter or energy, but they cannot be measured in the scientific laboratory. Indeed, scientific instruments are nothing but technological extensions of our five sense perceptions. Microscopes and telescopes are just bigger eyes. Microphones are bigger ears. What Bohm says is that these instruments operate only in the explicate order, and so they perceive only a tiny fraction of the totality of existence. Conventional science misses the implicate order altogether. Yet this is where the vast realm of consciousness dwells, and science is finally beginning to open itself to this domain of inquiry.

The other major characteristic of Bohm's model of reality, which for our purposes is crucial, is its holographic structure. To illustrate, consider an example from mathematical physics, fractal geometry, called the Mandelbrot set. The reader should rest assured: there is no need to understand any physics or mathematics to follow this narrative, the only requirement is an eye for beauty. An elegant example of a fractal is the Mandelbrot set displayed in Figure 1, and its detailed structure can be indicated by repeated magnification (Figures 2 through 5). If we trace this process of zooming in on Figure 1, and what do we find? Lo and behold, we discover in Figure 5 that the Mandelbrot set has a remarkable structure: embedded within it are miniature replicas k of itself. In Figure 5 we have come full circle, back to the original structure: the part contains the whole. Moreover, if we keep going with this magnification process, we find further embedded miniatures of the original set. In fact, there are billions of them, embedded throughout the Mandelbrot set, and no two are exactly alike. So structure of a fractal is something like a set of Russian dolls, where successively smaller dolls are stored inside the larger one, and each doll is painted slightly differently, so no two dolls are exactly alike.

In science, this holographic phenomenon is a recent discovery known as fractal geometry, which is characterized by "nested sets of self-similar structures." Yet this insight has been known to the mystics down through the ages: "As above, so below." The fractal is thus a modern scientific discovery of an ancient alchemical principle, which can also be stated: "As within, so without." The key insight is that deeply embedded within universal structures are a series of complete replicas of the original, on vastly smaller scales. The microcosm replicates the macrocosm.

The Fractal Nature of Consciousness

To pursue the spiritual implications of these ideas, let us now take a flight of fancy, and this is where things start getting interesting. Let us invoke our imagination to construct a simple model of the cosmos, using this Mandelbrot set. Now the equation which gives rise to the Mandelbrot set is this: $Zn+1 = Zn2 + Z0$. Again, the reader need not understand the mathematics here, (s)he need only understand that the Mandelbrot set doesn't come out of thin air, it comes from a very particular equation, which is itself a principle of mathematical ordering.[1] An equation doesn't live in the physical dimension, you can't see it, it's not possible to weigh it, smell it, or hold it in your hand. It doesn't exist in the manifest realm, but you can see its manifest effects, which are revealed in the Mandelbrot set, whose nature is entirely determined by this particular equation. So in Bohm's terminology, the equation represents the *implicate* order; it is the invisible ordering principle that actually creates the set. And the Mandelbrot set itself represents the *explicate* order, it is the manifest structure that results from the creative process of the implicate order. So the implicate order is the agency of creation, and the explicate order is what gets created. In this case, the equation (implicate order) creates the Mandelbrot set (explicate order).

Now back to our model of the cosmos. Imagine that the Mandelbrot set represents the entire physical universe, which is the explicate order, or matter-energy realm. This is the domain of traditional science. And the equation ($Zn+1 = Zn2 + Z0$) represents the implicate order, which is the realm of consciousness. Taken together, matter, energy, and consciousness, we have a model of the entire cosmos. Notice in this model that consciousness creates the matter-energy realm, not the other way around. The forms of matter and energy are projected from the implicate order into manifestation in space and time.

So in this model the physical universe is represented in Figure 1. Now imagine yourself, a single human being in this huge universe. Deeply embedded within the universe, billions of times smaller, there you are, a single human being with a yearning heart, as represented by the miniature Mandelbrot set in Figure 8. On the face of it, you are such a tiny speck amidst this vast expanse. Now, imagine that you explore your true nature, using perhaps meditation and other spiritual methods of inquiry, and through these practices you discover your true identity. You unveil the fundamental process that gives rise to your existence. In this metaphorical model, that would mean that you discover the underlying equation, or process, that created you and your particular form. Hence you discover that your interior essence, the truth of who you are, is not the tiny spec you thought you were, rather it is this mysterious process in the implicate order: $Zn+1 = Zn2 + Z0$. This is the source that created your being; it gave you all the awareness and knowledge you have, and sculpted your particular size, shape, and form. And then suddenly, you have a breakthrough realization, a major "Aha!" You realize that this fundamental truth of who you are (namely, $Zn+1 = Zn2 + Z0$) is *absolutely identical* to the fundamental truth of the entire cosmos (namely, $Zn+1 = Zn2 + Z0$). The process that creates you, and is your true identity, is none other than the very same process that creates the entire cosmos, and is *its* true identity. You and the cosmos are one!

As the mystical poet Rumi describes this realization, "The secret turning in your heart is the entire Universe turning!" Of course on the physical plane, the explicate order, your outer form is indeed a tiny spec, but even there, your form is a miniature version of the cosmos, you are made in the image of God, while on the consciousness level, the implicate order, your interior essence is one with the essence of the cosmos. So your outer form is a tiny spec, but your inner essence is the vast cosmos itself. And this is true not only for you, but for every other

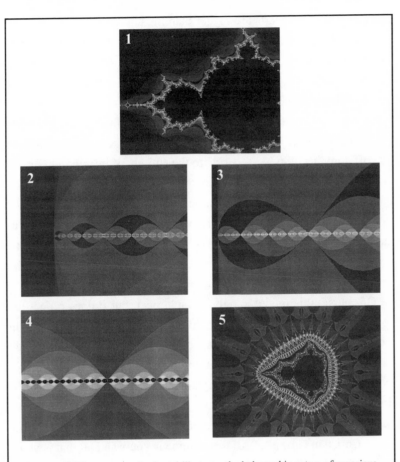

The remarkable structure of a fractal illustrates the holographic nature of consciousness. Figure 1 shows the Mandelbrot set. Let us zoom in on this figure to observe its structure more closely. We begin by magnifying the portion near the center left hand edge of Figure 1. The resulting enlargement is shown in Figure 2. Now, we repeat this process and zoom in on the center portion of Figure 2, which gives us Figure 3. Continuing in this fashion, we zoom in on the center of each figure to generate the next figure, and the next. After a successive process in this fashion, we discover something very remarkable: we arrive at a complete replica of the original structure we started off with back in Figure 1. We have come full circle; the part contains the whole! This particular replica in Figure 5 is 127 million times smaller than the original in Figure 1. And there are billions of other miniature replicas embedded throughout the set in Figure 1, as well as in Figure 5 if we keep zooming in. This intricate structure is called a fractal, and it mimics the holographic nature of consciousness.

[The author is indebted to Ben Levi for generating these figures.]

being as well. Our hearts are bigger than the universe.

The doorway to this universal consciousness is through our hearts, and the implicate order that links us all together can therefore be called the "inner net of the heart." The homonymic similarity to "internet" is intentional, because the computerized internet may be seen as an technological manifestation of this fractal principle in the explicate order. For every computer has access, apart from electronic firewalls that cordon off domains of cyber security, to the entirety of information on the internet. Any part of this vast cyberspace is only a few clicks away. Indeed the very existence of the internet is a consequence, in the explicate order, of a pre-existent and far more refined parallel principle in the implicate order. Just as every computer can access the entire universe of cyberspace through the internet, every heart can access the entire cosmos of consciousness through the inner net of the heart.

Of course, this model is only metaphorical, but it does reflect the character of spiritual realization in different traditions. For example, in Hinduism, the "Atman" represents the spiritual nature of the individual (sometimes called the Self), and "Brahman" is the spiritual nature of the cosmos. The fundamental enlightenment experience is the realization that Atman is Brahman – the two are identical. Or in the *Bhagavad Gita*, we "see the Self in every creature, and all of creation in the Self." In the Christian Gospels, "All that is mine is yours and all that is yours is mine" (John 17:10), and "The Father and I are one" (John 10.30). The Christian mystic, Julian of Norwich, tells us: "We are all in Him enclosed, and He is enclosed in us." In Islam, Allah says: "Heaven and Earth are too small to contain Me, but I fit easily inside the heart of my beloved devotee." In Zen, the great master Dogen says: "We study the self to forget the self, and when we forget the self, we become one with the ten thousand things." Here, the self we forget is just our physical and conditioned forms, our body, personality, ego, thoughts, family, vocation, all the attributes that characterize our manifest, temporal form. In the example above, it's represented by the tiny Mandelbrot structure in Figure 8. And when we forget this self, we become one with the "ten thousand things" because we become one with that which gives rise to all of existence. Similarly, according to the gnostic Gospel of Thomas, Jesus said: "When you make the two one, and when you make the inner as the outer and the outer as the inner and the above as the below, you enter the Kingdom." And finally, in Tantric Buddhism, the scholar Ajit Mukerjee says unequivocally: "The entire drama of the universe is replicated in the human body. When you come to know the truth of the body, you come to know the truth of the cosmos." And this is meant literally, but at a consciousness level, not a physical level. If you explore the nature of consciousness, you discover in your own being everything that goes on at the cosmic scale. As transpersonal psychologist Stanislav Grof emphasizes, "Each of us is everything."

Only on the physical level, the space-time plane, are you anything less than the whole of existence. If you identify with your form and attributes, you are but a speck in the cosmos. If you identify with your Being or essence, the whole of the Divine is merged into you, in all its depth and splendor. Your true identity is thus oneness with God. As Meister Eckhart put it "Nothing is hidden anymore in God which has not become manifest or mine. I become all things, as He is, and I am one and the same being with Him ... so entirely that 'He', and this 'I' become one, is, and act in this 'isness' as one."

Intention and Will in the Implicate Order

Thus far this model embodies a significant limitation in the way it is presented: it is static, like taking a snapshot of an evolving cosmos. But imagine now that the implicate order is changing over time, and the resulting explicate order also unfolds in time. And the two are coupled, so that each affects the other. Hence there is a coevolution of the implicate and explicate order.[2] This implies that by working in the implicate order, by working with spiritual laws in the invisible realms of consciousness, you can actually affect what takes place in the explicate order. This suggests that if you connect deeply to your core essence, and your actions are inspired from there, then not only does this shape your own destiny, but you may become an instrument for a profound impact on a much larger scale. The leaf can heal the tree. This holds because you are working on the plane of your essence identity, which transcends scale, so when your work translates back into the manifest plane, it does so on every conceivable scale.

This holds because you are working directly with the single, unitive process that underlies all of creation. "God is a simple essence," as Meister Eckhart put it. The process of creation takes place in consciousness first, and subsequently manifests in outward form. So if you want to make a change in your life or in the world, you work with it deeply in consciousness first, before anything "happens." In practical terms, you hold an intention or engage in a disciplined contemplative practice, and as you focus your attention and will in this way, it tends toward manifestation. In this model, when you focus your will and deep yearning of the heart in this way, you're effectively "sweeping" the implicate order and concentrating it, drawing it together to serve what it is you are seeking to manifest. As this energetic field becomes increasingly concentrated, there comes a point where suddenly it "condenses" out of the implicate order into explicate manifestation. If our physical eyes could see the implicate order, we could observe this dynamic process, but from our normal explicate point of view, the manifestation often appears to be quite sudden and magical. Note this also shows why faith is so important, faith defined as inherent trust in the unknown, because we must maintain the intention and work with the practice in our consciousness, despite the lack of observable evidence that it is making any difference. But if we could see into the implicate order, we would observe this energetic field of intention; how it gathers and intensifies and then becomes ever denser and more focused, until eventually it "pops" into explicate manifestation.

Implications of a Fractal Model of Consciousness
Of course this is a simple model, and our purpose is just to illustrate heuristically how science is beginning to embrace consciousness as

fundamental to reality, and also how consciousness radically transcends certain laws of matter, energy, space, and time. The physical universe is dwarfed by the consciousness universe, and science itself is opening to the possibility that consciousness may be fundamental. What are the implications of this?

First, consciousness has a fractal or holographic structure. This means that your consciousness is fundamentally one with the consciousness of the entire universe, and it is possible to access that universal consciousness. This is not a dreamy, poetic metaphor, it is a literal truth of consciousness. Mystics have known this for ages. As Rumi put it in the thirteenth century, "Let the drop of water that is you become a hundred mighty seas. But do not think that the drop alone becomes the Ocean. The Ocean, too, becomes the drop." It is our birthright to discover this "inner net of the heart" within ourselves, and live from that vast interior foundation of Being.

Second, this model points to the transformative power of serving the world from a spiritual foundation. When our actions are led by the larger wisdom of universal consciousness, and we serve the explicate world from our inner roots in the implicate order, then our work can become profound and transformative. This is what Gandhi, Mother Teresa, Martin Luther King, Aung Sang Su Kyi and other spiritual activists understand so deeply in their implementation of spiritual law in the secular world.

This doesn't necessarily mean you have to become a Gandhi to make a difference, just as you don't have to be an Einstein to be a good scientist. The transformative principles for social change and cultural evolution that Gandhi and King applied are accessible to us all, by transforming our selves through inner disciplines of consciousness, thereby becoming the instruments for a larger wisdom.

Third, this model also implies there is an amplified power of consciousness that operates in groups or communities who work with consciousness practices together through the inner net of the heart. Thich Nhat Hahn has said that the next Buddha will emerge not in the form of an individual, but rather in the form of a community of people living in loving kindness and mindful awareness. This is because such a community, people working together with their hearts and minds in alignment around a shared intention of the highest integrity, creates an amplified field of intentionality, like a laser beam of coherent consciousness that harnesses tremendous power from the implicate order. Taken far enough, this can tap into the core of the implicate order and begin working directly with the creative process of love itself. This dramatically increases the power and possibilities for manifestation in the explicate order.

Fourth, we are witnessing the dawning of a new science of consciousness and profound interconnection, or perhaps we should call it intercommunion. Thomas Berry observes that the universe is not a collection of objects, but a *communion of subjects* – a beautiful synonym for the inner net of the heart. However, before mainstream science can fully embrace the rich promise of these new developments, it will have to loosen its grip on cherished doctrines of materialism and rationalism, which excessively restrict both its epistemology and ontology. Physicist Ravi Ravindra has observed: "The greatest discovery of modern science is the discovery of its own limitations." Yet sadly, many scientists today still live as unwitting inmates in the conceptual prisons of a narrow orthodox worldview. As Mark Twain aptly sums up the consequences, "It ain't what you don't know that gets you into trouble, it's what you think you know that ain't so."

A brief thought experiment may shed some light in this regard. The following vignette overstates the case, but illustrates the problem, one that equally afflicts many fields beyond science as well. Imagine that the sum total of all scientific truth is represented by a complex conglomeration of sophisticated gears, pulleys, valves, pipes, switches, wires, computers, etc., a huge machine of sorts, with myriad interconnections, each one accurately representing some aspect of proven scientific fact. Now imagine this giant machine is floating in empty space somewhere, and that it's covered on all sides with mirrors. Then from anywhere inside, it appears that this complex structure extends to infinity in all directions. In other words, it appears from *within* science that the truths of science span the entirety of the universe. Whereas in fact, the mirrors, put it place by the mind, create a two-fold delusion: first the compelling appearance that scientific truth exhausts all possible truth, and second, a blindness to other forms of truth, because they are totally eclipsed. Fortunately in recent years, these mirrors are slowly being removed from the limitations of science, and unveiling the vast cosmos that lies beyond it.

What if Consciousness were Viewed as Fundamental?

Let us conclude with several reflections on this question. First, if consciousness were primary, then our primary work would be with consciousness. This means that we would focus on developing, purifying, deepening our consciousness as the first and foremost task in life. What are traditionally called "spiritual" laws are really laws or principles of consciousness. We would learn these and apply them directly in our lives. Rumi tells us, "there is one thing you must do, and if you remember this and forget everything else, there's nothing to worry about. But if you forget this, and remember everything else, your life will be utter waste." That one thing is to connect to the deepest core of our being, to return to the truth of who we are, and live from there. This is a task of transforming consciousness, and it is accomplished through contemplative disciplines that work with and through our consciousness.

Second, we would realize instinctively that, as Meister Eckhart put it, "What is received in contemplation is given out in love." Martin Luther King, Gandhi and Mother Teresa all lived this truth. Each of them achieved first in their individual consciousness the profound integration, love, and liberation which was later manifested through their work on a much larger scale in the world. The liberation of consciousness wrought in the heart of one individual was thereby transformed into a conscious liberation for many. This is the fractal of consciousness in action, the leaf can heal the tree. It's an application of "As above, so below" in reverse: As below, so above.

Third, we would move away from mistaken identity with our own thoughts. We would recognize the limitations of thought, and the crippling debilitation of incessant thinking all the time. As Bohm observed, "thought creates structures, and then pretends they exist independently of thought." We lead our lives within these thought structures as if they were immutable laws of nature. If consciousness were primary, we would see through thought itself to the subtle consciousness that underlies and creates it. Then our conceptual frameworks would appear as they are, elaborate (though often useful) props in the vast cosmic drama of life. We would then regard thought as just one powerful modality of consciousness, within a vastly larger, more subtle and ultimately more nourishing expanse. As Rumi puts it, "Thought gives off smoke to prove the existence of fire. The mystic sits within the burning."

Fourth, we would become increasingly free of our false selves. Einstein himself remarked: "The value of a human being is determined primarily by the measure and the sense in which he has attained liberation from the self." (*Ideas and Opinions*, 12). If consciousness were primary, there would be a natural progression away from identification with one's own personal selfhood, and an expanded alignment with the larger conscious purpose of life itself.

Fifth, there would be a greater plurality of voices in our society. Diversity in all its forms would be valued, as an explicate expression of the endlessly rich textures of consciousness in the implicate order.

Finally, and most important, we would love more. Eknath Easwaran has observed that in a healthy society, there is a natural tendency to love people and use objects, whereas in a materialistic society there is a reverse tendency, to love objects and use people. Our society has certainly erred in the latter direction. Yet as we connect more deeply to consciousness, love inevitably comes to the fore. As our consciousness becomes emptied of our selves, love rushes in to fill the void.

"By love has appeared everything that exists," Shebastari tells us, and "By love, that which does not exist, appears as existing." Love is indeed the greatest power in the universe. And divine love is the most powerful form of love. If we give ourselves to the transforming fire of this love, with its attendant demands of radical humility and spiritual surrender, our entire lives begin to burn with longing for the Divine, regardless of the path or tradition we approach it from. This takes us directly into the implicate order, where we reconnect with the Source of all life. At the core of the implicate order is the creative power of love, which initiates us into a mysterious alchemy that opens, from the inside, the inner net of the heart, the gateway to the Infinite. There is of course the question of whether any of this could ever be proven. My guess is probably so, in various forms, but this is not the point – the mystic has nothing to prove, and has moved beyond the need for proof in terms palatable to the rationalist and the skeptic. The mystic proves by his living, rather than living by his proofs. As Rumi put it, "If you are in love, that love is all the proof you need. If you are not in love, what good are all your proofs?"

Notes

1. This equation is the simplest form of what is called a non-linear iterative process, which is a technical term for complex evolving systems in which the future state of the system depends on its current state. Mathematical structures like these are used to model a wide range of natural phenomena.

2. This is oversimplified but suffices for our purposes. In refinements to his theory, Bohm proposed a hierarchy of several "superimplicate" orders. For Bohm, time is a particular type of explicate order that is unfolded from its own implicate order, which Bohm called the "eternal order." The eternal order unfolds into a succession of events that we experience as "time" in the explicate order. Bohm regards all of time to be enfolded in each particular moment of time, in alignment with mystical understanding of time. Eternity is present in each moment of time.

A METAPHYSICAL REVOLUTION? REFLECTIONS ON THE IDEA OF THE PRIMACY OF CONSCIOUSNESS

Anne Baring

The world is in the midst of a great metaphysical revolution which will shake the foundations of human thinking.
Ravi Ravindra[1]

We have the power to change the collective dream.
Paul Coelho

The greatest fairy tales are borne like seeds across the generations, carrying us with them by enchantment, connecting us to the dimension of the imagination that is so often neglected in our everyday lives. The story of the Sleeping Beauty tells of a hedge of thorns that grew up around a castle where a spell-bound princess lay sleeping for a hundred years. The story says that at the right time, for the right person, the hedge of thorns turns to roses: a way through it opens; a prince awakens the sleeping princess and restores the whole court to life...

Could the idea that Consciousness rather than matter is the ultimate reality – the ground of all being – initiate a metaphysical revolution which would shake the foundations of human thinking? Might it, like the prince in this fairy tale, open a way through the hedge of thorns thrown up by centuries of entrenched beliefs and habits of thought? Might it have the power to awaken our soul, nurture our poetic voice and our visionary imagination, and arouse in us a deeper capacity for relationship with each other and love for our planetary home? Could it restore to us the lost awareness of divine presence? Finally, could it stir to life the slumbering "court" of humanity? This essay is an attempt to reflect on these questions.

Long ago, in the Palaeolithic era, the rituals in the cave and the handprints on the cave wall put men and women in "touch" with an unseen source of life of which the darkness of the cave was the symbol. Now, 20,000 years later, at a new turn in the spiral of evolution, we are "touching" with our imagination the soul of the cosmos, the invisible fabric into which our lives are woven. I believe we are re-awakening to the awareness that we and the phenomenal world that we call nature are woven into a cosmic tapestry whose threads connect us not only with each other at the deepest level but with many dimensions of reality and multitudes of beings inhabiting those dimensions. As someone who has had a glimpse of these dimensions has written: "Far from living our lives unnoticed in a distant corner of an insentient universe, we are everywhere surrounded by orders of intelligence beyond reckoning."[2]

Beyond the present limits of our sight an immense, non-visible field of consciousness interacts with our own, asking to be recognised by us, embraced by us. The realisation that we participate in another level of being that is the source and ground of our own consciousness may eventually shatter the belief that this material reality is all there is; that we exist on a tiny planet in a lifeless universe and that there is no life beyond death. It may be that this field of consciousness has waited aeons for us to reach the point where more than a handful of individuals could awaken to this understanding. To respond to what is happening at the deepest level we have to leave the precinct of the rational mind and open the shuttered casement of the soul to revelation.

Just as it dawned on the early Portuguese explorers that the world was not flat but round so, incredulously, the realisation is dawning that the universe may not consist of dead, insentient matter but is conscious in every part of itself. Like fish in water, like birds in the air, we may, it seems, be immersed in a sea or field or web of energy so fine that as yet its existence can only be inferred by science. This sea of living energy embraces all universes. It is paradoxically at once "greater than the great" and "smaller than the small", co-inherent with the immensity of the galaxies of space and the most minute particles of matter. The sea is one of the oldest images of the soul and soul is a word that carries the resonance of the feminine principle, the connecting, containing, relating principle of the cosmos, the principle of love and wisdom. It is a word that evokes older cultures where soul in this cosmic, inclusive sense was a living reality.[3]

If we could see through the physical forms, including our own bodies which we experience as opaque and solid, we would see myriad patterns of energy interacting with each other and connecting us with the life around us. We would see light irradiating every cell of our bodies and radiating from us and from everything we perceive. We experience ourselves as distinct, separate entities, but if the whole universe is one integrated, living organism, one flowing, undivided energy, one symphony of cosmic sound, then we are part of this whole. As William James remarked, "We are like islands in the sea, separate on the surface, but connected in the deep."

The life we know appears to be an excitation on the surface of an immeasurable sea of energy that is continually surging, dancing, flowing into being. Every galaxy, every star, every planet, every cell of our being is the place where the universe is flaring forth into existence from this womb or sea of being. Brian Swimme writes of this revelation in his book, *The Hidden Heart of the Cosmos*: "Even in the darkest region beyond the Great Wall of galaxies, even in the void between the superclusters, even in the gaps between the synapses of the neurons in the brain, there occurs an incessant foaming, a flashing flame, a shining-forth-from and a dissolving-back-into."[4] But what does this mean for us? It means that when we are in touch with that inconceivable idea, each one of us becomes co-creator with that process, at one with our starry source.

Lynne McTaggart writes of new scientific discoveries in her book, *The Field*:

At our most elemental... we are not a chemical reaction, but an energetic charge. Human beings and all living things are a coalescence of energy in a field of energy connected to every other thing in the world. This pulsating energy field is the central engine of our being and our consciousness, the alpha and omega of our existence. There is no "me" and "not-me" duality to our bodies in relation to the universe, but one underlying energy field... At its most fundamental this new science answers questions that have perplexed scientists for hundreds of years. At its most profound, this is a science of the miraculous.[5]

One of the most exciting new theories in physics is the hypothesis of the mysterious all-containing eleventh dimension described as M-theory, which may hold within it any number of parallel universes. ("M" stands for Mother, Matrix, Mystery) . Physicists say that this dimension may be only a millimetre away from us yet we have no awareness of its existence.[6]

M-theory is presented in the objective language of science, but even this language is beginning, like the *corpus callosum* connecting the two hemispheres of our brain, to relate scientific concepts to the ancient metaphysical imagery of soul. Imagine this all-encompassing sea or web of being as a matrix of invisible relationships that underlies, permeates and contains the visible world. This limitless web or sea is an inconceivably complex, multi-levelled network of dimensions nested within dimensions, with information continually being exchanged between these dimensions – perhaps similar to the way we exchange information through websites and e-mails – at the molecular level, at the level of our own communication with each other, at the level of planetary life, and at the level of galaxies and perhaps any number of parallel universes of which, as yet, we know nothing.

These dimensions carry the memories of the entire experience of life on this planet: our individual memories and experience are encoded in a deeper field holding the memory of all orders of life over billions of years. We (or different aspects of us) may even be living simultaneously in other dimensions or worlds. Here, in these multi-levelled fields are benevolent and malevolent entities as well as hosts of discarnate souls, some of whom may be striving to contact us, to help us; others who, in their despair, hatred or fear, may affect us negatively in ways of which we are unaware.

It seems that whatever name we give this ground, whether we use scientific or metaphysical language – Quantum Vacuum, Zero-Point Field,[7] Creative Energy, Universal Intelligence, Ground of Being, Sacred Mind,[8] Cosmic Soul, God or Spirit – this Primal Consciousness is the origin or source of our being. All aspects of life, visible and invisible, are interconnected and interdependent: all life is one. Death is an illusion born of our fragmented consciousness: there is nothing beyond death but life.[9] In the light of this new understanding, the physical brain or even the entire mind/body organism is not the source of consciousness but the exquisitely fine-tuned vehicle of an invisible reality in which we all exist, the means through which it can come to awareness of itself in this material dimension. It could be said that this new vision marks the return of a very ancient insight known to the Vedic seers of India and summed up by the words in the *Bhagavad Gita*: "All is the Divine Being." (7:19)

To my knowledge, no one has described this new vision with such clarity and immediacy as Christopher Bache in his seminal book *Dark Night Early Dawn*:

What stood out for me in the early stages was the interconnectedness of everything to form a seamless whole. The entire universe is an undivided, totally unified, organic phenomenon. I saw various breakthroughs... as but the early phases of the scientific discovery of this wholeness. I knew that these discoveries would continue to mount until it would become impossible for us not to recognise the universe for what it was – a unified organism of extraordinary design reflecting a massive Creative Intelligence. The intelligence and love that was responsible for what I was seeing kept overwhelming me and filling me with reverential awe... As I moved deeper into it, all borders fell away, all appearances of division were ultimately illusory... No boundaries between incarnations, between human beings, between species, even between matter and spirit. The world of individuated existence was not collapsing into an amorphous mass... but rather was revealing itself to be an exquisitely diversified manifestation of a single entity... I came to discover that I was not exploring a universe "out there" but a universe that "I" in some essential way already was. Somehow these experiences of cosmic order led me into a deeper embrace of my own reality...[10]

Paolo Coelho, whose book, *The Alchemist*, enthralled so many of us, has said that we have the power to change the collective dream. Could the new vision of reality that is emerging into our awareness and is so beautifully conveyed by the passage above, enable us to change the collective dream, as he suggests? Can we fashion new bottles to assimilate the wine of such a radically different understanding of life? Can we hold the tension between the old vision and the new? It must have been like this two thousand years ago for the disciples of Jesus as they tried with every fibre of their being to assimilate and transmit what He was telling them, something so utterly different from anything they had heard before, which didn't "fit in" with the belief system or the values which governed the world of that time.

Now, as then, a radical new idea may be perceived as an "enemy" attacking territory that is known, proven, and therefore safe. Our pre-conscious survival instincts may be aroused to defend that territory from such a threat. It is these survival instincts which unconsciously give rise to the various forms of fundamentalism that are now increasingly encountered. The biggest challenge is how to dismantle the edifice of beliefs – a veritable hedge of thorns – that has been built as a defence against what has been designated by science as non-rational and what, in religion, is thought to threaten older revelations presented and accepted as incontrovertible truth.

Yet, because many people feel that we cannot continue much further along the old paths without inviting catastrophe, there is today a yearning for a new way of living and relating to each other and the cosmos. There is a longing to break free of old belief systems, old images of God, old concepts about nature and our own human nature. This longing, seeking expression through many different avenues, is urging us to break through the wall of beliefs that separates our consciousness from the Consciousness of the universe.

Einstein's great discoveries, William James's description of the varieties of religious experience, the pioneering work on the unexplored depths of the psyche done by Carl Jung and others, Rachel Carson's grave warning to us of a silent spring, the dazzling view of our planet seen from the moon and James Lovelock's naming of it as Gaia – all these events and the efforts of thousands of individuals have sown the seeds for a rise in consciousness, a soul awakening on a planetary scale, an awakening that could have the power to change the collective dream. At the same time, television has opened our eyes to the suffering caused by starvation, persecution and war and to the anguish we inflict on each other, even invoking the name of God to justify our unspeakable cruelty.

Fifty years ago, the readiness for a fundamental change of understanding, a paradigm shift, was inconceivable, although the advance preparation for it was, with hindsight, discernible. But now hundreds, even thousands of individuals who have been working in relative isolation along their own life paths for decades, are converging at the threshold of a breakthrough to a new image of reality. Physicists, cosmologists, transpersonal psychologists, individuals with experience of non-ordinary states of consciousness, poets, visionaries, healers, mediums, people working to protect the planet and avert ecological disaster, those disenchanted with the dogmatism of religion and the omnipotent stance of science in a secular culture, are connecting with each other, sharing the different facets of their vision. Increasingly, they are realising that they are being drawn together to participate in a

Great Work – the birthing of a new way of relating to life that would free humanity from the shackles of fear and ignorance that have so tragically prolonged its suffering. Thomas Berry, in his book, *The Dream of the Earth*, writes that this supremely important time is asking us for "possibly the most complete reversal of values that has taken place since the Neolithic period."[11]

A priceless treasury of ancient texts as well as methods of meditation and healing have been recovered during this same half-century from the great civilisations of the East, from the Egyptian desert (the gnostic texts of Nag Hammadi) and from the traditions and shamanic practices of older cultures. Widely disseminated among people hungry for a non-sectarian spirituality that would connect them directly with a deeper reality, these traditions and practices have helped to prepare the ground for a metaphysical revolution.

Shortly before he died in 1950, the great Indian seer, Sri Aurobindo, is said to have remarked, "If there is to be a future, it will wear the crown of female design." A strong element of this metaphysical revolution is the re-emergence of the long-repressed feminine principle, together with the mythology, imagery and texts that belong to it. The influence of the feminine principle is responsible for our growing concern for the integrity of the life systems of the planet and the attraction to the mythic, the spiritual, the visionary, the non-rational – all of which nourish the heart, the soul and the imagination, inviting new perspectives on life, new ways of reuniting the long-separated elements of body, soul and spirit.

Increasingly, there is becoming audible the voice of a feminine, receptive, caring consciousness in women and men who have opened their awareness to the reality of the great Web of Being and have discovered that we participate in the "marvellous melody of endless love" that is the life of the universe.[12] Increasingly, they are realising, in the words of the Dalai Lama, the greatest spiritual leader of our time, that our own heart is our temple and that the only religion we need is kindness. Through this insight, they have become channels for the increase of cosmic love and light in our world.

Because we are so deeply connected with each other, a change of understanding in one person facilitates change in others: a new way of responding to one issue, such as the pathology of war, the dangers of globalisation, or new methods of healing, accelerates change in others. Like leaven in bread, the awakening of a few individuals is raising the whole loaf. The pressure for change comes not only from the growing awareness of the threat to the planet from those aspects of science and technology that are dissociated from ethical concerns but also, increasingly, from the testimony of subjective revelatory experience as well as extraordinary discoveries in physics, astronomy and cosmology. It is as if a door is opening that previously was closed: a new way of living is becoming accessible to many. Thousands of people are crowding through this door, searching for a unified image of life.

New discoveries are pouring into the culture from every direction: the recognition that we have incredible powers to heal ourselves and our world; the fact that meditation, visualisation and prayer can effect remarkable changes in the neuro-chemistry of the body; the realisation that awareness of our connection to a deeper field of reality can increase our sensitivity and accelerate the pace of our comprehension of these mysteries. A vast new panorama is opening to our vision. There may come a time when such experiences will be so real and familiar to our culture that even as children we could become aware of them and learn to develop innate faculties that have atrophied for want of use.

Suppose we dared to tell our children from earliest childhood about this Web of Life, describing it as something that they belong to, participate in, so that they could attune their awareness to it, could learn how to listen to it, converse with it and develop a deepening relationship with it. Suppose parents and teachers told children that each one of them has a special gift, and that they can learn how to nourish and express that gift to the best of their ability. And that each one is unique and beloved, with the possibility of equal access to the source.

A hundred years ago there was a book called *Cosmic*

Consciousness, written by a remarkable man called Richard Bucke.[13] The state of consciousness that he describes in his book is manifesting now in a growing number of individuals who, whether by a personal experience of illumination or a process of intuitive deduction, are becoming aware of the oneness, interconnectedness and sacredness of all life. Many sense the presence of an Intelligence working within the depths of life; others have been made aware through personal experience that Light and Love are the primal ground of the universe and their own being. Bucke anticipated that this expanded state of consciousness would be experienced by more and more people until a "critical mass" was achieved, enabling the whole of humanity to enter a state of awareness that would allow us to transcend the fear, predatory behaviour and addiction to beliefs that have led us to destroy and desecrate what we have, until now, been unable to recognise as sacred and integral to our own being.

* * *

Enormous problems now confront us: the prospect of the irreversible ecological harm that we have inflicted on the biosphere of the Earth; famine and genocide in Africa; the relentless spread of Aids there and elsewhere; the destitution and suffering of millions of orphans created by these catastrophes and the devastation, suffering and pollution caused by the escalation of military technology and by innumerable conflicts. Over all hangs the spectre of the shortage of food and water created by global warming and an increase in population that the earth cannot sustain. And this is apart from governments and rogue groups of individuals arming to the teeth with the most devastating weapons of mass murder ever devised by man. Yet certain significant ideas are developing:

1. The idea that all aspects of life are interconnected and interdependent.

2. The idea that we have a responsibility to act in defence of nature; and that this responsibility requires a global strategy for radical change.

3. The idea that change may not come from governments (who are elected to protect the national interest) but from the pressure on governments of people demanding and effecting change from below.

4. The idea that our values and our concept of good and evil need a new definition in relation to a new and unified image of spirit and nature and a new awareness of responsibility towards planetary life.

These ideas invite the convergence of a mature spirituality, ecological awareness and a more comprehensive and responsible science that would support and further such a paradigm shift. How might this consensus be reflected and embodied in our society?

If, for example, with Sri Aurobindo in his book *The Life Divine*, we came to understand that "apparent Nature is secret God,"[14] the idea that matter is dead and insentient would be replaced by the idea that nature and matter belong to the great Web of Life, and are conscious or sentient by the manner of their organisation and their participation in this living organism. As Aurobindo writes elsewhere, "Spirit is the soul and reality of that which we sense as Matter; Matter is a form and body of that which we realise as Spirit."[15] Or, in the words of Christian de Quincey, "Matter is inherently sentient all the way down. Therefore, nature, the cosmos – matter itself – is inherently and thoroughly meaningful, purposeful and valuable in and for itself. Nature, we must see, is sacred."[16] If this revolutionary idea were incorporated into the teaching of science, together with the idea that both observer and what is observed are part of this Web, feeling would not be dissociated from thinking. It would become more difficult to treat whatever seems "other" – whether matter, different species or other people – as something separate from ourselves and as a potential object for our control.

If matter were seen translucently in this way, we might realise that the manipulation of matter – as in the genetic modification of food and plants – without regard for the long-term dangerous effects of our actions, is not only irresponsible and ecologically unsound, but may be acting against what might be called the sacred order of life. With a sense of extreme urgency, we would renounce the invention, manufacture and sale of weapons which desecrate that order, recognising that the effects of depleted uranium, for example, not only inflict calamitous suffering on human beings but contaminate the soil for millions of years.[17] We would no longer breed deadly viruses or develop chemicals with which to destroy our enemies, since we would realise that in killing others and preparing for war by the invention and testing of ever more terrible weapons we are desecrating the physical "form" of spirit and inviting our own destruction.

It is possible that if we really understood that we cannot die, that each one of us is eternally held within the embrace of the light and love of the divine ground, we could abandon the need to kill others. This insight could eventually make war obsolete. Thousands are already aware that we cannot continue indefinitely to act as if nations or individuals were autonomous units with the right to destroy life on an apocalyptic scale. But it is immensely difficult to relinquish this pathology: deeply unconscious survival instincts hold us bound to the belief that we can only protect ourselves by arming to the teeth against potential enemies, even by attacking them in order to pre-empt an attack on ourselves or the belief that we can eradicate evil by eliminating an enemy.

Those who invoke death for others may be driven by the need to overcome a deeply unconscious fear of death: if there is nothing beyond death, then death itself becomes the ultimate aggressor and the unconscious need to defend ourselves against it by sacrificing others is projected into all our conflicts with each other. If, on the other hand, it were realised that death for consciousness is an illusion, this primordial fear could be relinquished and we could begin to change old habits.[18]

* * *

The issues are steadily becoming clearer: if the sacredness, oneness and interconnectedness of life were truly perceived, we would have a new ethical and moral framework within which to assess our actions. Evil arises from the illusion of our separateness from nature and the life of the cosmos. As we became more aware of the interconnection of everything, we might designate as evil those actions and technologies which harm and pollute the fabric of life, and focus on developing technologies that protect and cherish life. We would renounce the omnipotence that strives to dominate, control and exploit any aspect of life for the sole benefit of our species. The naturalist, David Attenborough, has commented: "The current impact of mankind on the bio-diversity of the planet can be compared to the impact of a ten mile wide meteor on earth 65 million years ago."[19] It is becoming clear that our own immediate future and that of generations to come depends on the ability of the planet to nurture and maintain life in all its diversity. If we destroy that ability, we destroy our habitat and with it, ourselves. Al Gore puts it this way:

> We have the opportunity to join together to experience what very few generations in history have had the privilege of knowing: a generation mission, a compelling moral purpose, a shared and uni-fying cause, and an opportunity to work together to choose a future for which our children will thank us instead of cursing our failure to protect them against a clear and present danger with equally clear and devastating future consequences.[20]

Out of respect for the finite resources of the planet and in the interests of the survival of our own and other species, we would aim to maintain the size of our families at replacement level so that we don't exacer-bate the pollution and depletion of resources that derive from over-population – a population that is estimated to increase by twenty-one percent, from 6.2 to 7.5 billion over the next two decades and to reach 9 billion by 2050.

We would choose to develop those kinds of energy which do not leave lethal residues in the earth, sea or air to poison our own and future generations. We would abandon nuclear technology because of its dangers, and concentrate all our efforts on developing a benign global energy system that has lower greenhouse gas emissions than the current ones and does not pollute planetary life systems.[21] It would no longer be a question of which technology to develop but of whether that technology was beneficial or harmful to the planetary organism. What was beneficial for the planet would be beneficial for every living creature on it, including ourselves.

We would curtail the predatory greed that treats the Earth's resources as commodities to be exploited for the financial benefit of the few. The very term "exploitation" would become obsolete as attitudes changed. We could use the wealth saved from our obscene expenditure on weapons to feed, house and educate the world's poor, particularly the destitute, desperate and abandoned children who roam the streets of our cities. We would open our hearts to heal the suffering we have unwittingly brought into being.

We would cease exporting poisonous chemicals and the products of dubious technologies to the Third World – taking no responsibility for the lethal effects of these on its defenceless people – and focus on the long-term aim of growing organic food world-wide that is free of the pesticides and toxic agro-chemicals which inflict long-term damage on the immune systems of all species, and have already seriously depleted the soil of vital nutrients. We would focus on the prevention of disease by ensuring a balanced diet during pregnancy and protecting the embryo and foetus from the long-term negative effects of toxic chemicals, anti-biotics, alcohol and drugs.[22]

The role of the feminine in this arduous endeavour is to bring together ideas, inuitions, insights and discoveries, as well as to connect people with each other. As it increasingly informs and transforms our thinking and draws us together to act on behalf of life, so we will become more able to understand the underlying relationship of all aspects of life to each other. The impulse for change seems to invite a programme that might be called "The Restoration of Nature to the Realm of Spirit." Only when we truly see that the Earth and everything that belongs to it is sacred and intrinsic to the Whole, will we be able to relinquish the arrogance that permitted us to act as if we had the right to conquer and dominate nature, outer space and each other.

At this dark time when the spectre of hatred and terror stalks the Earth, and many are succumbing to fear and despair, the emerging vision of reality is taking us beyond an outworn paradigm where we were held in bondage to beliefs and attitudes that belong to the past. It is a vision that invites a new concept of God or Spirit as a cosmic Sea of Being, a Web of Life – as well as the organising intelligence of that sea or web, and a new concept of ourselves as belonging to and partic-ipating in that intelligence. It is a vision that recognises the sacredness and indissoluble unity of life and imposes on us the responsibility of becoming far more sensitive to the effects of our decisions and our actions. It invites our recognition of the needs of the planet and the life it sustains as primary, with ourselves as the conscious servants of those needs. Above all, it is a vision that asks that we relinquish our addic-tion to violence and the pursuit of power; that we become more aware of the dark shadow cast by this addiction which threatens us with ever more barbarism, bloodshed and suffering.

The crisis of our times is not only a political and ecological crisis but a soul crisis. The answers we seek will not come from the limited consciousness which now rules the world but will emerge from a deep-er understanding born of the union of heart and head, bringing the recognition that each one of us is a marvel, an atom in a cosmic body of immeasurable extent. The urgent need for this psychic balance, this profound intelligence and insight, this wholeness, is helping us recover a perspective on life that has been increasingly lost until we have come to live without it – and without even noticing it has gone –

recognising nothing beyond the human mind. It is a dangerous time because it involves discarding entrenched belief systems and habits of behaviour that are rooted in fear and the greed and desire for power that are born of fear. But it is also an immense opportunity for evolutionary advance, if only we can understand what is happening and why.[23]

The consciousness of the universe is urging us to open our minds to the revelation of all cosmic, planetary and human life as a divine unity. For those awakened to this vision, to be born a human being is to be born into a world lit with an invisible radiance, ensouled by divine presence, graced and sustained by incandescent Light and Love.

References and Notes

1. Ravindra, R., *Science and the Sacred: Eternal Wisdom in a Changing World*, Wheaton, Ill: Quest Books, 2002.

2. Bache, C., *Dark Night, Early Dawn*, New York: Suny Press Inc., 2000; p. 4.

3. Baring, A., and Cashford, J., *The Myth of the Goddess: Evolution of an Image*, London: Penguin Books Ltd., 1993.

4. Swimme, B., *The Hidden Heart of the Cosmos*, Maryknoll, New York: Orbis Books, 1996; p. 101 and *passim*.

5. McTaggart, L., *The Field*, London: HarperCollins, 2001.

6. Horizon programme, London: BBC2, February 2002.

7. The term used by Ervin Laszlo, *The Interconnected Universe, Conceptual Foundations of Transdisciplinary Unified Theory*, Singapore: World Scientific, 1995.

8. The phrase used by Christopher Bache in *Dark Night, Early Dawn*.

9. Kovács, B.J., *The Miracle of Death*, Claremont, CA: The Kamlak Center, 2003.

10. *Dark Night, Early Dawn*, p. 74.

11. Berry, T., *The Dream of the Earth*, San Francisco: Sierra Club, 1988. See also *The Great Work*, Random House Inc. 1999

12. Julian of Norwich.

13. Bucke, W.M., *Cosmic Consciousness, A Study in the Evolution of the Human Mind*, New York: Innes & Sons, 1901 and Dutton & Company, Inc., 1923.

14. *The Life Divine*, Wilmot, WI: Lotus Light Publications, 1990; p. 4. "If it be true that Spirit is involved in Matter and apparent Nature is secret God, then the manifestation of the divine in himself and the realisation of God within and without are the highest and most legitimate aim possible to man upon earth."

15. Ibid, p. 241

16. Christian de Quincey, *Radical Nature: Rediscovering the Soul of Matter*, Montpelier, Vermont: Invisible Cities Press, 2002; p. 260.

17. Helen Caldicott M.D., Founder and President of The Nuclear Policy Research Institute. *The New Nuclear Danger: George W. Bush's Military-Industrial Complex*, The New Press, 2002. Also Dr Rosalie Bertell, *Planet Earth, The Latest Weapon of War*, London: The Woman's Press, 2000.

18. See Kovács, B.J., *The Miracle of Death*.

19. David Attenborough in a 3-part television series called *State of the Planet*, London, BBC1, November/December 2000.

20. From an article in the Sunday Telegraph, UK, November 19th, 2006.

21. See *The Global Climate and Energy Project*, Stanford University. Report, Herald Tribune, December 5th, 2002.

22. See Ridgeway, R. and House, S., *The Unborn Child*, London: Karnac Books Ltd., 2006

23. See Tarnas, R., *Cosmos and Psyche*, New York: Viking, 2006. This book gives an extraordinary overview of the importance and significance of our time.

* * *

I would recommend anyone who wishes to be informed about the neg-

255

ative aspect of our science and technology to read *Our Final Century* by Sir Martin Rees, the British Astronomer-Royal. (London: William Heinemann, 2003)

I would like to express my thanks to Amit Goswami for his book *The Visionary Window* (Wheaton, Ill.: Quest Books, 2000) and to all the other men and women of this and other times, who have helped me to understand something of the mystery that I am and the Consciousness I participate in.

THOUGHTS ON A WORLD IN WHICH CONSCIOUSNESS IS REALITY

Rose von Thater-Braan

There is a dual challenge in writing about consciousness in English – the writing and the English. For I must attempt to translate into a noun-based language a world learned, known, experienced and described orally in process-based languages. To write about consciousness is an experience a friend described as like talking about talking. Having accepted the invitation it will now require what everyone I know, knows to help me keep my word. It is fortunate that in the Native world, knowledge belongs to the people as a collective. It is our lega-cy and is gathered, shared and contributed for the good of all. So I begin these writings with thanks and gratitude to all my relations for their knowledge, wisdom and generosity.

What follows are a collage of thoughts that though related are not set in a linear progression. This form more closely models my way of perceiving. It reflects notions of relationship and interdependence. I invite you to walk the circle of these thoughts with me in the hope it will make visible my view of consciousness. An additional note to the reader: Though these words come to you in written form, they are pre-sented following an oral tradition. The thoughts and words are meant to be heard and they follow the breath. After that perhaps, they may meet up with the usual rules of grammar punctuation and tense.

* * *

The universe to which I belong is conscious, animate and interactive. Time is movement. An unending shifting of patterns that appear and disappear in multiple layers of rhythms. Concepts of a linear and finite time are foreign and are superimposed over an innate and different experience of time. Space is a chaotic flux that is constantly transforming. From this view of the world, "relationship" best describes the core of consciousness. In this universe, it is relationship to place that lies at the heart of learning, and where we discover the pleasures, obligations, kindnesses and duties of self in community. In this exploration of relationship and interdependence we can immerse our sensibilities, integrate wordless knowing and within the spontaneous patterns of time, create and share our expressions of what we have come to know and how we have come to know it.

The voices of consciousness are heard through our senses. Through feeling, they become known. In a purely material perception of reality, one that suppresses or dismisses feeling, it is a simple step to isolate or limit meaning from thought, choice from action or to feed spiraling levels of excess and conflict that deny the spirit. Human creativity that falls into these slender channels and aspects of consciousness shape society and define its values, institutions, and expression. A purely material reality is without balance and is malnourished. This malnourishment sustains the many loops of addiction.

To live in relationship with a conscious world is to live a practice of the art of listening. It is in the internal world where we find the connection to the creation and to that which created it. That internal place of connection is the place of hearing and understanding and the place from which to listen. It is not possible to have a good relationship without permitting the intimacy of hearing what is being spoken in whatever languages are used. What is heard and how it is heard when confined to the intellect delivers too narrow an understanding to allow full comprehension.

Through nourishing the internal connection to the creation the voices of that which creates comes to meet the senses and using the physical world as teacher can be heard, understood and interacted with. Through these interactions one is formed as a person of community. It is the same as the way water forms the land, or the wind forms the feather, bringing intelligence, meaning, shape and function. The English words "person" and "community" infer separate worlds, an inference unique to the Eurocentric paradigm and it is in this language of dividing and holding in place where fragmentation is born. Inversely, this noun language also fuels the desire for connection and wholeness, but it is a frightening, dangerous and lonely journey when feeling and meaning are discarded or left by the side of the path.

Developing oneself in good relationship with life is the first responsibility of a person of community. It is through our contributions that the dance of relationship is learned. Living as kin, in an animate reality opens understandings and realizations about the place of humans in the creation. The place of humans is equal, not elevated. Humans have their duties as do the plants, the stones, and the darkness. The concept of hierarchy and "other-ness" are intellectual/social constructs that have been devised to create and further a material reality.

The primary relationship from which we learn about the creation of life is the relationship between the male and female principles as they engage one another in nature. If I speak about the Sun as an embodiment of the male principle and the Earth as an embodiment of the female principle then it is easy to see how the meeting of these two forces and the quality of their meeting determines that which emerges from their coming together. The warmth of the sun attracted to the dark fecundity of a receptive Earth travels to her and in their meeting activates her power to give life. Learning the qualities of the female and male principles as they express throughout the natural world brings us to the essence of these principles and the opportunity to re-discover knowings and meanings, boundaries and purposes that are inherent in these powers. The core of a conscious world rests in dancing the balance that brings these two principles into harmony over and over and over again. By appreciating, sustaining, restoring and renewing these principles we attract a creative relationship between the living universe and the person, the couple, the family, the community and the society. By living aware that we are of the Earth, we come to recognize and respect our interdependence.

Learning the essence and expressions of these two principles is a life-long journey. We must understand both, of course, since both male and female live inside us. I first explore the consciousness of the feminine, its interplay and expressions as one of my duties as a woman. In a matriarchal society, such as the Haudenosaunee, known as the Iriquois Confederacy, one of the primary expressions of the feminine principle is to animate, model, guide and influence ethical social conduct. This is done in many ways, one of them is the preservation of culture and traditions, which promote harmony among the people, and serve and defend life. This confederacy has continued unbroken since its founding on the Great Law of Peace in about 1000 AD, ending war among the Mohawk, Onondaga, Oneida, Seneca, Cayuga and later the Tuscarora tribes. To the present day it is the responsibility of the Clan Mothers to select or remove the fifty coequal chiefs that make up the Grand Council of the confederacy as well as the presiding moderator, (Tadodaho) who presides over them.[1]

The female principle with its power to attract is intended to influence and provide structure to the potent force of the male principle, why else would it have such power to attract? The strength of the feminine capacity for vision, intuition and the realms of emotion provide guidance and protection to our societies as well as inspiration and innovation. It is difficult to write about these matters in the present culture where the word "feminine" is heard as a challenge, and in an environment where the feminine has been fragmented, commodified, politicized, pathologized and marginalized. Nevertheless, in a world that is awake, distortions fall away and deeper, richer and wiser understandings of the feminine and masculine return to view. Essential meanings and purpose are once again respected as gifts, skills and capacities, and known as sacred components for the nurturance, flowering and continuance of life.

When something is innately equal, struggling to prove that it is so creates a dynamic that includes a dependence on the oppression against which one is struggling. The need to be heard, to be visible and respected as a valued part of life is a basic need and originates in what is called by some the Great Mystery or, in the *I Ching*, the Creative. Authenticity and a sense of validity emerge from the internal world to be reflected in the external world. In a society that is unbalanced and dominated by a single worldview, the act of "proving" is rooted in an assumption that only what is defined as rational within that worldview can be real. But if you look to the Earth, you see that what manifests remains invisible until it is birthed from the internal into a temporal reality. From the internal place of learning, proof of equity is the embodiment and expression of principles congruent with the natural laws of harmony and balance. Those laws are, of course, subject to constant transformation. Expressions of equality generated from an internal knowing contain discernment and constant questioning which strengthens and broadens the capacity to experience a sense of related-ness and enhances the ability to generate harmony, and to cultivate per-severance, respect, humor and humility.

When feminine and masculine principles are out of balance there is oppression. Not oppression just of the feminine, but oppression of the masculine as well because you cannot oppress one without distorting both. Oppression does not discriminate. It oppresses all. Its invisible and pervasive force constricts the heart, suppresses the spirit and cen-sors expression. When the focus of our attention lives in stillness and animates balance and renewal, there is an endless breadth of possibili-ties that nourish heart, spirit and creativity. There is coherence in a process that encourages the sharing of different understandings which add to the body of knowledge and meaning in support of life. The pro-found aspects of the feminine and masculine principles are sensible in a conscious world. All is interconnected and the wheel of movement, process and performance continues its spin, coming together and mov-ing apart, emerging and disappearing in the chaos of flux.

I envision a conscious world evolving through the healing and restoration of the masculine and feminine to their place of symmetry and cohesion. And because they are inextricably joined I see this accomplished through the restoration of the feminine to its place of respect. It is a task in which many people are deeply engaged, this recovery and revitalization of the essential powers of the feminine and masculine principles. The dominance and distortion of male power has abused men and the spirits of men, warping their creative drive. It has brought loneliness to men, to women and to our children. And it has brought grief and suffering to the Earth. Men and women who have nurtured their knowledge of the female and male principles project an understanding of the sacredness of life and a deep commitment to the visible inclusion of the profoundly feminine into mundane life. With courage these ones look into the face of violence and the brutalities that have resulted from dominance and control. These ones act to learn what must be known about the mutations and their terrors. It is said that we carry our wounds as medicine for the healing. These ones use their consciousness to hold the stillness while they stand, speak and act with reverence for life and for the compelling need for a humility that is consistent with our limited view as humans. These are the ones who monitor their ambitions, master their desires, and examine their weaknesses to find the way to wisdom and compassion. These ones explore their mistakes, recognizing them as learning, and use their knowledge to devise inclusive strategies, demonstrate productive collaborations and construct questions to draw out deeper answers that have the potential to move all to health and renewal.

In a conscious world, we are introduced from infancy to our duties and responsibilities to the creation. We understand the critical necessity for strengthening the best parts of our nature and the cultivation of our creativity as a contribution for the good of all. The taking of life, whether it is plant, animal, element or human requires the restoration of balance through performance of ceremony, reconciliation, and embodied acts of conscious responsibility. Acquisitiveness and force are not symbols of strength or leadership but clear signals of a weakness of spirit and character.

* * *

If you look at an internalized, embodied understanding of consciousness there is a shift from a hierarchical perception, as in levels of consciousness, to the perception of a geography of consciousness. An ecology of interdependent relationships. Living practically within a world that is conscious calls for a different understanding of time. Here, time reveals itself as *the* essence, not *of* the essence. As essence it is innately creative. This is a fundamental understanding. Living with time as the creative power in action cultivates the ability to distinguish different patterns, harmonies and rhythms and invigorates perception and perseverance. It builds courage because the sisters of illusion, confusion and delusion, are encountered in waiting.

Waiting well means waiting happily in the core of stillness while living fully in the assault of distractions that suffuse society. Waiting is not a peripheral ability, but is central to a way of being that links us to time and the worlds of Earth and Water, Air and Skies, of the visible and the invisible, of sound and silence. Within waiting lives the potential for fulfillment. Waiting well combines with listening well to breed a way of seeing that cultivates thoughts and actions that harmonize with place, life and the Mystery. With our desires comes the rush of ambition. Ambition, unmediated, fears time and feeds the demand for solutions that appear absolute and that soothe anxieties with fantasies of control.

Waiting is a part of movement: To prevent waiting from becoming paralysis entails trust, a knowledge of self and of the languages consciousness uses. In waiting we surrender to following the processes that are in play, looking to see where beauty will make itself visible, attracting our attention to the knowledge it contains. The heart recognizes pure beauty, beauty uncommodified, as harmonized expressions of the consciousness of the creation, the perceiver and perceived.

Waiting is not passive. There is a lot to do while waiting. Mastering balance and spontaneity, polishing discernment, perceiving movement and patterns, fostering humor, deepening appreciation and flexibility and practicing kindness. The fulfillment of vision is in the preparation and in learning the patterns of time. The longer one ignores the consequences of impatience, the greater the distance grows between vision and fulfillment. The reward for impatience is time.

In the world I describe, time is not a commodity. To mechanize time and attempt to contain it within a singular framework is an undertaking with implications and consequences that have revealed themselves as destructive and dangerous. Time is movement and movement is constant and chaotic. Discerning the myriad movements of time and its overlapping layers of diverse rhythms is one of the great pleasures of consciousness. Within the human body, just as in the natural world, there are many different times and rhythms. It is useful to agree on a type of time for certain purposes, just as nouns are useful in naming. However imagining that an intellectual agreement describes what time is in its entirety, especially when that description does not match with what we observe and experience within ourselves, is comparable to wearing your shoes on the wrong feet – it is a strange, disorienting experience. The effect of living with an artificial definition of time imposed over natural time works like an addictive drug causing people to function and believe in a social reality separate from the movement of the creation of life. If the theory of linear time were accepted as a tool for measuring movement, an intellectual construct devised for certain practical purposes like a chair, and if that understanding of time was commonly known and practiced within the acceptance of many different perceptions of time, then time in the wider society, would no longer wear the mask of adversary and commodity. It would not have the ill effects that have resulted from the singular perception of time as linear. The belief in linear time and its imposition has distorted, mechanized and limited life. And in so doing, separates humans from that on which they depend, the heartbeat of the mother Earth to whom we belong and to whom we owe kindnesses, as well as duties and obligations.

* * *

It is profoundly intimate to listen, to listen to the sunlight, or to someone, or to yourself. Automatically your breathing blends with what you are listening to (or for) and your listening is an opening to feeling. Listening is skill, art and capaciousness. The skill comes in distinguishing, refining, clarifying, and tuning to that which resonates inside you. When you think about communication in terms of different consciousnesses, listening is more important than speaking and speaking is exposed as the least refined of the means of communication. It is said that at one time the animals, the stones, the many forms of life and humans all spoke the same language. This changed and the animals and the other forms of life stopped speaking to aid humans in their learning of many things, among them, listening.

Tumult and stimulation fill the material world and it can appear that choice and selectivity are the answers to overwhelm, yet selectivity carries its own consequences and isolation is an extreme that leads away from the human need for connection. In a world, where many more voices and languages are audible and visible, discernment is high art but what or who to listen to is a lesser question. *Where* to listen from is of greater importance.

Knowing where to listen from provides a compass through the flux to find the pathway to clarity or resonant answers. Vision emerges from stillness and stillness precedes clarity. Clarity must guide action in an interrelated, interdependent world. If it is true for you, as it is posited by many, that the external world is the reflection of the internal world, then our listening choices determine which parts of our nature we value and wish to nourish. If illness and disease are understood as imbalances in a living system, then the task is to restore balance. Balance by its nature can be restored, and from this we know that there is a medicine for each ill. Yet medicine when isolated from the fullness of its song can catalyze further imbalance or become poison. The practice of deconstructing medicine plants to a mathematical formula of components fractures the unity of the natural structure and what is discarded is the medicine's song. It is that song that invokes a harmony that can transform poison into medicine. The alchemy that transforms poison into medicine is learned through listening and feeling. In listening and feeling the song being sung, we open the transformative portal, offer our respect and honor that which creates, strengthening its presence. In listening we may hear what asks to be restored, renewed, strengthened. The alchemy is in the resolve to maintain our humility and kindness, generosity of spirit and integrity as we listen for the medicine. This is not the world of simple dualism, straight paths from "a" to "b" and the false hope of absolutes, it is the world of process and performance of knowledge and exploration of paradox. It is the understanding that impeccability in performance of ritual and of following of process only determines the quality of the offering. Restoration remains in the realm of the Mystery and only with its participation can healing or passage to deeper realms of understanding occur.

Humor and good character mature with listening and vision improves over time. Humility is the doorway to listening and respect is the core. Hearing is a full body sport. I never fail to notice where in my body I hear someone or something or silence. When I am with an accomplished listener I know my name will be safe in their mouth or moving across their lips. Dancing the flux of paradox breeds lightness and virtuosity. Listening makes great dancers.

* * *

Human consciousness shares in the most intimate of ways the consciousness of the Earth. The Earth's consciousness is made visible through her beauty. It is the mystery of that beauty and the longing to reflect and answer it that teaches us.

There is intimacy in the transmission of knowledge. Listening and learning are intimate. It is a falling in love. When a learning is for you, you fall in love and your attention travels over and over to the paths that lead to that which is loved, discovering and exploring aspects, pitfalls, anomalies, practices, performance, reflection, possibility.

Listening opens the senses. When the teacher you are learning from is the Earth awareness develops. The intellect becomes a fine and useful tool for integration like a softly leaded pencil moving smoothly, guided by many intelligences to write your song, make your medicine, offer your contribution.

The manner in which knowledge is transmitted has far-reaching consequences. In the Native paradigm the forms, the processes by which education is gained, its uses and refinement cannot be separated from place and relationship. Sense of place equals land, family, community, and traditions. Learning is not bounded by a physical structure or confined to a designated set of people, nor is it restricted to interactions with humans or linear definitions of time. The transmission of knowledge is not confined to words, it comes through our relationships. In the Native paradigm, knowledge is catalogued in holistic symbols that embody principles and experiences. These symbols describe the unity between people, animals, plants, air, water, sky, etc. They describe the ecology of relationship and the principles, ceremonies and ways of living in a sustainable community. This knowledge has become highly valued and sought after in a modern world that faces the consequences of excess. However, the consciousness that diminishes feeling, creates excess, that caters to acquisitiveness, and separates knowledge from service cannot successfully expropriate the Earth's intelligence and hope to apply it for benefit of one over another or even for the broadest of altruistic purposes. In the Native paradigm, the gateway and safe passage to deeper realms of perception, comprehension and ultimately to wisdom rest in our traditional values. Indigenous knowledge cannot be learned through writings and photographs, nor can it be bought or sold by an individual. This knowledge of process and performance requires sharing. It demands humility, discipline, perseverance and patience, each a quality that takes copious amounts of time to develop. The tempo of the passage to learning, the enhancement of perception and the ability to transmit and share knowledge is inextricably linked to the development and refinement of character. Indigenous knowledge lives in the unity of the people, the land, and that which created all. There is a coherence in a conscious world to which we must be attuned. Distinguishing that coherence and aligning your life to it is a governing principle of animating consciousness.

* * *

The United Nations designated 1996 The Year of Indigenous Peoples. That July an International Summer Institute was convened at the University of Saskatchewan in Saskatoon, Canada. The attendees represented Indigenous people from around the globe. From lands that colonizers called Australia, New Zealand, South America, Europe and North America. Among them were the first generation of post-colonial Indigenous scholars, artists, traditional knowledge holders and allies of Indigenous people.

The Summer Institute met to share perspectives and gain a holistic view of colonization. They came together to map and diagnose colonization, to share and evolve processes and strategies to heal the colonized and to imagine and invoke a new society. "Through sharing, feeling, listening and analyzing we engaged in a critique of the trauma of colonization…We came to understand that it is the systemic nature of colonization that creates cognitive imperialism, our cognitive prisons."[2]

In Western science and in traditional educational institutions students are taught in a Eurocentric educational model. What is taught has been drawn from a limited sample, projected as universal and normed on a limited sample of experience and ways of knowing which exclude the majority of women, diverse culture and Indigenous people. Children enter school with open minds and a sense of discovery, yet the longer their education the narrower their view becomes. By the time they reach the doctoral level their knowledge of a fragment of a specific subject will have grown and deepened but their perspective of knowledge itself has become narrow. I remember being in school and realizing that what was being presented did not reflect or honor my innate knowledge. It was then that I turned to look out the window at my teacher and never again took as whole the fragments presented in the Eurocentric educational system. Many have had experiences of pure intelligence. Its purity gives a nourishment that bathes and feeds the entire being and passes itself through the mind, the body and the spirit to express itself in thought, action and creativity that are marked by a congruence with and devotion to life.

The systemic nature of cognitive imperialism remains, for the most part, invisible and inviolate. As human consciousness evolves, an educational model that divides and oppresses grows in its destructive force. For instance, medical training which focuses on localized treatment of specific symptoms and ignores the matrix in which an imbalance occurs, devises medical interventions which often cause deeper imbalance. By dividing and isolating, Western medicine has unwittingly separated itself from its own healing songs in the same way that by imposing a singular system of thought, Eurocentric education has isolated itself from traditional knowledge, the learning inherent in community, and the wisdom contained in feeling.

I recently heard an Ojibway man speak of teaching his children about wild rice. He took them out to the waters where the wild rice grows so that they would hear the sound it made when it touched the canoe. It is a good example of a transmission of knowledge that includes process, performance, community and timelessness. It is a teaching method that brings the learners into the presence of pure intelligence.

To think about the need for cognitive pluralism as if it were a matter of social justice, is to minimize it. Valuing cognitive pluralism is not an act of social justice, it is the recognizing and valuing of consciousness. The validity of cognitive pluralism is beyond the artificial constructs of a social system. Cognitive pluralism is consistent with natural law and its meanings which we see expressed throughout the creation. Part of the human journey is learning the geography, voices and languages of consciousness. The imposition of a series of assumptions, as practiced in colonialism, and its pervasive, incessant demands for assimilation is an assault on the human spirit and on consciousness itself.

A transformed and transformative educational system will reflect, embody and teach the skills and capacities that nourish consciousness and the ability to value it in its infinity of expressions. As long as a colonizer's consciousness remains invisible to both the colonizers and the colonized, the thinking, methods and possibilities for change that are brought forward remain within the systems of thought and consciousness that produced the disease and you cannot be the doctor if you are the disease.

* * *

To attempt to separate knowledge and power from service and meaning is a known path to failure of purpose and the wounding of the spirit. Ultimately the achievements, lacking integrity at their core, cannot be sustained and eventually must reflect in the external world, an internal disintegration of character. In a reality where the material is held as primary and time is linear, human accomplishments beguile and seduce. Fortunately, transformation is a constant and false steps a part of learning. In a reality experienced as transformative and interdependent, our embodiment of learning and its expressions into daily life carry the potential for improving the quality of our relationships and ultimately the quality of our communities, societies and institutions.

Valuing what is known outside the context of relationship limits further our already limited view. Knowledge is only potential and when disconnected from meaning, from its relational context and from the Mystery, creates excesses which destroy balance and harmony. Unlimited excess that occurs in the human body is called cancer. When excess occurs in the natural world inevitably there is a re-orientation, adaptation and change to support the restoration of balance with time. Excess starves the spirit and the being. It triggers desires and hungers that cannot be sated or slowed by the material. In a conscious society it is understood that the value is in the quality of the question, the constancy of attention, the clarity of discernment, the fullness of observation, the capaciousness of listening and the generosity of spirit. The power of the invisible is dismissed by the foolish; actions taken whether they are innocent or contrived that ignore the power of the invisible generate consequences. These consequences are known as fate.

* * *

Leadership is the responsibility of each person. We must be able to lead ourselves away from that which feeds the lesser parts of our nature, toward that which nourishes and strengthens the good. What is "good"? In this notion of kinship and interdependence "good" holds a meaning of fitting in the natural order, of causing Creativity to continue itself, of preserving cultural integrity while mirroring the diversity of the natural world.

"Good" is something which serves the whole. Among the leadership qualities that generate and strengthen the good are kindness, generosity, humor, humility, compassion and truthfulness. These words sound so "soft" – how could such gentle sounding qualities lead a people to nurturance and safety in a terrorist world?

Terror has always been available in the world. In pre-history it was found as it is now in the unknown, the unexpected. And so it seemed that a powerful leader was one who controlled and dominated threatening forces. That characterized the unknown as threatening, cruel, unfeeling. Yet with the constant practice of control and domination, century after century, terror never left. It was magic that went underground. Terror stayed above ground and became a tool of power. A tool like a chainsaw or a jet engine and in its noise and harshness, deadened the senses, stimulated fear and re-focused resolve to narrow corridors of survival and supremacy. If you deny the power of ethical conduct to disperse fear, you deny the power of the Creative to expand the ways in which the invisible resolves the impossible. By denying the importance of the internal world, and trading the knowledge of the deeper realms of perception for trinkets large and small, one ends up with an illusion of safety that rests on foundations so flimsy that they threaten to shake to pieces at the very thought of loss or change. It is a poor trade.

It is in recognizing the manner in which life moves from the primordial to the temporal that we find our opportunity to collaborate with and contribute to life. Learning these cycles requires the cultivation of those soft-sounding qualities because they compel a person to build a strong and flexible mind, courage, humility, resolve and dependence on the Great Mystery. This is the power of the gentle.

To return power to that which creates it is in alignment with life. This is seen clearly in the circle of relationship between Mother Earth and Father Sky. It is seen in the life of water as mist, rain, river and ocean, the warmth of the sun quickening its transformations. It is seen in the life of a tree, its nourishment rising from the Earth to activate the seed, feed the bud, blossom, the fruit and then return to ground. Each transformative change, alive, performing an act of beauty, power and continuance.

It has been said so often that it has become a cliché that power corrupts. But the Earth has immeasurable power. Consider the way a volcano builds an island. It is only Earth's human children who attempt to actively hold power over one another. How does this happen? Aboriginal scholar, Leroy Little Bear, once posed these questions: What is it in the nature of a consciousness that causes it to impose itself on others? And what is it in the nature of a consciousness that would allow itself to be imposed upon? One hundred people sat together and reflected on those questions for ten days. The answers provided both a map and a re-visioning of Indigenous voice and vision.

My observation is that power (energy) distorts and corrupts when the intention is to gather it and hold on to it. In the natural world energy is movement and it returns to its source in a constant cycle. In that cycle of constant transformation are the processes of pure intelligence. In that movement there is a place for the Mystery to serve the good. The movement of the Mystery lies beyond usual human perception. Great thinkers, women and men of knowledge, spend their lives hoping to glimpse the Unknowable, and always what they express in the end is awe, humility and gratitude. At the heart of ritual and ceremony is the deep need to express gratitude to the Unknowable to acknowledge our helplessness and the infinite love that has allowed us to continue our learning.

* * *

I offer you these thoughts with respect and the wish that they will bring beauty, strength and a smile to your heart.

All my relations.

References

1. Hall, S. & Arden, H., Interview with Leon Shenandoah, in *Wisdomkeepers*, 1990; p. 102.

2. Battiste, M., Introduction, *Unfolding Lessons of Colonization, Reclaiming Indigenious Voice and Vision*, University of Columbia Press, 2000.

COMMUNION

Christopher Bache

If we lived in a world that affirmed the primacy of consciousness, by which I mean one that affirmed the vision that behind and saturating this extravagantly beautiful universe lives another equally resplendent world, a Mother Universe, source of this world, Primary Matrix of this world, a Cosmic Womb, if we lived in this understanding instead of the belief system we presently live in, how would our lives be changed? My response to this question is: What would not be changed if we lived in such a world?

Like many today, I believe that humanity is swiftly moving toward such a worldview. The implications of living in a multi-dimensional universe that is truly alive in the deepest sense of the word, in which the qualities of "mind" are just as fundamental as the qualities of "matter," are beginning to emerge in our collective awareness. In many disciplines we are beginning to see signs of this basic shift in perspective. In psychological and philosophical circles, we are beginning to recognize the fundamental difference it would make if we saw ourselves living in an ensouled universe, a universe suffused with soul, with passion, feeling, intelligence, and choice.

The invitation of this anthology is to describe what we think is emerging on the curve of history as we make this pivot. The reader will understand that this is not an assignment that calls for caution and timid formulations, but one which invites us to throw ourselves as far as possible into the world we see emerging. What might the future look like if we transition to living consciously in a physical universe surrounded by a Cosmic Womb universe, a Meta-universe, a Spirit universe, to use the old language; if we saw everything about ourselves – our bodies, our hearts and our minds – as birthed out of this Primary Matrix? More importantly, perhaps, what would it *feel* like to live in such a world?

I think it might feel and look like *communion*. Communion is what we are sorely lacking today, and for good reason. Face it, who wants to enter into communion with a dead universe? Who in his or her right mind wants to enter into communion with, to become intimate with, to exchange the juices of life with a mechanical universe which can't feel me, or a blind universe which does not see me, or a universe which grows itself through random chance, making my very existence a lucky accident. That we would isolate ourselves from such a universe makes perfect sense. When we confine the qualities we find within ourselves to our kind alone, when we deny that these qualities or something like them flow through the larger matrix of life, then it makes sense to seek communion with only our own kind, with other humans and near-humans. But how terribly we shrink the world when we do so.

If we came to believe that the universe was not composed of "dead matter" but living, intelligent, self-emergent energy-matter, if we came to believe that inside the creative pulse of evolution was not simply blind luck and patient sifting but ingenuity and even forethought, this might be a universe that we would want to enter into communion with. If we felt that our individual creativity had a counterpart, a silent part-ner, hidden in the surrounding Meta-universe, this might be a partner-ship we would seek to deepen. If we felt that the love we feel for our children were mirrored in a love the universe feels for her *sapiens child*, this might be an embrace that we would seek to cultivate.

Is this just a dream, a wild speculation from those unwilling or unfit to live in the cold truths of the scientific era? Is it a fantasy compensat-ing us for the loss of the divine parent we suffered in the seventeenth and eighteenth centuries?

How much easier it would be if it were only this. How much sim-pler, for then all we would lack is courage and courage can be found. Courage to take back what in our youth we gave away to Father Jehovah, Father Allah, Father Vishnu, and all the other Old Boys who held sway over us for the past four thousand years. How much easier if it were simply a matter of braving it through this last step away from the medieval home, setting up our own planet, an ideal site for commerce and trade, brave new world, all that. But it won't work.

What fades in the rear view mirror of history is easier to describe than what approaches – the vision of the universe as Gardener, patiently growing crops on a scale seldom imagined before now. An intelligent gardener who has invested 13.7 billion years tilling the ground, preparing the soil of multi-galactic fields destined to burst with life. Who invests 4.6 billion years on a single planet, patiently drawing forth from its waters increasingly complex life forms hosting increasingly subtle forms of awareness. We have seen but the first shoots poking through the surface. Thirteen billion years preparing the ground – what lies a mere million years hence?

When we look for the signs of whether this Gardener be cruel or kind, we should not be lulled with fairy tales of romance. If this Gardener loves her children, it is a fierce love indeed. Kali, the goddess of destruction, caresses with a hard hand, seemingly without mercy. One must reach deep into the plan of life to recognize compassion in her touch. Goddess Kali, symbol of life's continual self-regeneration, is sometimes pictured surrounded by gore. Shattering the old forms in order to liberate the new, she cuts away last year's crop to make way for the next generation. "She eats her children," the ancient scriptures say. What kind of mother eats her children, shreds one species to make room for another? And yet, said Ramakrishna, if we want to know God, we must be willing to look evil in the face. We must look deeply into the complete experience of being alive in this untamed, constantly shifting, constantly expanding universe, and not flinch at what we see. This world eats her children. This vision is not for the faint of heart.

If we became convinced of the primacy of a living, conscious, intentional, genius-laden Cosmic Womb, if we came to feel our full post-enlightenment, post-modern selves to be part of an extended birth process, we would naturally want to cultivate communion with this Womb. We would begin to cultivate the practice of communing with the source of our being, and as this communion deepened, so would our self-understanding.

It would only be a matter of time before we would collectively begin to pierce the veil of amnesia and penetrate the storehouse consciousness that holds the memories of our former lives, the echoes of all our former adventures and residences. With this discovery, the bottom would fall out of time and with it our collective fear of death. We would no longer experience ourselves as trapped in time, consigned to one brief temporal slice, but instead as swimming in time, playing in its waves, plunging repeatedly into its waters. Fear of death would be replaced by awe as we took in the profound achievement of the continuous recycling of life, folding each accomplishment into ever more complex patterns, the brilliant wisdom of the relentless turnover of comparatively short life cycles accelerating the development of that deeper "something" in us we have called soul.

Soul, such a frail name for that extraordinary consciousness that imbibes a thousand incarnations, fusing their energies into a brilliant singularity, a shining star that once birthed lives forever. First glimpsed several thousand years ago, the Soul, the Atman, the Divine Self, the Kingdom Within was first thought to be so extraordinary a creature that it could not make its home on this poor planet. The Hindus named its discovery *moksha*, "escape" from *samsara*, escape from this world of sorrow. It was thought that the true home of such a glorious thing as the Soul could only be with Vishnu in paradise, or with Christ in Heaven, or with Amitabha in the Pure Land. Even when Buddhism replaced the "up and out" ideal of the *arahat* with the *bodhisattva* ideal of repeated return, the goal still tended to be framed in terms of emptying the earth of her awakening children. Only slowly, perhaps only now, do we begin to grasp the larger arc of our evolutionary trajectory. *Samsara* is not a place but a state of consciousness. Though slower and harder to liberate than mind, matter itself must eventually yield to the patient and relentless infusion of the Divine.

As our communion with the Mother Universe deepens, we would begin to recognize the deeper pattern of the evolutionary potential awakening inside the form we already are. Only after we had absorbed Darwin and recalculated the age of the universe, only after the vision of fixed life forms had been replaced by a vision of fluid processes flexing across vast tracts of time, only then could we dare to guess the immensity of the symphony we are part of.

When communion deepens to the point that we break through the shell of our egoic identity and release the solar identity that has been incubating inside us these many millennia, and when this awakening is wedded to the new cosmological story of a dynamic, unfolding universe, we will begin to see that the Soul's true destiny is not escape back into the Mother Universe but flourishing here on a transformed Earth, pulling more and more of the Mother's vitality into cells of flesh and bone. *Star children will one day walk this planet in full consciousness, an abiding co-mingling of Heaven and Earth.* Involution precedes evolution, and evolution opens the gate to more potent forms of communion between matter and spirit. As we enter more deeply into this communion, we will begin to discover a deeper meaning to the hymns that sing of creating heaven on earth.

Once the door to the Mother is opened through communion, there is no predicting where humanity could go. No matter how farsighted the vision we may hold of our future, it will likely fall short of the reality. When we look to the future, we are always trapped within the limitations of our assumptions, and the most basic of these assumptions is the very form of the being we are at this present moment in our evolutionary development. Our individual imagination is constrained by the boundaries of our collective psyche, but this collective psyche is itself changing and evolving.

If we make the shift to living in a Living Universe, we will practice the arts of communion with this Universe, making conscious what has up to now been largely an unconscious relationship. The flow of vitality and insight that had previously seeped into us from the hidden recesses of our innermost minds would become a conscious stream. Inspiration dished out by fickle Muses would become a conscious dialogue with the source of mind itself. Our psychological and spiritual evolution would compound itself exponentially, and with that shift our social and cultural evolution would accelerate. If this happens, how could it not also happen that we would eventually remake the planet in greater harmony and peace? Could such a revolution fail to be part of the historical crisis bearing down upon us now?

If we felt the world to be saturated with intelligence, creativity, and consciousness, we would spend more time listening to her. We would listen to our stream of consciousness until we located its source. We would listen for the larger voice that surrounds and saturates our personal voice. If we did this, our culture would re-discover what all inward-listening cultures have discovered, that Nature truly is alive and speaking. She speaks but it is we who have forgotten the language she uses. If we came to believe that the universe was truly speaking to us, we would learn how to learn from her.

I don't think we should expect persons with advanced degrees in physics, chemistry, biology, anthropology, and psychology to hear the same messages heard by the primal peoples of the ancient world. Do not expect physicians with PET scans and MRIs at their disposal to hear the same healing songs as pre-literate shamans. I am not minimizing the wisdom of indigenous peoples, but what marvelous songs will the current generation of *sapiens children* hear when they turn their educated ears inward? What new conversations will spring up between the Mother Universe and us, conversations that could never have taken place before now?

Surely there will be continuities with the past. Surely we will hear again the ancient message of embracing love, the imperatives of compassion, and the promise of reward for labor well spent. And surely we will hear truths that will lead us to have greater respect for the wisdom preserved by older cultures. But equally surely we will engage in conversations that could not have taken place before this century, not because the Mother Universe was lacking but because her children were not ready. We were still crawling in the dust counting our toes and calling it higher math.

In deep nonordinary states of consciousness, one enters into intimate dialogue with the infinite resources of the Mother Cosmos. The conversations that arise in these states are a subtle interaction between our *sapiens mind* and an Infinite Intelligence. What one takes away from this dialogue is a function of what one is capable of comprehending. With degrees in religious studies, my conversations have tended to focus on the evolutionary progression of humanity arching through time and slicing through *bardos*. With degrees in biology, Rupert Sheldrake returned with penetrating insights into the process of formative causation and structures he called morphogenetic fields. With degrees in clinical psychiatry, Stanislav Grof discovered the perinatal roots of various forms of psychopathology and the transpersonal well of healing. The point is that when our culture evolves to the point of generating focused and sustained conversations with the Mother Universe, the outflow will be as diversified as the minds we bring to the encounter. The answers will be as sophisticated as the questions each of us is holding.

It comes down to this. Thinking we are the most intelligent, most evolved life form thrown up by a foaming, mechanical universe, we commune only with ourselves and keep the cold world at bay. But if we were to open to a world in which we recognized the blazing intelligence of the cosmic womb that birthed us and everything we see around us, if we began to glimpse the scale and scope of her project and the depth of love that underwrites it, we would turn and face this mysterious world. We would send out emissaries and establish outposts. We would build up commerce with it until contact deepened into communion, and communion is a sacramental exchange that transforms both parties.

With this pivot, history would turn. We would begin to value and cultivate the *skills of alignment*. We would begin to recognize the symptoms of misalignment in individuals, in institutions and ideologies. We would begin to recognize the pattern of half-truths that have been popping through history, fragmented bits and pieces of insight, brief glimpses of sunlight overwhelming eyes accustomed to shadows, the passionate but brief kiss of lovers too soon parted by the re-descending darkness. So long and confusing our love affair with this other world. So many misunderstandings mixed with genius. As communion deepens, we would realize what of our cultural past needs to be surrendered and what held onto. We would learn to separate what was immature and pre-mature from the higher calling that draws us ever forward into fuller and more complete expression. The tensions and mystery of a universe committed to perpetual growth would fill us with compassion for our long and bloody history, and forgiveness would follow.

Forgiveness is a frequent sign that a true breakthrough has taken place in awareness. When one sees more, one spontaneously forgives oneself and others for seeing less, and we have much to be forgiven. As humanity's communion with the Mother Universe deepens, we would own the damage we did to her planet in ignorance and greed. If we had waked sooner, so many species might have been spared, but now there is time only to rescue those remaining and to restore the balance of our bio-systems.

As our communion with the Mother Universe deepens, we would ask forgiveness from the four-legged ones and the winged branches of our family. We would ask forgiveness from our own brothers and sisters of different skin colors and faiths, forgiveness from the mothers of children killed by poverty, greed, and hatred. And only when this bitter cup had been drunk could we turn with reasonable hope to create a saner, safer, and more balanced world. As communion deepened, the tragedy and illogic of our social pathologies of isolation would tear through the remaining barriers, giving birth to new beginnings round the globe.

"Get practical! Be real!" the chant rises from the skeptics. "What you're proposing is preposterous fantasy!" I understand their cry. It seems impossible. But such cries rise from a species stuck in that terrible and precarious moment in its evolution when we are aware enough to be self-conscious but not yet aware enough to be conscious of the patterns that weave individual lives into larger wholes. We are like leaves not yet able to see the tree that we belong to. Only half-awake, we are conscious enough to value the talents we find bubbling up within ourselves, but not sufficiently conscious to recognize the true source of these talents. Not recognizing their source, we claim all we find as our own, as children always do. Meanwhile, the parent watches fondly and waits.

But the Mother Universe seems not to be waiting any longer. Her waters have broken, signally the beginning of humanity's collective labor. The mushroom columns of fire rising around the globe, the falling skyscrapers, the creeping blight of industrial poison and rising global temperatures signal the inevitable ending of the old order and the beginning of a new order. The imperative that will birth us into this new order is simple – "Change or die." We simply can no longer afford the luxury of our divisions or the scavenging greed of corporate culture. The birth of this new planetary child may be perilous and costly, but how precious is its call.

Pictures of our planet from space, the blue marble, mesmerize us, calling us toward some goal each of us can feel but perhaps not yet articulate clearly – a goal not likely to be realized in one generation but a pivot that must be made now or not at all. As we are given fewer and fewer options in the years ahead, the only option remaining will require that we step through this portal quickly, not looking back. A burning house stands behind us. Communion beckons us.

BOOKS

O books
O is a symbol of the world, of
oneness and unity. In different
cultures it also means the
"eye", symbolizing knowledge
and insight, and in Old English it
means "place of love or home".
O books explores the many
paths of understanding which
different traditions have
developed down the ages,
particularly those today that
express respect for the planet
and all of life.

For more information on the full list of over 300 titles
please visit our website
www.O-books.net

SOME RECENT O BOOKS

Punk Science
Inside the mind of God

Manjir Samanta-Laughton

Wow! Punk Science is an extraordinary journey from the microcosm of the atom to the macrocosm of the Universe and all stops in between. Manjir Samanta-Laughton's synthesis of cosmology and consciousness is sheer genius. It is elegant, simple and, as an added bonus, makes great reading. **Dr Bruce H. Lipton**, author of *The Biology of Belief*
1905047932 320pp **£12.95 $22.95**

Is There An Afterlife?
A comprehensive overview of the evidence, from east and west

David Fontana

2nd printing

An extensive, authoritative and detailed survey of the best of the evidence supporting survival after death. It will surely become a classic not only of parapsychology literature in general but also of survival literature in particular. **Universalist**
1903816904 496pp 230/153mm **£14.99 $24.95**

The Science of Oneness
A world view for the twenty-first century

Malcolm Hollick

A comprehensive and multi-faceted guide to the emerging world view. Malcolm Hollick brilliantly guides the reader intellectually and intuitively through the varied terrains of the sciences, psychology, philosophy and religion and builds up a vibrant picture that amounts to a new vision of reality for the 21st century. A veritable tour de force. **David Lorimer**, Programme Director, Scientific and Medical Network
1905047711 464pp 230/153mm **£14.99 $29.95**

The Thoughtful Guide to God
Making sense of the world's biggest idea
Howard Jones
The wide scope of this fusion of theology, philosophy and science makes this an important contribution to a study of the divine that is easily readable by the non-specialist. **Dr Verena Tschudin**, author of *Seeing the Invisible*
1905047703 400pp **£19.99 $39.95**

The Thoughtful Guide to Religion
Why it began, how it works, and where it's going
Ivor Morrish
This is a comprehensive and sympathetic approach to all religions of the world, including the lesser-known ones, sects, cults and ideologies. Broader than "comparative religion", it uses philosophy, psychology, anthropology and other disciplines to answer the key questions, and provides a holistic approach for anyone interested in religious or philosophical ideas.
190504769X 384pp **£24.99 $24.95**

The Thoughtful Guide to Science and Religion
Using science, experience and religion to discover your own destiny
Michael Meredith
This is a rich book that weaves science, experience and religion together with significant experiences from the author's own life. It ranges widely through the sciences and different religious traditions. A gem for the modern spiritual seeker. **Scientific and Medical Network Review**
1905047169 208pp **£10.99 $19.95**

Mysticism and Science
A call to reconciliation
S. Abhayananda
A lucid and inspiring contribution to the great philosophical task of our age

- the marriage of the perennial gnosis with modern science. **Timothy Freke** author of *The Jesus Mysteries*
184694032X 144pp **£9.99 $19.95**

Back to the Truth
5,000 years of Advaita
Dennis Waite

A wonderful book. Encyclopedic in nature, and destined to become a classic. **James Braha**

Absolutely brilliant...an ease of writing with a water-tight argument outlining the great universal truths. This book will become a modern classic. A milestone in the history of Advaita. **Paula Marvelly**
1905047614 500pp **£19.95 $29.95**

The Fall
The evidence for a Golden Age, 6,000 years of insanity, and the dawning of a new era
Steve Taylor

Taylor provides us with the most overwhelming evidence of the existence of an Age of Perfection at the onset of human evolution, and of the fact that human spiritual, social and cultural evolution and history have been a process of degeneration. The Fall is one of the most notable works of the first years of our century, and I am convinced it will be one of the most important books of the whole century. **Elias Capriles** International Journal of Transpersonal Studies.

Important and fascinating, highly readable and enlightening. **Eckhart Tolle**
1905047207 352pp **£12.99 $24.95**

The Wave
A life-changing insight into the heart and mind of the cosmos
Jude Currivan

2nd printing

Rarely does a book as fine as The Wave come along - this is a true treasure trove of ancient and current learning, covering a wide variety of interests. Accessible, interesting, educational and inspiring. The reader will find that both the intellect and the heart are gratified with this book, and that on a deeper level, much of it feels right - and that may be the best kind of knowledge. **Merlian News**
1905047339 320pp **£11.99 $19.95**

The History of Now
A guide to higher yearnings
Andy Nathan

This is all about the spark of optimism that gets us out of bed in the morning, and the different ways it has flared to life during the time of humanity. A "who's who" of the world religions.
1903816289 160pp 250/153mm **£9.99**

Islam and the West
Robert van de Weyer

2nd printing

Argues that though in the sphere of economics and politics relationships between Islam and the West have often been hostile, in the area of ideas and philosophy the two have much in common, indeed are interdependent.

A military and financial jihad against global terrorism cannot be won. Bit a jihad for peace can, and will render the first jihad unnecessary.
1903816149 128pp **£6.99**

Trading Faith
Global religion in an age of rapid change
David Hart

Argues boldly that the metaphor of trading provides the most useful model for religious exchanges in a world of rapid change. It is the inspiring biography of an intensely spiritual man with a great sense of humour who has chosen an unusual and courageous religious path. **Dr Anna King**, Lecturer in Hinduism, University of Winchester
1905047967 260pp £10.99 $24.95

You Are the Light
Rediscovering the Eastern Jesus
John Martin Shajananda
2nd printing

Closed systems, structures and beliefs have prevailed over the last 2000 years, cutting off the majority from direct contact with God and sharing Jesus's own insight on non-duality. This is an inspiring new contemplative vision. **Scientific and Medical Network Review**
1903816300 224pp **£9.99 $15.95**

The Bhagavad Gita
Alan Jacobs

Alan Jacobs has succeeded in revitalising the ancient text of the Bhagavad Gita into a form which reveals the full majesty of this magnificent Hindu scripture, as well as its practical message for today's seekers. His incisive philosophic commentary dusts off all the archaism of 1500 years and restores the text as a transforming instrument pointing the way to Self Realization. **Cygnus Review**
1903816513 320pp **£12.99 $19.95**

Everyday Buddha
A contemporary rendering of the Buddhist classic, the Dhammapada
Karma Yonten Senge (Lawrence Ellyard)
Foreword by **His Holiness the 14th Dalai Lama**
*Excellent. Whether you already have a copy of the Dhammapada or not, I
recommend you get this. I congratulate all involved in this project and have
put the book on my recommended list.* **Jeremy Ball** Nova Magazine
1905047304 144pp **£9.99 $19.95**

The Ocean of Wisdom
**The most comprehensive compendium of worldly and spiritual wisdom
this century**
Alan Jacobs
This anthology of 5,000 passages of spiritual wisdom is an awesome collection of prose and poetry, offering profound truths to everyday guidance.
A valuable reference for any writer or historian, but it also makes for a good
fireside or bedside book. **Academy of Religion and Psychical Research**
190504707X 744pp 230/153mm **£17.99 $29.95**

Good As New
A radical retelling of the scriptures
John Henson
*An immensely valuable addition to scriptural understanding and apprecia-
tion.* **Methodist Recorder**
   *A short review cannot begin to persuade readers of the value of this
book. Buy it and read it. But only if you are brave enough.* **Renew**
2nd printing in hardback
1903816734 448pp **£19.99 $24.95** cl
1905047118 448pp **£11.99 $19.95** pb

Popol Vuh: The Sacred Book of the Maya
The Mayan creation story
Allen J. Christenson

The most accurate and comprehensive translation ever produced. His work is an extraordinary masterpiece of scholarly analysis. **Karen Bassie-Sweet**, University of Calgary.

Clear, vital and entrancingly true...a brilliant exegesis, worthy of the treasure it unpacks. **David Freidel**, Southern Methodist University
190381653X 320pp 230/153mm **£19.99 $29.95**

Popol Vuh II
A literal, line by line translation
Allen J. Christenson

A definitive document of rhetorical brilliance. **Stephen Houston**, Jesse Knight University Professor, Brigham Young Univ.

*An invaluable contribution...***Justin Kerr**, author of *The Maya Vase* books.
1903816572 280pp 230/153mm **£25.00 $37.50**

The Principal Upanishads
Alan Jacobs

Alan Jacobs has produced yet another literary masterpiece in his transcreation of the 'Principal Upanishads', which together with his 'Bhagavad Gita', aim to convey the nondualist teaching (Advaita Vedanta) of the ancient Indian scriptures as well as explore the author's own poetic expression. **Paula Marvelly**
1903816505 384pp **£12.99 $19.95**

The Spiritual Wisdom of Marcus Aurelius
Practical philosophy from an ancient master
Alan Jacobs

Most translations are literal and arid but Jacobs has paraphrased a selection of the best of Aurelius' meditations so as to give more force to the essential truths of his philosophy. **The Light**

There's an uncanny appropriateness of this work to current times so this book is bound to resonate with many. **Wave**

1903816742 260pp **£9.99 $14.95**

A World Religions Bible

Robert van de Weyer

An admirable book to own personally for reflection and meditation, with the possibility of contemplating a different extract a day over an entire year. It is our hope that the use of this splendid anthology will grow. We recommend it to all for their personal enrichment. **The Friend**

Outstanding collection of religious wisdom...never has so much wisdom been concentrated in such a small space. **New Age Retailer**

1903816157 432pp full colour throughout 180/120mm **£19.99 $28.95**

A Heart for the World
The interfaith alternative

Marcus Braybrooke

This book is really needed. This is the blueprint. It has to be cherished. Faith in Jesus is not about creeds or homilies. It is a willingness to imitate Christ-as the Hindu guru Gandhi did so well. A must book to buy. Peacelinks, **IFOR**

1905047436 168pp **£12.99 $24.95**

Bringing God Back to Earth

John Hunt

Knowledgeable in theology, philosophy, science and history. Time and again it is remarkable how he brings the important issues into relation with one another... thought provoking in almost every sentence, difficult to put down. **Faith and Freedom**

An absorbing and highly readable book, profound and wide ranging. **The Unitarian**

1903816815 320pp **£9.99 $14.95**

Christ Across the Ganges
Hindu responses to Jesus
Sandy Bharat

This is a fascinating and wide-ranging overview of a subject of great importance. It is a must for anyone interested in the history of religious traditions and in the interaction between faiths. **Marianne Rankin,** Alister Hardy Society

1846940001 224pp 230/153mm 6x9 **£14.99 $29.95**

A Global Guide to Interfaith
Reflections from around the world
Sandy and Jael Bharat

For those who are new to interfaith this amazing book will give a wonderful picture of the variety and excitement of this journey of discovery. It tells us something about the world religions, about interfaith history and organizations, how to plan an interfaith meeting and much more - mostly through the words of practitioners. **Marcus Braybrooke**

1905047975 336pp 230/153mm 6x9 £19.99 $34.95

The Hindu Christ
Jesus' message through Eastern eyes
John Martin Sahajananda

To the conventional theologian steeped in the Judaeo-Christian tradition, this book is challenging and may even be shocking at times. For mature Christians and thinkers from other faiths, it makes its contribution to an emerging Christian theology from the East that brings in a new perspective to Christian thought and vision. **Westminster Interfaith**

190504755X 128pp **£9.99 $19.95**

Trading Faith
Global religion in an age of rapid change
David Hart

Argues boldly that the metaphor of trading provides the most useful model for religious exchanges in a world of rapid change. It is the inspiring biography of an intensely spiritual man with a great sense of humour who has chosen an unusual and courageous religious path. **Dr Anna King**, Lecturer in Hinduism, University of Winchester
1905047967 260pp **£10.99 $24.95**

You Are the Light
Rediscovering the Eastern Jesus
John Martin Shajananda
2nd printing

Closed systems, structures and beliefs have prevailed over the last 2000 years, cutting off the majority from direct contact with God and sharing Jesus's own insight on non-duality. This is an inspiring new contemplative vision. **Scientific and Medical Network Review**
1903816300 224pp **£9.99 $15.95**

Rosslyn Revealed
A secret library in stone
Alan Butler

Rosslyn Revealed gets to the bottom of the mystery of the chapel featured in the Da Vinci Code. The results of a lifetime of careful research and study demonstrate that truth really is stranger than fiction; a library of philosophical ideas and mystery rites, that were heresy in their time, have been disguised in the extraordinarily elaborate stone carvings.
1905047924 260pp b/w + colour illustrations **£19.95 $29.95** cl

The Way of Thomas
Nine Insights for Enlightened Living from the Secret Sayings of Jesus
John R. Mabry

What is the real story of early Christianity? Can we find a Jesus that is relevant as a spiritual guide for people today?

These and many other questions are addressed in this popular presentation of the teachings of this mystical Christian text. Includes a reader-friendly version of the gospel.

1846940303 196pp £10.99 $19.95

The Way Things Are
A Living Approach to Buddhism
Lama Ole Nydahl

An up-to-date and revised edition of a seminal work in the Diamond Way Buddhist tradition (three times the original length), that makes the timeless wisdom of Buddhism accessible to western audiences. Lama Ole has established more than 450 centres in 43 countries.

1846940427 240pp **£9.99 $19.95**

The 7 Ahas! of Highly Enlightened Souls
How to free yourself from ALL forms of stress
Mike George

7th printing

A very profound, self empowering book. Each page bursting with wisdom and insight. One you will need to read and reread over and over again! Paradigm Shift. I totally love this book, a wonderful nugget of inspiration.
PlanetStarz

1903816319 128pp 190/135mm **£5.99 $11.95**

God Calling
A Devotional Diary
A. J. Russell
46th printing
"When supply seems to have failed, you must know that it has not done so. But you must look around to see what you can give away. Give away something." One of the best-selling devotional books of all time, with over 6 million copies sold.
1905047428 280pp 135/95mm **£7.99** cl.
US rights sold

The Goddess, the Grail and the Lodge
The Da Vinci code and the real origins of religion
Alan Butler
5th printing
This book rings through with the integrity of sharing time-honoured revelations. As a historical detective, following a golden thread from the great Megalithic cultures, Alan Butler vividly presents a compelling picture of the fight for life of a great secret and one that we simply can't afford to ignore.
Lynn Picknett & Clive Prince
1903816696 360pp 230/152mm **£12.99 $19.95**

The Heart of Tantric Sex
A unique guide to love and sexual fulfilment
Diana Richardson
3rd printing
The art of keeping love fresh and new long after the honeymoon is over. Tantra for modern Western lovers adapted in a practical, refreshing and sympathetic way.

One of the most revolutionary books on sexuality ever written. **Ruth Ostrow**, News Ltd.
1903816378 256pp **£9.99 $14.95**

I Am With You

The best-selling modern inspirational classic

John Woolley

14th printing hardback

Will bring peace and consolation to all who read it. **Cardinal Cormac Murphy-O'Connor**

0853053413 280pp 150x100mm **£9.99** cl

4th printing paperback

1903816998 280pp 150/100mm **£6.99 $12.95**

In the Light of Meditation

The art and practice of meditation in 10 lessons

Mike George

2nd printing

A classy book. A gentle yet satisfying pace and is beautifully illustrated. Complete with a CD or guided meditation commentaries, this is a true gem among meditation guides. **Brainwave**

In-depth approach, accessible and clearly written, a convincing map of the overall territory and a practical path for the journey. **The Light**

1903816610 224pp 235/165mm full colour throughout +CD **£11.99 $19.95**

The Instant Astrologer

A revolutionary new book and software package for the astrological seeker

Lyn Birkbeck

2nd printing

The brilliant Lyn Birkbeck's new book and CD package, The Instant Astrologer, combines modern technology and the wisdom of the ancients, creating an invitation to enlightenment for the masses, just when we need it most! Astrologer **Jenny Lynch**, Host of NYC's StarPower Astrology Television Show

1903816491 628pp full colour throughout with CD ROM 240/180 **£39 $69** cl

Is There An Afterlife?

A comprehensive overview of the evidence, from east and west

David Fontana

2nd printing

An extensive, authoritative and detailed survey of the best of the evidence supporting survival after death. It will surely become a classic not only of parapsychology literature in general but also of survival literature in particular. **Universalist**

1903816904 496pp 230/153mm **£14.99 $24.95**

The Reiki Sourcebook

Bronwen and Frans Stiene

5th printing

It captures everything a Reiki practitioner will ever need to know about the ancient art. This book is hailed by most Reiki professionals as the best guide to Reiki. For an average reader, it's also highly enjoyable and a good way to learn to understand Buddhism, therapy and healing. **Michelle Bakar**, Beauty magazine

1903816556 384pp **£12.99 $19.95**

Soul Power

The transformation that happens when you know

Nikki de Carteret

4th printing

One of the finest books in its genre today. Using scenes from her own life and growth, Nikki de Carteret weaves wisdom about soul growth and the power of love and transcendent wisdom gleaned from the writings of the mystics. This is a book that I will read gain and again as a reference for my own soul growth. **Barnes and Noble review**

190381636X 240pp **£9.99 $15.95**